D0722568

TALENT MANAGEMENT SYSTEMS

TALENT MANAGEMENT SYSTEMS

Best Practices in Technology Solutions for Recruitment, Retention and Workforce Planning

ALLAN SCHWEYER

EXECUTIVE DIRECTOR, HUMAN CAPITAL INSTITUTE

Foreword by

CONNIE PASCAL

PRINCIPAL, THE TALENT MARKET GROUP

WILEY

John Wiley & Sons Canada, Ltd.

Copyright © 2004 by Allan Schweyer

National Library of Canada Cataloguing in Publication

Schweyer, Allan
    Talent management systems : best practices in technology solutions
for recruitment, retention and workforce planning / Allan Schweyer.

Includes index.
ISBN 0-470-83386-6

    1. Manpower planning--Computer network resources.
2. Employees--Recruiting--Computer network resources. I. Title.

HF5549.A27S38 2004   658.3'00285'4678   C2003-906700-9

Production Credits
Cover and interior design: Interrobang Graphic Design Inc.
Printer: Tri-Graphic Printing

Printed in Canada
10 9 8 7 6 5 4 3 2 1

Contents

꿘

The Role of Talent and Technology in the Organization

We live in an information economy powered by the human capacity to create value out of knowledge—an intangible asset that has come to be known as human capital. The only way to create human capital is to build and support a workforce. Every organization, large and small, has its unique workforce. At the heart of the workforce is the human capital engine, the manifestation of an organization's talent management system.

When the human capital engine is in working order and tuned to its environment, the organization has the capacity to support growth, produce innovation and gain competitive advantage. Talent is the fuel of the human capital engine. As fuel, talent becomes a strategic natural resource. It must be in steady supply for the organization to grow and prosper. It must flow to the right places and at the right time. It must return on the investment that organizations put into it by producing innovation and competitive advantage. In the world today, organizations are at an intersection of three major forces—the Internet, the global organization and rapidly changing workforce demographics. Talent *management* involves managing the supply, demand and flow of talent through the human capital engine.

With effective talent management, the human capital engine can deliver the right talent at the right time. *Without* talent management, the organization puts productivity at risk...in a perfect position to run out of gas. Effective talent management increases the value of the enterprise, mitigates risk and fuels workforce productivity and innovation. It is impossible to separate these outcomes from the strategic success of any organization. For almost every organization, effective talent management is impossible in the absence of the right technologies.

Talent Management as a System in the Organization

Talent management as a systems concept had its beginnings in the late 1980s when client/server technology, optical character recognition software and equal employment opportunity (EEO) reporting made applicant tracking possible and necessary for most large corporations. It took off in the mid-1990s with the advent of the Internet, Web browsers and database technology. It went mainstream in the late '90s with the explosion of online job boards, e-recruiting companies and corporate employment Web sites. Today, we see some form of technology-based talent management system in use throughout every one of the Global 2000 group of companies, whether simply posting requirements online or implementing multi-million-dollar enterprise software packages and formal talent management best practices.

In this book, the author aims to bring talent systems in organizations into better view and recommend methods and technologies to facilitate effective talent management. When the talent management system is working, individuals find career opportunities that meet their work/life balance needs, organizations increase in value and the economy improves around both the individual and the organization. When it is *not* working, there are unexpected layoffs, underemployment and career stagnation; the organization decreases in value and the economy around both the individual and organization suffers.

For all organizations, whether public or private—government, military or academic—talent management should be viewed as a strategic challenge, not a tactical problem.

The Systems Approach to Talent Management

Taking a systems approach to talent management makes it easier to conceptualize how the organization goes about creating demand, attracting jobseekers, producing candidates, filling jobs, deploying staff and developing human potential. This approach is far from new. From general systems theory[1], we know that

- systems can be observed;
- systems are in a constant state of change, decay and renewal;
- systems tend to fail;
- systems produce unintended results;
- systems must interact, respond and depend on other systems to exist.

We also know that healthy systems produce innovation, improve productivity, shrink or scale depending on the demands being made of them, and increase in value over time. A systems approach to talent management requires a holistic and pragmatic mind-set. It is necessary to view the organization through the "eyes" of the system. In the systems definition of talent management this includes

- full-time employees, i.e., the direct workforce;
- the contingency workforce—temps, contractors, consultants and outsourced workers;
- the potential workforce—external jobseekers, candidates and applicants.

It is only by pulling in both contingent and potential talent that the complete talent management system and life cycle come

---

[1]To summarize and paraphrase Stephen G. Haines in *Systems Thinking and Learning Styles* (Amherst, Md: HRD Press, 1998), 8–9. General systems theory began in the 1920s with biologist Ludwig Von Bertalanffy and others. They proposed the idea of a general theory of systems that could operate at all levels of science, from the study of a single cell to the study of society and the planet as a whole. What they did was create a set of scientific principles that can be applied to virtually any body of work. This theory becomes an excellent framework for describing systems and being able to classify subject matter and understand relationships and interdependencies between systems and the environment.

into view. It is this view of talent as holistic, collaborative and flowing that makes the talent management system unique from other human capital management systems such as the human resource management system (HRMS) or payroll. Once this view is brought into focus, it becomes clear which best practices suggested in this book will be most useful to you and meaningful to the system.

The Talent Management System— Building Block of the Human Capital Asset

A systems approach to talent management begins by thinking of people as investments that add value, not as costs that shrink the income statement. This concept is based on the idea that if people are our number one asset, it should be true on the balance sheet as well. The talent management system is integral to increasing the value of human capital in the organization. Cost-based accounting does a poor job at valuing intangible assets. When the question becomes "what do we need to invest in a person to create the most value for the organization?" instead of "what did it cost to replace that skilled worker with a new hire?" the importance of the talent management system is easily recognized as an asset.

In the not-too-distant future, talent management systems (TMSs) will measure and define workers' performance through a new generation of metrics designed to quantify intangible assets. The ability to measure these assets and create shareholder value forms the core of an effective TMS. In 1990, 50 percent of the value of U.S. corporations came from tangible assets such as factories and facilities and 50 percent came from intangible assets including patents, royalties and licensing agreements. During the irrational exuberance of the dot-com era, the value of intangible assets on the books of American corporations shot up to over 70 percent. Now, even after September 11, 2001, recession and the Iraq War, over 60 percent of the value in Fortune 1000 companies is still based in intangible assets.[2] This number is rising as the U.S. moves increasingly towards an intellectual property (IP)-based economy.

---

[2] IC Growth Inc., www.icgrowth.com.

In addition, outsourcing and globalization are dramatically and irreversibly changing the business models of most large organizations. This is creating the urgent need for a view of talent flow on a global basis. Organizations are coming to realize that it's important to measure the contribution of all systems within the enterprise, including the TMS.

It is the human capital capacity of an organization that actually drives the growth and sustainability of other intellectual capital assets (ICAs), and it is the talent management system that fuels this capacity. ICAs include such things as intellectual property, customer capital and organizational capital. In this model, human capital becomes an investment and can be linked directly to the incremental value it bestows on the organization. A strong talent management systems approach aligns the interests of investors with those of management and of employees.

Talent management is just emerging as its own budget item. A groundswell of early adapters are becoming talent management organizations (TMOs), organizations that, among other things, can understand their talent management needs as far ahead as the next twenty years.

What Makes Talent Management Possible?

In a sentence, Web-based technology is what shapes the talent management system. It is the combination of browsers, search engines, e-mail and database technology that allows talent management data[3] to be gathered, analyzed and measured. Technology gives us the ability to peel back the onion of our organizations and uncover the underlying talent systems in operation. It makes possible the gathering of data, the processing of transactions and the analysis of mass quantities of information. For example, organizations are now able to create private talent databases (searchable repositories of candidate records) using sophisticated extraction

---

[3]Talent management data includes job requirements, source information, workforce plans, resume data, assessment data, contact information, testing results, background/reference data, job application history, performance data, interview results, etc. The goal is to create a talent record that is collecting data across the talent management life cycle, thus creating a more complete picture or profile of the person's talents, aspirations and performance.

and database technology to mine information from resumes and job requirements. They are combining this information with other data to create candidate and workforce profiles. This data can be used to measure the depth of talent in a particular demographic region, for example, or to match staff and external candidates to the right assignments at the right time, in order to align the workforce with the objectives of the business.

Talent as an intangible asset can be viewed like an inventory—an inventory to be acquired, qualified and made available. Workforce planning technology can tell us when we'll need critical talent resources in place, how much of an investment we'll have to make to get the talent productive and even where the talent is most likely to physically reside.

From a technology perspective, 80 percent of the business requirements for a talent management system are the same regardless of the size of the organization. The 20 percent of the business requirements unique in each organization center around scalability—the volume of demand and capacity the organization needs to differentiate itself among its competitors.

Talent management strategy has to be in alignment with business goals, not with software standards. Technology is an integral part of talent management, but in talent management the technology should be transparent to the user. The talent management approach is designed to optimize the people and process components of the system, while technology delivers business intelligence, processes transactions and serves up content and information.

The importance of having a holistic view of the TMS cannot be overstated, especially if you are going to invest the time and money necessary to implement the talent management best practices described in this book. Conceptual models should be used to help create a shared vision of talent management. Once there is a shared vision, people can agree on a comprehensive approach, share responsibility for the different elements of the system and use a common language to discuss the different choices that have to be made. Best practices will help bridge the gaps and fill in the blanks.

Talent management is the number one ingredient of organizational success, more than money, market share, or the track record of the management team. The value of an enterprise is directly related to its success in talent management and the growth of human capital as an asset. The more that organizations pay attention to the strategic importance of managing how the right talent flows through their company, the better off our entire society will be. In fact, the entire world would be a better place if more people found the right jobs—jobs that allow them to exploit their best talent willingly—through a highly symbiotic relationship with their employer or clients, and the economy in general.

It is impossible to argue against the idea that if more people were able to make a living best suited to their own unique talents, the world would turn a little bit easier. Talent management is a worthy goal for any organization. It puts the right person in the right job at the right time, and it also attracts growth and builds opportunity. However, superior talent management not only produces the right talent at the right time for the organization, it also sparks innovation and spawns new industries, and creates brighter futures and sustainable improvements in the standard of living for everyone in the organization.

This book contains strategic, practical and proven best practices for designing, implementing and optimizing complex Web-based talent management systems at the organizational level. Many of the approaches and strategies suggested are basic requirements for organizations of almost every size and type. Others represent leading-edge strategies that will provide early adopters with a head start in the quest for competitiveness through exemplary talent management.

Connie Pascal
Principal, The Talent Market Group

Introduction

There has been a marked evolution in the critical factors that enable organizations to compete—from factories, equipment, land and capital since before the industrial revolution, to ideas, creativity, problem solving and innovation today. From things to people and from fixed assets to mobile assets.

In the July 2003 edition of *Harvard Business Review*, business professors Roger Martin and Mihnea Moldoveanu state: "In our knowledge-based economy, value is the product of knowledge and information. Companies cannot generate profits without the ideas, skills, and talent of knowledge workers, and they have to bet on people—not technologies, not factories, and certainly not capital."[1] To survive in the knowledge economy over the long term, organizations must become focused on and capable of managing employees as their most critical resource.

Workforce Dynamics

Knowledge and information workers now account for more than two-thirds of the U.S. workforce and that share is growing faster

---

[1] "Capital Versus Talent: The Battle That's Reshaping Business," *Harvard Business Review* (July 2003), 36.

than any other segment of the labor force. There is increasing recognition that the more knowledge- and information-intensive the industry, the more the reliance on its workforce as the key ingredient for success. In addition, workforce costs account for the largest component of U.S. business expenditures today.[2] In this context, industry competitiveness means that a great deal of attention must be paid to managing human capital assets exceptionally well in order to be successful.

But what does this mean? To date, despite plenty of CEOs claiming that talent is their most valuable resource, few companies operate as though talent and talent management are paramount. Organizations have found talent management—the ability to expertly attract, recruit, motivate, develop and retain staff—to be an intricate and complicated matter, and the majority, despite good intentions, have failed to develop enterprise-wide skills to do so. Almost nowhere has the notion of "talent first" penetrated the corporate culture, yet the prevailing environment indicates it must eventually *define* that culture.

As developed world economies have become increasingly information- and knowledge-oriented, job requirements have grown more demanding. Workers now require more education and skills than ever before as positions become more knowledge-based and information-intensive. Long gone are the days when most workers could be dealt with in bulk, like commodities. Today, virtually every full-time hire requires a search followed by careful screening and selection. Staffing takes more time because the consequences of good and bad hires are magnified. Recruiting, training and replacement costs are higher than ever. The cost of turnover is a staggering two to three times most knowledge workers' annual salary.

Beyond staffing, talent has to be managed throughout the entire employee life cycle. This means from hire through retire. Learning and development, performance and incentive management, employee retention, workforce planning and worker redeployment are all part of the new workforce science.

To make a difficult situation worse, the talent required by organizations is often in very short supply. Even during recent economic downturns, unemployment in the U.S. among college

---

[2]U.S. Census Bureau, Business Expenses Survey 1997, 14.

Introduction

graduates has averaged about 3 percent compared to well over 6 percent for the general population.[3] A rebound in the economy with a return to an overall unemployment rate of approximately 4 percent would bring with it a skills and talent shortage potentially worse than that of the late 1990s, and one that might persist for decades if demographic forecasts are accurate.

According to many demographers and labor market economists, including those at the Bureau of Labor Statistics, reduced growth in the labor force due to large-scale retirements and fewer youth entering the job market, combined with a sustained economic upswing and the inexorable demand for higher skills and knowledge, could produce a "perfect storm" in the labor markets later this decade or next.[4] As with most trends, this will occur gradually and there will be plateaus and dips in general and specific worker demand along the way. Given this emerging environment, workers will eventually become more secure about their prospects and the future due to greater demand for their talents. The result is that abundant opportunities fueled by pent-up demand will lead to a readiness to jump ship. Workers will likely be more connected to job boards and recruiters than they were in the tight labor markets of late 1990s. This will facilitate the exodus of talent from organizations that have not taken measures to stem the tide.

E-recruitment, workforce planning and other talent management technologies will be important, but they won't solve the problem. Organizations that routinely institute learning from best practices—especially those that fully know and understand their workforce and are familiar with the external labor market (potential candidates for positions who are presently not employed with the organization); those that practice aggressive (and selective) employee retention strategies (measures to keep the best staff); those that take a "total workforce" (all workers—external, salaried, hourly, temporary, independent contractors, etc.) approach to workforce development; and those that cultivate relationships with staff, alumni (former employees that it would like to rehire) and potential candidates—will have a significant advantage.

---

[3] Bureau of Labor Statistics historic unemployment rate tables. See www.bls.gov.

[4] See Nicole Stata: http://www4.hr.com/HRcom/index.cfm/116/5067F265-F624-4082-8E6A17BA6AEC04FD?ost=feature.

However, preparations must be made early to realize this advantage.

The premise of this book is twofold. First, because talent has become the most critical and important factor in competitiveness, it must be managed at least as carefully as any physical asset. Second, because becoming a talent management organization is so complex and difficult, it cannot be attempted without the aid of today's talent management technologies.

Talent management technologies come in various flavors. Some remain DOS-based or client-server oriented, meaning in part that they are delivered on an organization's network with software on the user's desktop. However, software to assist organizations in their efforts to recruit workers has evolved swiftly since the inception of the Web in 1994. Today, nearly every major vendor of e-recruitment solutions and talent management systems (TMSs) advertises a Web-based toolset that users can access easily through standard browsers like Netscape and Internet Explorer.

No industry has made better use of the Web and remote services delivery (otherwise known as application service provider or ASP) than human resources. This is particularly true of recruitment. Some of the Internet's best-known and most successful brands (for example, Monster, CareerBuilder and Yahoo! HotJobs) are career sites used by millions of job seekers and hundreds of thousands of employers. Where software solutions suppliers in many industries have failed or faltered in trying to deliver their products remotely via the Web, niche staffing software companies like Recruitsoft, IQNavigator and Recruitmax have proven the viability of delivering complex HR tools on the vendor-hosted/Web-delivery model most commonly referred to as ASP. Even the large enterprise resource planning (ERP) vendors that provide broad business software solutions, including PeopleSoft, Oracle and SAP, have made the move from client/server to fully Web-based platforms in the delivery of their talent management and most other HR products.

Despite unfavorable economic conditions in recent years, e-recruit and other human capital management (HCM) software companies have continued to push the envelope. Most notably, it is becoming possible for organizations to license or lease solutions that can help manage talent from the planning stages through recruitment, learning, performance and incentive management and beyond to redeployment, outplacement and alumni relations. These products offer a wide array of options and can interface with other Web-based and legacy HR solutions to automate and leverage increasingly more of an organization's HR processes.

By 2003, virtually every North American organization of at least 250 employees used one or more e-recruiting methods. Worldwide, 94 percent of Fortune 500 companies operated a corporate career site for recruiting.[5] Many mid-to-large-size companies, not-for-profits, and government departments have also discovered the efficiencies to be achieved by instituting best practices in total workforce management automation, including e-recruitment.

This book focuses on technologies, methods and best practices in staffing, retention and elements of learning, performance and workforce planning. Web services and protocols that facilitate data sharing and integration between disparate Web-based software at lower costs are examined. (We have included screenshots in the book. If you want to investigate the specific screenshot yourself by visiting the Wbsite, the URL has been provided to help you.) Also addressed is how ERP providers, TMS providers and others are designing products that attempt to address all aspects of the HR value chain, from candidate sourcing to hire, right through retirement and beyond. Solutions built through partnerships in which different suppliers' products and services are integrated and vendors, who through partnerships or acquisitions, are attempting to build comprehensive talent management solutions on their own, are explored in detail.

The Talent Management Process

Leading organizations view the talent management process as an ongoing, holistic and proactive exercise. Internet-based HCM products are supporting this philosophy in a number of ways. The best solutions are enabling the creation of tiered and pre-qualified talent pools (structured and screened candidate databases) to help turn recruiting into a longer-term, continuous

[5] See HR.com research results in Chapter 3 and iLogos Research (a division of Recruitsoft) at www.iLogos.com: "Global 500 Web Site Recruiting" 2003

and proactive relationship-building exercise for both internal and external talent.

While talent management is about all components of the workforce, including the potential workforce that exists outside the organization, it is principally an internally focused discipline. Unfortunately, most organizations currently pay too little attention to internal job mobility that can boost their competitiveness, efficiency and employee-retention efforts. Effective deployment and redeployment of employees is an emerging area of specialization within HR that requires solid workforce planning, analysis and skills/aptitude/interest tracking. It is essential that organizations develop the capacity to analyze their workforce and redeploy staff effectively. The typical company's growing requirements for workforce flexibility and its need to develop employee skills through developmental assignments means that people change jobs and careers inside organizations as frequently as they do outside.

TMS solutions are a necessary infrastructure to facilitate effective internal deployment of staff. By providing a forum for job postings and a means to capture employees' skills, competencies, aspirations, performance reviews, results from testing and so on, the organization gains knowledge that transforms redeployments from a guessing game to a fine-tuned process.

Another often-overlooked component of the workforce is contingent labor, normally defined as temporary help, contractors and some professional services. Software used for the recruitment and management of the contingent workforce is known as vendor management systems (VMSs) or contingent workforce management systems (CWMSs). These solutions are beginning to merge with those that help recruit and retain the permanent, salaried workforce and those that specialize in the acquisition of the hourly workforce. Integrated total workforce acquisition software will enable organizations to do all of their hiring, worker time and expense management and reporting from one solution. In the same vein, leading vendors are embedding workforce analytics (software to analyze data generated by TMS about the workforce) into e-recruit solutions so that companies can forecast and plan using accurate skills inventories, historical trend data and predictive models, giving them a near 360° view of their internal and external talent pools.

Trends

The concepts of proactive workforce planning, applicant screening and sorting, candidate assessment and acquisition, and talent retention, along with end-to-end HCM and integrated technologies and services, are shaping emerging best practices in talent management. Customers will be less inclined to purchase technologies that operate in isolation and are difficult to plug into their plans for integrated workforce optimization (the process of putting the right person in the right job at the right time). Progress in the development and adoption of data exchange standards like HR-XML (Human Resource-Extensible Markup Language) and greater migration to Web services platforms, including the use of .Net and J2EE (which assist in making disparate systems compatible for information sharing), will facilitate the trend.[6]

Established best practices from previous years will continue to influence consumers. Organizations will still look to vendors that have proven track records in their industry and in satisfying clients of similar size and needs. Buyers will still require vendors to satisfy concerns about their solutions, including functionality, implementation, integration and data security, and about their business stability, including economic viability and customer service questions. Customers will want ever-increasing control over the solutions they purchase, including powerful configuration tools that can be operated by trained, non-IT staff. Increasingly, buyers will not only ask for and check references, they will arrange on-site visits to see how solutions impact return on investment (ROI) and affect various users including HR professionals, recruiters, hiring managers and staff. Finally, when choosing ASPs, customers will request tours of data facilities to ensure that the vendor offers adequate network, physical and personnel security.

---

[6] Extensible Markup Language, or XML, is a coding language that describes data and is used to set standards across and between industries. For instance, in a resume, XML tags can describe the various possible fields captured so that HR technology developers can build their solutions to a common standard that will recognize a resume and its contents across all platforms and solutions. Once completed and universally adopted, HR-XML or a similar standard will facilitate document sharing and systems integration in the HR industry.

With few exceptions, and in contrast to the late 1990s, the fore-most staffing problem so far this decade is not sourcing candidates, but the screening, sorting and processing of a flood of applications. This may not change dramatically in the short-term, but should gradually give way to a more balanced challenge between screening and sourcing candidates if demographic projections of worker and skills shortages prove accurate. Still, even when the economy improves, organizations will have realized the ROI in advanced automated selection tools and they will not look back. The pressure on e-recruit vendors to develop additional and better screening, candidate self-selection and automated (i.e., online) assessment/testing tools will continue. Much of the ROI in e-recruitment today is found in methods by which companies accurately, fairly and ethically reduce the number of applicants they receive to a manageable list. The coming months and years will see rapid advances in scientific and valid screening and assessment technologies.

For large organizations that have implemented human resource management systems from ERP vendors like PeopleSoft, Oracle, SAP, Lawson and others, the question has been when and if these suppliers will offer first-rate talent management software that can truly challenge the solutions offered by niche vendors known as "pure plays" or "best of breed," who typically specialize in TMS solutions and offer nothing else. It is difficult to predict when pressure from ERP vendors, continued economic stagnation and/or other factors will produce consolidation among pure-play and best-of-breed e-recruitment vendors. As such, buyers must remain vigilant in selecting vendors that can demonstrate viability. In the same vein, they should not blindly, or by default, select their ERP vendor's e-recruitment and other TMS solutions. Nor should they look only at solutions from the biggest and best-known pure-play vendors when there may be opportunities for better fit and greater value from smaller, less-known suppliers.

Risks

It is clear that while e-recruitment and TMS technology can save time and money, much of it, and many of its vendors, will never gain a permanent foothold. Organizations run a substantial risk of wasting resources by pursuing the wrong solutions and/or vendors, or getting caught up in poorly planned and executed implementations. The following chapters discuss strategies to ensure companies perform proper due diligence in selecting technologies and processes that hold the most promise without constantly trailing the early adopters and suffering competitively as a result. Ideas and tools are identified that have either gained traction or will do so as a result of delivering real return on investment and giving their users some insurance against the future.

CHAPTER 1

卍

The New Primacy of Talent

Throughout history the bulk of human capital has been employed in physical labor. For centuries, a small, educated elite occupied positions of authority and leadership. There was little demand for knowledge workers[1] because wealth and prosperity were gained on the basis of physical resources and inexpensive, abundant and disposable labor. Assets were hard and fixed. They could be counted, touched, felt and controlled. More importantly, they could be managed using principles and techniques developed over the centuries, as evidenced by the difficulty of gaining wealth from a position of poverty and the reasonable assurance of preserving it for generations once it was obtained.

The birth of the modern age, with the French and American revolutions followed by British anti-slavery laws and the U.S. Civil War, hastened the end of centuries of feudalism and servitude. But it wasn't until the balance of western economic activity tipped away from repetitive factory and farm work and toward value-added goods and services and creative knowledge work that the demand for a better-educated workforce emerged. The trend away from manual skills to knowledge and creative abilities appeared in Europe and North America after World War II

---

[1] Knowledge workers are commonly defined as those with bachelor degrees or higher.

and has accelerated since. The implications for economies world-wide can be seen clearly in the differences between the idea-driven, value-added industries in developed countries today versus the primary, resource-intensive and labor-intensive industries that continue to predominate in the less-developed world.

As compensation for skilled workers has grown with demand, however, disparities in wealth have mushroomed everywhere. Not since the end of slavery have Americans been so divided along socio-economic lines.[2] Despite a still strong middle class, there is a striking similarity between the wealth and poverty of individuals today and in centuries past, and in the success and failure of organizations and nations themselves. Consider how closely aligned the well off and the poor were to possession or dispossession of land and financial inheritance in centuries past. Today, economic success is closely correlated with possession of skills and knowledge, which are the new currencies. Democratic, developed nations like the U.S. are meritocracies. Few of today's new upper class, or bourgeois bohemians (Bobos), as David Brooks refers to them in his best-selling book *Bobos in Paradise*, came by their status (status has implications beyond wealth) the old fashioned way—through inheritance.[3] Today's yuppies, Bobos and movers and shakers are invariably innovative, creative, skilled and likely to be very well educated. And, according to Brooks, their influence on nations greatly exceeds that of all other elements of society.

Just as knowledge work has grown in developed economies, industrial, manufacturing, agriculture, textiles, and many services have steadily moved offshore to developing economies that can still compete on low wages, long hours and poor working conditions. Take textiles, for example. The old mill towns that were once the backbone of both New England and old England have virtually disappeared (an ironic example can be found in Maynard, Massachusetts where Monster.com, the world's largest job board, now occupies a massive old mill complex that once

---

[2] Marion Wright Edelman, President of the Children's Defense Fund, "Following, Not Just Honoring King's Dream," *The Sacramento Observer* (September 5, 2003).

[3] BOBOs is a contraction of "bourgeois" and "bohemian." Brooks finds that America's new upper class is comprised of highly skilled and creative people with bohemian values and bourgeois tastes. *Bobos in Paradise: The New Upper Class and How They Got There* (New York: Simon & Schuster, 2000).

employed hundreds of textile workers). The manufacturing industry that remains in Europe and North America depends on fewer, more-skilled workers, while rote assembly is left to the machines. By contrast, knowledge work has grown dramatically in developed countries and will continue to do so, eventually expanding to dominate every economy on earth.[4]

Impact on Organizations

Organizations that once managed hard assets (land, factories, etc.) using time-proven methods and possessing the confidence that comes with intergenerational experience and knowledge find themselves today managing less of this type of asset and more of the fluid kind (ideas, knowledge, people and talent).

Unfortunately, the mantra that "our people are our most valuable asset" has become trite. This is so not because it isn't true for most organizations, but because it is often perceived by its intended audience as little more than lip service. Employees and others look for evidence where they know it counts—in annual reports, stock valuations and management actions. The problem is that no one really knows how to quantify human asset return on investment (ROI) for balance sheets. What is its precise and measured impact on organizational success as reflected in the stock market, for example? When analysts learn that a gold mining operation has a number of known and potential reserves in its properties, they know what to do with that information in terms of advising the investor community. But beyond the CEO and key executives, how can a company be compared with others in terms of its human assets? There is no good answer yet.

Some assets, particularly commodities, are easy to manage and measure. Human assets, at least today in advanced economies, are very rarely commodities. A true commodity is a product or service that is indistinguishable from supplier to supplier except on price, terms of delivery and other non-product

---

[4] U.S. Bureau of Labor Statistics data shows an increase in managerial and professional workers of almost 100 percent between 1940 and 2002 (from 18 percent to 32 percent of the total workforce), while manufacturing-related jobs declined from 48 percent of all positions to 28 percent over the same period.

quality-related factors. Pulp, various grades of fruit and vegetables, and industrial diamonds are examples. Some forms of labor are hired in a manner similar to purchasing commodities. Fruit and tobacco farmers in North America, for example, import labor from the Caribbean and Central America each year. In Jamaica, where participation in the farm workers' programs can make the difference between a year of poverty and one of comparative wealth, workers have historically been chosen not for their harvesting skills but for their political affiliations. If their party is in power, they might be chosen (depending on their level of support); if not, they stay home.

The important point is that the farmers who receive the workers have no guarantees of whom they're getting and to a large degree it doesn't matter. They know the average output they can expect from a group of workers and they plan accordingly. The work itself is manual and monotonous and it requires no special skills or aptitudes. Farmers have no need to receive or screen resumes, conduct interviews or compare references. In work such as this, one pair of hands is much like another. Farmers know that some workers will be unproductive or careless, some exceptional and the majority average. A farmer may offer incentives for the most productive workers, but for the most part it doesn't matter. Workers are valued not for their individual attributes but for their predictability as a group.

This used to be a very common labor scenario. Nowadays, examples of commodity labor this clear cut are becoming much harder to find. As economies in the developed world move away from their old manufacturing and natural resource bases and toward a growing dependency on skills, problem solving, innovation and knowledge, differentiation between workers widens.

The importance of choosing each worker as though he or she alone were a critical component of success becomes vital. Increasingly, organizations must be strategic about workforce management because the talent they find, attract, develop and retain is in almost every sense their only competitive advantage. Ironically, many organizations have become like commodities themselves, distinguished almost entirely by the quality of their workforce. For example, consider Southwest Airlines or Starbucks

Coffee, both highly profitable within their respective industries. Both companies are consistently voted by their employees as among the top companies to work for in the United States. Employees have responsibility for problem solving, for generating creative ideas, and for directly contributing to the way the company is run and how it operates. In a conference in Baltimore in early November 2003, Southwest Airlines' chairman and co-founder, Herb Kelleher described his company's approach to value creation. "If employees come first, they'll treat the customers well and everybody wins. That's how you create shareholder value." The differences between companies like Southwest and their competitors are manifested in their balance sheets and brands. Southwest, once a tiny regional player, is now worth more than all of its competitors combined.[5]

The impact of this paradigm shift on organizations, even though it is occurring gradually, is immense. Until very recently, large corporations recruited all workers, even white-collar professionals, for attributes that had little to do with their ability to leverage the company's competitiveness. Loyalty, the willingness to follow orders, patience and an ability to fit within a rigid hierarchy were most sought after. Workers conformed, for the most part, making recruitment, selection and retention largely administrative functions performed by personnel departments. Gradually, as individual skills and capacity to contribute grew in importance, the field of human resources was born. Soon, human resources may be eclipsed itself as organizations realize that the management of talent must be elevated in importance again, such that it becomes the first priority for all supervisors, managers and executives throughout the organization. Indeed, a recent trend to promote managers from other disciplines into the most senior human resources positions is indicative.

Today, in most industries, the majority of hiring requires a great deal of planning, analysis, sourcing and careful selection, followed by the necessity to motivate, develop, reward and retain top talent after hiring. No HR department can be responsible for all of it. Rather, it is the HR department's responsibility to lead the entire organization along the path of becoming a strategic talent management organization.

[5] Eric Reguly, *The Globe and Mail Report on Business*, November 15, 2003.

The Talent Management Organization

Organizations today are blazing paths for their counterparts of the future. It may sound exciting, but in the trenches of most companies it is a tough slog. As frustrating as it is for organizations to manage their talent, the fact that talent can't be controlled and kept like many other resources is more challenging still. Talent is fluid; it is the type of resource that can leave whenever it desires.

If talent can be shown to drive company valuations, it should be evident in professional sports franchises. Consider the New York Yankees, one of sports' most valuable franchises, recently valued at almost US$1 billion.[6] At first glance, one might look at its roster of superstars and conclude that its value is tied entirely to its talent. But this is not so. The Yankees are valuable for their mythology, their history of winning, their sales of merchandise and a loyal fan base—their brand, in other words. The talent is mobile, it can leave of its own free will (even despite contracts) and it does so frequently. Its contribution is immense but it only adds to overall franchise value over time and only if it performs at consistently high levels.

The fact that the Yankees are worth so much today has as much to do with the team's superstars of the past century as its current talent. The Yankees have a history of winning thanks to the culture of talent the organization has developed and nurtured over the decades. However, the talent at any given time is only worth the sum of the team's payroll. If more convincing evidence is required, consider the correlation of baseball talent (as measured by payroll) to team success in Major League Baseball (MLB). Across the entire league from 1995 to 2002 the analysis shows a positive correlation (a direct causation) of less than .5. A correlation score of 1.0 indicates a perfect positive correlation, or a direct cause and effect, while a score of 0 means a perfect negative correlation (no relationship whatsoever). This means that those teams with the highest payroll, which is an excellent indication of talent in baseball, had an above-average but not overwhelming propensity to succeed according to a correlation analysis using seven years of recent win/loss data.[7] Payroll is certainly an indicator of success in MLB, but it is hardly convincing.

---

[6] See Forbes annual survey of MLB's finances, 2003.

[7] See http://twinstakes.bonnes.com.

Yet professional sports franchises are extremely careful about who they recruit. Few CEOs, let alone other employees, are scouted and studied as carefully with respect to their potential role in the organization as the least important pitcher on a Major League Baseball team. Baseball's talent scouts spend their careers getting to know each of their prospects in exacting detail, from the speed of their fastballs to what they eat for breakfast and everything in between.

If even the most obvious and meticulous markets for talent can't provide examples for business, then what can? The key does not appear to be in trying to fit talent assets into the mold of immediately quantifiable value that applies to physical, financial and other assets. Take a step back and consider MLB as a whole. It is valuable based on its talent across all the franchises. There are numerous professional baseball leagues worldwide, offering very high levels of play. None, however, compares with MLB in quality. This is for one reason only—the best in Japan, Latin America and even Cuba want nothing more than to play and prove themselves in the big leagues. MLB has established itself as the preeminent baseball league to such a degree that there are no challengers. It has done so by always finding room for the best and by mercilessly culling those that can no longer contribute at the required levels. This model of talent management may appear primitive and basic, but it is elegant and advanced at the same time. It is effective at the franchise level and extremely effective at the league level, yet it may be impossible to pull off outside of professional sports and entertainment.

Baseball is far less complex than the business environment that most organizations operate in. In baseball, teams that manage and motivate their talent most effectively usually have winning seasons, barring the bad luck of injuries. In business, there are many more pitfalls. Organizations cannot just hire great talent and solid leaders and expect to become great. Yet this does not mean that the management, motivation, development and retention of talent are not worthwhile. Part of the problem is that there are few examples of organizations that manage talent effectively. Those that do, such as General Electric and SAS have outperformed their rivals significantly in the past decade or so. GE and SAS are vastly different, but each in its own way manages its talent extraordinarily well compared to others. They have been recognized for it and featured in everything from business magazines and books to television newsmagazines. Better still, both have built measurable and systematic value through talent management.

The lessons from the New York Yankees, MLB, and companies like GE and SAS are that talent should not be expected to carry an immediately quantifiable asset value in the same sense that a gold mine or even the prospect of one does. Organizations can be valued for their talent, but not as the sum of the "scores" each of their employees measures on some fictional talent meter. Rather, an organization should be assessed on its ability to manage talent—on its effectiveness in becoming a talent management organization. The benefits of an organization's success in talent management can only be determined and realized over time.

Talent is the most important asset in knowledge-based organizations because only talent can build the brand equity that creates value in the long run. While we may not be able to point to precise ROI in talent management as far as the bottom line, we can safely say that talent builds world-class products and services, nurtures customer relationships and invents new processes and improves existing ones. Talent inspires, coaches and leads. Talent builds the organization's reputation, and over time companies and organizations of all stripes will or won't become valuable because of talent.

Asset: A Valuable Item That Is Owned

People are complex and unique. Even if such a thing as a vacuum removing all external, non-work-related stimuli could be created, it would be impossible to predict a person's success. When you take an "A" player from one organization to another and add new environments, a different work culture, unfamiliar managerial styles, new colleagues and a new supervisor (in particular), any number of factors can influence performance, and the negative impacts on a person are generally thought to be cumulative. That is, a poor manager on top of a new and incompatible culture can easily turn a star into a struggler.

Yet hiring top performers depends largely on one's ability to make predictions of future success based on past performance. This brings us back to the Major League Baseball example. It is very likely that if the average person (one who does not follow baseball very closely) were asked to predict which teams would have the most success in a coming season, almost everyone would do the same thing—they would simply refer to the previous year's results and make their predictions accordingly. To a baseball aficionado, comparing each team's current roster of talent might seem to be a better approach (though not overly predictive as we've seen above).

In fact, both approaches would produce poorer than expected predictions. Again, using data from 1995 to 2002 there is only a .42 correlation between previous year success and current year success.[8] This is an even worse predictor than examining the depth of talent a team possesses. Again, the sports industry represents a far less complicated field than everyday workplaces. In sports, the goals are clear, the majority of players love their jobs and all players have highly specialized roles that they know well, having most likely performed them since early childhood. The players follow a relatively small number of signals or patterns in a playbook. Culture differs somewhat, but in comparison to the business world, is relatively similar from team to team. Teammates have a great deal in common professionally and in many other respects, making movement to another organization much less bewildering. Why, then, can a team go from "first to worst" in one season (or the opposite), even when much of the talent remains the same? Why if I recruit last year's most valuable player is there a strong possibility that he or she will become merely good or even average in the space of one year?

In the business world, top performers often become average (or worse) after they move to another company. Sometimes their performance deteriorates even when they stay put. The employment dynamic, combined with human complexity, is too volatile to lend itself to predictability. Excellent leadership and motivation has proven to be the best method to cope, but the truth is that star performers become so (and cease to be) for hundreds of different reasons, some of which the employer has no control over. Employees, being unpredictable and mobile, should therefore *not* be considered an organization's most valuable "asset" in

---

[8] Ibid.

the sense that if I gather the best talent I will necessarily have the most successful organization. Talent must be viewed as the most indispensable ingredient for success, but success also depends on how that talent is managed.

But Can Talent Be Managed as a Resource?

Talent can be managed like assets, but requires a substantially different approach, and one that has not been fully defined. Talent management techniques will never be as precise and predictable as hard asset management. However, the central argument of this book, and much other research, is that for an organization to survive the challenges of business cycles, global competition and shifting demographics, it *must* manage its talent at least as well as its competitors. To become a market leader, it must become expert at talent management.

Talent management cannot be measured against the same thin error tolerance and metrics used elsewhere in business, but much of the technique is the same. For example, like asset management, talent management begins with planning.

The workforce must first be analyzed. Its growth or reduction and its development and redeployment must be planned. The first step in talent management is to gain a solid understanding of the internal workforce. In a knowledge economy where skills requirements change frequently and are rising inexorably, finding and deploying the right talent for the task, at the right time, can be incredibly challenging. In large organizations with thousands of employees and hundreds of discrete jobs, just knowing the collective skill set and aspirations of employees is something few organizations can claim. Worse still, jobs are posted and candidates are hired for them without anyone ever looking to determine the full blend of skills and other characteristics needed for success. That can only mean that hiring in these circumstances is done based on other considerations such as first impressions, nepotism or flawed, reactive hiring processes. This is due to the absence of technologies and practices that are necessary for quality hiring and repeatable, ever-improving talent management processes.

Many will argue that external candidates should be hired for company fit rather than job fit. This idea has merit, but what about people already hired? How should they be redeployed to develop their careers and to optimize talent internally?

The further an organization is on the scale of requiring brains over brawn and skilled workers over commodities in its workforce, the more sophisticated its talent management capabilities must be. And, insofar as talent is the greatest competitive instrument, skills, competencies and aspirations are its building blocks. If skills are to talent as investments are to wealth, then why can most investors list their holdings in detail, often from memory, while human resource departments usually don't have even a basic concept of the skills at their organizations' disposal?

As harsh as that sounds, it is not meant as criticism. Large organizations possess thousands, even hundreds of thousands of collective skills and competencies. Each employee has his or her own career aspirations and may not share them with the organization unless prompted to do so (and, if not invited to, may seek career fulfillment elsewhere). In large organizations it would be impossible to collect and track information of this magnitude without the aid of technology.

With the data collected by talent management technologies, workforce planning becomes possible. Planning is continuous. It is the umbrella under which the rest of talent management occurs, including the sourcing, selection, development, retention and redeployment best practices discussed throughout this book.

Figure 1.1: The Talent Management Continuum

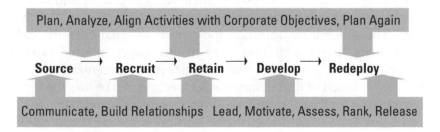

The talent management continuum suggests the need to view workforce management as an ongoing process that repeats, starting with planning. A workforce plan is a variable instrument that differs from organization to organization depending on their needs and structure. However, it should always include a means to map available and potential talent to broad and precise business objectives. For example, it should include a forecast of external recruitment (including positions and skills), training, redeployment, developmental assignments, succession plans and promotions, and elimination of positions. Forecasts should be in alignment with the organization's plan for expansion or contraction corporately and also at departmental and unit levels.

What happens after a strategic workforce plan is in place? In an ideal world, this is when sourcing new hires, training and redeployment should begin. In the real world, an organization that decides to become strategic with respect to talent management will have to do so in the midst of legacy processes and ongoing cycles. In other words, people will be hired and others will leave, some will find new jobs inside the organization, training will progress and so on. The good news is that there is no wrong time to transform the processes. Talent management (and mismanagement) is a continuum, whether it is done well or not.

If an organization is growing, the workforce plan will inform better sourcing and hiring decisions. Talent will be selected based on its ability to help deliver on corporate objectives. Retention of key existing talent (top and above-average performers) will be paramount. Most organizations recruit externally before even considering inside talent, due to factors such as a corporate culture in which managers don't want to fight to hold on to their best performers and other managers' attempts to recruit these performers are seen as "poaching." The strategic organization looks at its internal capacity and individuals' career aspirations and it encourages internal career mobility. The sophisticated talent management organization will know how much of the organization's objectives can be met through redeployment of staff, employee development and external recruitment (full-time or contingent) and it will understand the tangible and intangible (hard and soft) costs associated with its decisions. Wherever possible, it will encourage employees to fulfill their career aspirations inside the organization by giving them the opportunity to compete for promotions, lateral moves and developmental assignments freely. This is about achieving balance, however, between fostering internal career mobility and external recruitment in order to build and manage a workforce on the best available talent. In meeting overall workforce planning needs, a process unfolds that recognizes internal skills gaps in relation to staffing needs and informs external recruitment strategies as well as internal redeployment.

The Talent Management Imperative: People and Technology

Human resources is evolving as organizations place greater and greater emphasis on talent. It is becoming a more vital function in organizations, and with advances in metrics and human capital value equations, one that will soon be able to quantify its contribution to the bottom line. Nevertheless, it is apparent that most HR departments are not getting larger, despite there being a great deal more to be done in most companies in order to compete on talent now and in future.

Excellence in talent management is complex; the data collection and management elements are enormous and proper analysis of the data is even more challenging. Recruitment management, performance management, learning management and incentive management are multifaceted initiatives deserving of their own full-time specialists. Even if the goal of world-class talent management is removed, most organizations expect HR to improve efficiencies and "do more with less." In either case, HR departments have no choice but to acquire and use modern HR technologies. Streamlined processes and efficiency gains are obviously possible in the absence of technology but are just as obviously severely restricted in potential. The only question is what technology to choose and how best to leverage that technology both tactically and strategically.

This is not to say that technology is the greater part of the equation. In fact, the 80/20 rule (80 percent human effort versus 20 percent technology) applies equally well to talent management as it does to other disciplines. HR technology is necessary in order for many small and all mid-to-large-size organizations to compete nowadays, but capacity must exist within the organization to deploy and use the technologies effectively.

The Evolution of HR in the Organization

The need for human resources specialists arises as organizations grow and become more complex. Normally the HR function evolves along with the sophistication of the organization in general. In other words, the new HR department almost always focuses on handling transactional and administrative tasks that mushroom as the organization grows. These tasks include payroll and benefits administration; regulatory compliance issues (employment equity, etc.); on-boarding of new hires; terminations; pension administration; relocation; grievance administration; and training administration to name just a few. Gradually, the department broadens its focus to include consultation with hiring managers on staff selection, performance evaluation, discipline and termination.

In most large and established organizations, the HR department has also evolved to include a strategic component. This division concerns itself with research, benchmarking and best practices so that it can guide the organization in critical matters involving strategic staffing; targeted retention; variable compensation tied to business objectives, performance and retention; employment branding (positioning the image of the company with current and potential employees); incentive management; and workforce analytics and planning, among other things.

All HR departments in mid- to large-size organizations should have a strategic component. Indeed, among very large organizations there is a slight but distinctly growing trend to HR business process outsourcing (BPO), in which the entire HR department (except strategy and consultative activities) is handed off to a third party to operate under service level agreements and negotiated metrics or targets. HR departments have been outsourcing components of the discipline for several decades, most frequently including payroll and benefits, staffing, and health and welfare, but the HR BPO trend is different. The BPO decision is taken in part to save money and improve processes, but also in the explicit expectation that HR should offload all transactional and administrative work so that it can focus exclusively on strategy, playing a consultative role to other departments and managing vendor relationships (i.e., with the human resource outsourcer [HRO] or HR BPO).

Strategic thinking and planning, combined with expert consultative capacity, represents the ultimate evolution of the modern human resources function in large organizations. For organizations that ignore it and those that have no capacity for strategic workforce analysis and management, the future will hit hard. Like deer caught in the headlights, HR will look up from its databases and forms to see a juggernaut called "retention crisis," or perhaps even "talent crisis," hurtling toward them. They will be unprepared to manage the crises and the organization will be rudderless because no one foresaw and planned for inevitable change.

Demographic Certainties

The labor force is composed of workers within defined age groups roughly made up of people between the ages of sixteen and sixty-five. Demographers can predict how many youth will be entering the workforce and how many seniors will be leaving in any given period with high accuracy. Immigration levels are more volatile but can also be predicted accurately. It is a demographic certainty that, due to declining birth rates and an aging population, workforce growth will decline for the next several decades across North America and the workforce will actually contract in Japan and in much of western Europe. This will take place even if, as appears very likely, more seniors put off retirement for several years beyond age sixty-five, immigration levels remain constant and the trend to offshore outsourcing accelerates.

The number of new jobs created by the economy and the number of jobs lost are far less predictable. Productivity improvements, which reduce the need for workers, are also subject to unpredictable forces such as technology breakthroughs or their absence. Historically, productivity has been trending up sharply since the end of World War II. In fact, despite an economy that has grown eight times in size since 1948, the U.S. workforce has merely doubled in size. Worker productivity growth of 400 percent since 1948 has made up the slack.[9]

---

[9] U.S. Department of Labor, Bureau of Labor Statistics.

As unlikely as a general worker shortage seems, there is a near unanimous belief among government, academia and other analysts that a labor shortage is looming, and that it will begin within the next few years, gradually worsening through at least 2030. Whether or not a broad, general talent crisis is in the cards, it is certain that specific skills shortages will continue and probably expand.

In good and poor economies over the past fifteen to twenty years, unemployment among professionals and others that are considered knowledge workers has been below that which many economists agree is the "natural" rate of unemployment—that caused by workers transitioning from one job to the next or from school to work (usually defined as 4 percent of the workforce).

There are already serious shortages in the health care industry and across many professions and skilled trades. Despite the hit the manufacturing industry has taken in the last few years, the U.S. National Association of Manufacturers has recently warned that "manufacturing could soon experience a shift from merely having a talent shortage to facing a serious labor crisis." The premier of Alberta, Canada has stated that skilled worker shortages are the greatest threat to developing the local tar sands oil reserves (deposits that rival those in Saudi Arabia)—and this at a time when North America desperately needs alternatives to Middle Eastern oil. In the neighboring province of Saskatchewan, a 2003 report on immigration concluded that in order to stem the tide of a shrinking labor force and population, it would need to adopt immigration policies the province had in place a century ago—a period during which Saskatchewan welcomed hundreds of thousands of immigrants into what was then a near-empty land.[10] It is very likely that skills shortages will become labor shortages in some pockets, perhaps at the municipal, regional or even national levels (such as Spain, Italy and possibly Japan) in years to come.

In North America, there are industries and occupations in which a talent crisis is the norm. The reasons for this aren't as important as the fact itself. The economic laws of supply and demand might eliminate shortages in occupations quickly in completely free markets, but some industries, such as health care,

---

[10] The Canadian Press, "Sask. must adopt bold immigration strategies: Report" (October 1, 2003).

are regulated to varying degrees and budgets are always constrained, keeping salaries for nurses and others artificially low. Other occupations, such as in the skilled trades, suffer from perception problems and well-meaning but unhelpful advice from parents and guidance counselors who encourage nearly every young person to pursue professional aspirations.

In general, worker shortages and surpluses follow economic cycles, not demographics. The bigger question then, is what will happen in the next cycle of broad economic expansion. Scanning back through the pundits' predictions in 1998 through 2000, one would have thought the good times would last forever. Economists and futurists were declaring an end to economic boom and bust cycles that had characterized western economies for over 150 years. Needless to say, they were wrong. Officially, the recession that began in 2000 was mild, yet the rebound has been termed by the press a "job-loss recovery." Although unemployment rates were low between 2000 and 2003 (at about 6 percent to 6.5 percent) relative to other bust cycles, workers in the United States were increasingly concerned for their jobs. This was demonstrated by a steady decline in consumer confidence and spending (which, despite historically low interest rates, reached its lowest point in over ten years in 2003).

The expectation is that because economies are cyclical, they will gradually come out of their malaise into new periods of expansion (and vice versa). However, given the current geopolitical situation, horrendous consumer debt, a massive trade deficit, and deep U.S. federal and state budget deficits, the chance of a quick return to an economy rivaling the boom years between 1997 and 2000 is compromised. Nevertheless, there is no reason to believe that the first recession of the new millennium will be the one that marks the end of cyclical economies. A strong recovery including a rebound in worker demand will arrive whether in 2004 or beyond, and when it does it will bring new demands for talent as fast-expanding economies always have.

The problem for employers, however, is that the next prosperous period may overlap with a demographic-driven shortage of workers. In his novel *The Perfect Storm*, Sebastian Junger describes how independent meteorological phenomena converged on the same place at the same time, creating the storm of the century and punishing many who were caught unaware.

Experts are now warning employers and policy makers that a similar convergence of independent economic factors might contribute to the labor market's storm of the century within a few years. Fears of an impending shortage of workers, despite general labor surpluses at present, have their roots in the latter part of the last decade.

Over 20 million jobs were added to the U.S. economy between 1990 and 2000, but growth in the labor force could not keep pace and the shortfall in skilled workers was made up only through the recruitment of foreign talent. Recruiters will recall just how tight the labor market became. Many companies, and some industries in general, were held back due to their inability to field enough talent in the right places at the right times. Wages, bonuses, benefits and other incentives skyrocketed, particularly in industries such as IT and locations like Silicon Valley and Boston where workers were most in demand.

In 2001, this period of heightened demand gave way to an era of mass layoffs among many of the same skilled workers who were in such demand only months earlier. No one knows for sure what scenario to expect this decade. In its projections released in December 2001 for 2000–2010 net new job growth, the U.S. Bureau of Labor Statistics (BLS) estimated a 15 percent increase. That is slightly less than the 17 percent growth in net new jobs recorded between 1990 and 2000.[11] Nevertheless, this would account for over 22 million net new jobs this decade—mostly in the knowledge worker portion of the economy.

The same report stated that overall labor force growth between 2000 and 2010 in the U.S. is expected to account for an additional 17 million workers (slightly more than were added in the 1990 to 2000 period). Using simple math, and ignoring numerous factors that are impossible to predict (such as prolonged or recurring economic stagnation), this suggests that the gap between the number of jobs and the number of workers will increase by about 5 million between 2000 and 2010. Since 2000 BLS statistics showed 145.5 million jobs and a labor force of only 140.9 million workers, the total shortage becomes about 10 million workers.

It is important to remember that the number of available workers does not equate to the number of employed individuals,

---

[11] See www.bls.gov.

however. An unemployment rate of 4 percent in 2000 meant that there would have been about 5.7 million more jobs unfilled. However, this number was more than offset by the millions of workers who held two or more jobs, which, in part, accounts for the overall gap. Most of the remaining difference between the number of jobs and number of workers consists, as seems logical, of jobs that employers would fill if they could find people to do them for the compensation they are willing to pay. As Dr. Peter Cappelli of the Wharton School of the University of Pennsylvania states in a recent article entitled *Will There Really Be a Labor Shortage?*, surveys indicating that employers have job openings that they have not filled are sometimes used inappropriately to suggest that there is a labor shortage. Cappelli is referring to the manner in which statistics are gathered concerning employers' hiring intentions. Employers aren't always asked to estimate how many workers they intend to hire; rather they are often asked how many they would like to hire for the amount of work they have—a significant difference. Cappelli uses himself as an example by saying he would have a cook, a maid and a gardener if they were willing to work for the trifling wages he could pay. Similarly, most employers would take on additional workers if they could obtain them for next to nothing.

The BLS projections may also be compromised in other ways. Economic prospects for this decade were damaged by the events of September 11, 2001 and may be further affected by domestic and geopolitical events (such as the Iraq War) and beyond. The BLS projections for the decade were prepared before September 11, 2001 and are almost certainly optimistic (in terms of net new jobs added) as a result. However, despite this and the concerns raised above, if the BLS projections are close, and if present retirement trends continue, it appears more likely than not that there will be broader skills shortages and even pockets of general worker shortages in some industries and regions by 2010 and that these shortages will be greater than those leading up to 2000.

Leading up to 2010, we are likely to see wider skills shortages across more occupations and industries. Large numbers of youth will be entering the labor force throughout this decade and the percentage of workers aged forty-five to sixty-four and beyond will grow. In the first decade of the twenty-first century, there may be a dearth of talent in the mid-career ranges (roughly thirty-five- to forty-five-year olds). Thus, finding experienced professionals and middle managers may become much more difficult. However, filling entry-level positions should be somewhat easier through 2010 than during the period from 1990 to 2000.

As is almost always true, workers with the right skills in hot industries, whether in IT, health care, education, biotech or something new, will be extremely difficult to recruit. A full-blown talent crisis will occur only when the shortages become widespread across most occupations and industries, rather than just a few. This partly describes the situation in most of the latter part of the 1990s and into 2000 when unemployment rates fell well below 4 percent across the United States. During that period, record numbers of skilled workers, particularly in engineering and IT, were recruited from outside the U.S. to fill the gaps. However, recruiters may not be able to tap into foreign talent markets as easily or in the same manner this decade as they did during the last.

Competition for Foreign Skilled Workers

Despite potential worker shortages, the United States is in the best shape of all Organisation for Economic Co-operation and Development (OECD) countries in terms of workforce growth. In the U.S., labor force growth has only slowed, while in other OECD countries it has declined precipitously. Soon, that growth will stop altogether. In a few countries, the labor force will actually shrink. Canada and Great Britain are only slightly worse off than the U.S., but parts of western Europe and Japan may face grave problems very soon. This means that American employers can expect more competition for skilled workers from supply countries like China and India, particularly if Japan loosens its rigid barriers to foreign workers.

The U.S. is a magnet for would-be immigrants from all over the world, and the BLS predicts that net migration will continue to account for a significant portion of U.S. labor force growth. But, it also predicts that immigration will fall from about 980,000 in 2002 to 720,000 in 2010. When governments from Germany to Italy and from Canada to Australia start providing more and better incentives, attracting the best and brightest to the U.S. will not be as easy as it has been in the past, especially in the quantities needed for particular skills. Furthermore, the governments of "talent supply" countries have already decried the brain drain they experienced during the last labor shortage. They will resist an exodus of their best and brightest in the next round and will be better prepared to defend their resources through intervention with demand countries and, more significantly, by positioning themselves to attract work that can be done in the home country on behalf of firms that might have required skilled migrants otherwise. As a result, and to save money, North American and European companies will outsource a greater proportion of their work offshore, a trend that has accelerated sharply since 2001.

Assuming that technological breakthroughs do not vastly increase worker productivity, employers may have to work harder to entice more of the population into the workforce. Older workers, aged forty-five to sixty-four, for example, will constitute the largest growth segment in the labor market between 2000 to 2010. The U.S government is slowly raising the age at which social security can be accessed, to sixty-seven from sixty-five. This will keep some older workers in the labor force longer. Already, men aged sixty-five to seventy-four are remaining in the labor market in greater numbers. The participation of older workers in the labor force will likely grow even faster this decade given the erosion of private pension plans due to the stock market collapse of 2001, the lower percentage of employers offering generous, fixed benefit pension schemes (money *and* health coverage), and the unprecedented level of debt carried by the American worker. Should a severe talent shortage occur, better incentives and compensation will keep older workers engaged longer and will entice many others out of retirement. As Dr. Cappelli advises, even a small increase in the number of older workers choosing to remain in the workforce will have a large effect on any potential labor shortages due to the sheer size of the cohort.[12]

At the other end of the spectrum, as alluded to above, recruiters should have fewer problems attracting entry-level workers this

---

[12] Peter Cappelli, "Will There Really be a Labor Shortage?" *Organizational Dynamics* (September 2003).

decade. Young workers, those aged sixteen to twenty-four, are expected to increase by 2.4 million between 2000 and 2010, which is a much higher figure than in the previous two decades. Nevertheless, employers may find the next generation of workers to be a fickle and less committed group. They have seen their parents and older siblings downsized and have been told throughout their young lives to expect to have several careers with many different employers. Moreover, surveys of this generation reveal an attitude toward work/life balance that may have some "old school" managers shaking their heads at an apparent lack of ambition and commitment. And, according to broad surveys of the workforce done by Spherion in 1999 and in 2003, workers' attitudes are shifting quickly toward a theme of career self-reliance and loyalty to coworkers rather than employers.[13] Like the generation before it, this generation will become the best-educated cohort in history. Higher education, particularly in knowledge-based economies, translates to higher worker productivity. Thus, they might get more done in less time once they do start work, but many will not enter the labor market until their mid- to late 20s because of their pursuit of advanced degrees and diplomas.

Finding educated and experienced mid-career workers may be the biggest challenge. The BLS predicts workers aged thirty-five to forty-four will decline by 3.8 million and those aged forty-five to fifty-four will grow only very slightly in number through 2010. The lifeblood of many organizations are its thirty-five- to forty-four-year olds. This group contains the majority of future senior managers and leaders and is usually the age range at which workers are the most productive. As the next economic expansion heats up, competition for talent in this age range—mid-career professionals, in other words—may be intense.

Much of the hype surrounding pending labor shortages in the media is exaggerated. Nevertheless, the BLS and the majority of other rigorous demographic analysis points to a problem beginning in the first decade of the twenty-first century that has the potential to be worse in scope and length than the shortages experienced in the late 1990s. Even under the more depressing

---

[13] Spherion Emerging Workforce Study, 1999, 2003.

scenario, in which 6 percent or higher unemployment becomes the norm with talent surpluses in many areas, organizations will still benefit from knowing their workforce thoroughly. The more that is known about the skills and attributes required and which contribute the most to employee success in the organization, the easier it will be to apply strategic staffing, retention initiatives and intelligent screening filters so that the right talent can be hired, trained, retained and deployed both in times of talent surplus and talent shortages.

If, as is more likely, the economy improves and talent is harder to come by, solid workforce planning and analysis begun today will position organizations well. Those that continuously monitor and develop the talent they possess, and establish relationships with external talent, will have the knowledge and means to recruit and retain strategically and in alignment with corporate objectives. For organizations that do not address the problem, the future may be bleak, even if talent shortages do not materialize to the extent forecast. An article in *BusinessWeek* magazine in October 2003 offered several opinions of the coming talent retention problem: Sibson Consulting was quoted as saying one out of six workers in the U.S. is ready to bolt. And Accenture was quoted as saying that half of all U.S. middle managers are actively looking for new jobs or will be soon.[14]

Organizations will be compelled to adjust to changing workforce demographics and the shifting priorities of workers. If, as seems likely, the trend to later retirement grows, the workplace will be composed not only of more fifty- and sixty-year olds but also more sixty-five- and seventy-year olds. Demand for flexible schedules, part-time work, telecommuting, phased retirement and other benefits will grow. At the same time, youth will likely demand a separate roster of benefits centered on work/life balance and developmental opportunities.

---

[14] Louis Lavelle, "Coming Next: A War For Talent," *Business Week* (October 1, 2003).

Conclusions

Talent is the most critical component of success in today's economy, yet no proven formula exists to manage it or even measure its precise impact. Nevertheless, the challenges of this decade and those to come require that in order to become or stay competitive, organizations and their human resources departments in particular must become strategic where the selection, development and retention of talent is concerned. HR must take the lead in becoming a "talent management organization," and to do so it must invest in and leverage modern HR technologies to the fullest.

Purchases of technology to aid in recruitment, retention and other talent management processes should be based on documented strategies and plans that are revisited as often as necessary. No mid- to large-size employer should select a talent management solution vendor that does not demonstrate a commitment to the development of strategic software to aid in workforce optimization. A frictionless, organization-wide labor market can be made possible only by using end-to-end talent management technologies, and doing so expertly.

A recruitment and retention strategy that is informed by a deep understanding of what skills, competencies and potential the organization possesses and those that it needs to execute on its strategy is a must in order to face whatever challenges arise in future. This includes a general knowledge of the external talent market and an expert knowledge of where the types of workers required can be found and how they can be brought into the organization when required.

Some industries and some employers face talent supply crises now. Specific worker shortages will increase, and, at some point, may give way to a more generalized problem. It is safe to predict that almost all employers of skilled workers, professionals, knowledge workers, and even hourly and unskilled labor will face periods in which they cannot, without great effort, find all the talent they need when they need it. Despite the unlikelihood of a sudden, critical labor shortage, organizations must plan for specific hiring needs and put in place the technology and methods to make their talent management processes as efficient and competitive as possible.

CHAPTER 2

꿿

Best Practices in Technology-Enabled Talent Management

In Chapter 1, we examined the historic, economic and demographic evidence that talent has become the prime lever in competitiveness for modern business. We concluded that the focus of today's human resources challenges have moved beyond processing payroll and benefits toward that of strategic talent management. Like payroll and benefits processing, though, talent can be managed much more effectively with modern HR technologies. This chapter attempts to summarize the best practices in selecting, implementing and using those technologies. Subsequent chapters will look at each type of technology in greater detail.

Online Recruiting and the Birth of Talent Management Systems

Electronic recruitment is a constantly changing field, driven by fast-evolving technologies and new methods. Online recruiting dates from around 1994, but e-recruitment technologies have been on the market for almost twenty years. Early technology included client-server applications and the use of BBS systems (electronic bulletin boards).

In 1981, J. Paul Costello and Lars Perkins produced the world's first applicant tracking system, called Restrac. This early tool was followed into the marketplace by Resumix in 1988. Restrac and Resumix were the first truly automated and commercial resume-tracking tools. By scanning paper and e-mailed resumes and using optical character recognition (OCR), it became possible for organizations to warehouse thousands of resumes for retrieval at a later date using search tools.

Restrac and Resumix worked by extracting skills and other information from each resume scanned into the database, and allowing recruiters to perform keyword matches to generate candidate lists from the database. Time and hiring costs decreased overnight and sales ranging from US$50,000 to over US$1,000,000 per implementation in corporations and government agencies mushroomed for both companies.

Though these client/server resume-tracking applications were advanced in their day (and are still in use), they had many shortcomings. Among them was the softwares' inability to recognize patterns or to exhibit intelligence of any sort in search results. When job seekers were advised about how to make effective applications to companies that used such technology, they were told to throw out the old rules. Nicely formatted resumes were out of fashion. Instead applicants were advised to cram as much skill information and as many skill-type keywords into their resumes as possible. They were told not to worry about appearance because the main hurdle was getting past the computer, not a person.

First-generation e-recruit/applicant tracking tools could not reliably retrieve the best candidates from a large resume database, however. One problem was the way they were used by most organizations. After candidates entered the database (applying for an advertised position) they were told they would be contacted if a position suitable to their skills/qualifications arose. Unfortunately, if the software did not extract the precise skill the organization was looking for from a resume, that person would not be screened in. For example, a skilled technical writer might describe his or her experience as follows: "wrote users' manual for accounting software package" or "developed manual for servicing industrial lathe component," but unless the applicant specifically listed "technical writer" as a skill or competency, he or she would not be returned in the search.

Beyond too literal a search, first-generation e-recruit tools suffered from the necessity that all resumes had to be processed either by scanning and OCR, or by data extraction tools, an inaccurate process that still requires much manual intervention. Client server tools also tend to require high initial costs (software license and servers, for example) and entail a high cost of ownership because they must be learned by users and maintained by IT staff.

With the advent of the World Wide Web, it became possible to solicit resumes from candidates anywhere in the world, require them to complete structured resume templates and process them into a local or remote resume database in real time.

The World Wide Web

As North America emerged from the recession of the early 1990s, it was fortuitous that the Web arrived and brought with it technologies that helped employers to source and manage job candidates. First came the job boards. By 1995/96 there were already hundreds of Internet sites that posted job advertisements on behalf of employers and let candidates browse and apply for them online. The early job boards, including Monster.com and Career Mosaic, became the first to popularize the concept of candidate profiling so that employers would receive standardized and structured profiles rather than resumes with candidate personal information, skills and experience information in the same format. This meant that candidates could be compared more easily and searched more accurately.

Corporate career sites were the next recruiting tool to develop out of the Web as companies reasoned that they should be promoting themselves and attracting candidates directly. Technologies like Junglee facilitated the link between corporate Web site recruiting and job boards by automatically copying jobs from client career sites to the job boards the company subscribed to. RecruitUSA and eQuest got into the business of enabling automated job distribution so that recruiters could send their postings to their corporate career sites and multiple job boards all at once.

In the mid-to-late 1990s, companies like Alexus, Personic and Icarian developed Web-based applicant tracking systems—tools that manage applications and candidates. Dozens quickly followed, including Peopleclick in 1997, Recruitsoft and BrassRing in 1999, Hire.com and Webhire (Restrac) in 2001 and the major enterprise resource planning (ERP) vendors in 2002 and 2003. Today, there are well over one hundred talent management system (TMS) solutions providers, a number that is still growing.

The Internet has seen the advent of additional advanced recruiting tools like "deep Web mining" from AIRS, infoGIST and more recently Eliyon. These tools enable recruiters to search across the Internet for "candidates" who may or may not be actively seeking work. Advanced resume processing from Mohomine and Resume Mirror allows organizations to collect resumes in any format (paper, fax, e-mail, etc.) and deposit all of them into a single database that is part of an applicant tracking system. Job and resume blasting from vendors like eQuest and ResumeXpress, and advanced, conceptual resume searching from Engenium, Burning Glass and others have added to the technology arsenal recruiters now have at their disposal.

Career networks—CareerBuilder, for example—built from dozens of specialty job boards assist employers in exposing their requisitions to larger, more diverse audiences. Supply chain partners for background checks and assessments have used the Web to integrate their services and software within talent management systems. New global standards like XML (Extensible Markup Language) and Web services protocols are enabling disparate systems to speak to each other more easily and less expensively.

Developments in talent management technology are fast paced. Organizations that stay abreast of the field will be prepared to apply the technologies to the challenges they may face in the next few years. Many of the preparations begun now will build the foundation for success in the future

Talent Management Defined

Talent management can be defined as encompassing all HR processes, administration and technologies. For the purposes of this discussion, however, a more common and specific definition will be used. Talent management commonly refers to the sourcing (finding talent); screening (sorting of qualified and unqualified applicants); selection (assessment/testing, interviewing, reference/background checking, etc., of applicants); on-boarding (offer generation/acceptance, badging/security, payroll, facilities, etc.); retention (measures to keep the talent that contributes to the success of the organization); development (training, growth assignments, etc.); deployment (optimal assignment of staff to projects, lateral opportunities, promotions, etc.) and renewal of the workforce with analysis and planning as the adhesive, over-arching ingredient. In other words, talent management is what occurs at the nexus of the hiring, development and workforce management processes and can be described alternatively as talent optimization.

Summary of Best Practices in Talent Management

Since their inception in about 1994, Web-based TMSs have changed the way employers and job seekers find each other and interact before, during and after engagement. Today, for example, virtually every North American organization uses one or more electronic recruiting methods for talent acquisition. In the near future, we will see more widespread integration with other talent management technologies, such as candidate and applicant management solutions, retention tools like performance and incentive management software, and workforce analytics and planning engines. Better applicant screening capacity and "internationalization" of product capabilities will continue so that systems can be deployed globally by multinationals and sold into foreign markets.

The purpose of this review of talent management technologies and methods is to describe and determine which technologies and accompanying uses constitute proven and emerging best practices and trends. Corporate adoption of talent management technologies is gaining traction such that today, well over 90 percent of large companies use corporate career sites on the Web to connect internal and external job seekers to positions in the organization. A smaller but growing number of organizations have connected their corporate career sites to applicant and candidate management systems that help screen, process, store and track candidates through the hiring process. However, few organizations so far have attempted to connect their candidate sourcing and tracking tools to systems that help them plan, manage, rate and retain their workforce in an optimal manner.

Given the primacy of talent, even conservative organizations that are slow to adopt new technologies should avoid placing themselves at a disadvantage by ignoring proven best practices in automated talent management. Organizations looking for clear competitive advantage in talent optimization should consider early adoption of talent management technologies and integrated platforms that hold promise but are as yet untested by a critical mass of users.

Best practices in automated talent management can be divided roughly into two types: those that have been in use for several years by thousands of organizations and those that are at or near the cutting edge and have not yet withstood the tests of mass usage and time.

The findings of this review can be summarized as follows:

Basic Best Practices

1. At minimum, organizations should operate a corporate career site with the following elements:
   - one-click links from all corporate Web pages
   - a link to corporate career site prominently displayed on the organization's home page and on key secondary pages (divisional and subsidiary home pages)
   - all postings on external job boards and newsgroups route candidates through the corporate career page to apply
   - URL advertised on all print-based postings
   - information on benefits, corporate culture, work/life philosophy, training/education and advancement opportunities
   - a separate section or site for the recruitment of students and recent graduates
   - clear and detailed job descriptions with information on the salary range
   - compelling employment branding and messaging (rich and detailed information on corporate culture and why the organization is a great place to work)

- ability to create and store multiple profiles/resumes and cover letters that can be maintained and edited for future use by the job seeker
- ability to apply online
- personalized e-mail acknowledgements to applicants
- ability for candidates to refer a friend/colleague
- ability for candidates to register for automated job alerts that automatically e-mail positions of interest to the candidate
- help tools, such as contextual help pages or online guides to assist job seekers in using the site
- a privacy policy and statement for candidates
- information and/or interactive exercises that help candidates determine their eligibility, aptitude and interest in positions
- prescreening questionnaires at the individual job posting level to help screen candidates and assist them in determining their fit for positions

2. In order to manage applications efficiently, reduce time and cost per hire and collect vital data for workforce planning, organizations must connect their corporate career site to a candidate/applicant management system with the following base features:

    - resume/profile database
    - ability for managers and recruiters to create requisitions and track them and applicants through the hiring procedure
    - powerful search tools that allow keyword and field-based searching at a minimum
    - a job posting distribution mechanism that streamlines the process of sending job requisitions to the internal and external corporate career sites and to multiple Web-based job boards
    - extensive do-it-yourself configuration tools that allow trained administrators to change elements of the solution after it has been implemented (e.g., for workflow, job and resume templates, career site look and feel, custom reports, etc.)
    - ROI-based reporting and ad hoc reporting capability that gives administrators the tools to create whatever reports are

necessary from the data collected by the system

- advanced screening, sorting and ranking tools
- available, proven ability to integrate with human resource management systems (HRMSs) and ERP solutions
- solid business partners and/or XML APIs (extensible markup language application program interface, i.e., plug-ins and adaptors) to facilitate the integration of background checking, resume processing, online assessment/testing tools and more
- capability of integrating with workforce analytics/planning tools (systems that process and display data for the purposes of examining and modeling the workforce in support of planning
- integrated employee referral plan software (tools that automate the process of recommending friends and ex-colleagues to positions in the organization)
- hiring manager and recruiter desktops (role-based interfaces for key users of the solution)

Advanced Best Practices

Leading organizations are looking at the recruiting end of the talent management process as an ongoing and proactive exercise. Talent management systems are supporting this philosophy in numerous ways, such as by enabling the creation of partially prequalified talent pools. Talent pools house the profiles of promising candidates that have been screened in as qualified by the system and/or recruiters. Employers can nurture relationships with these individuals in much the same manner as they might with customers or potential customers, through the use of personalized and automated e-mail, for example. The database must include, in addition to external candidates, current employees, candidates that current employees refer and select alumni—past employees that the organization would like to bring back.

Large, multinational organizations are looking for solutions they can deploy worldwide that will accommodate differences in language, culture, law (protection of personal information), currencies and various local idiosyncrasies. Organizations want solutions that can stand alone *and* integrate with ERP software (e.g., PeopleSoft,

Oracle and SAP), HRMS and other HR technologies. The use of Web services architectures and XML APIs, and the concept of combining hiring management systems for use in recruiting the permanent and hourly workforce with contingent workforce management systems (often referred to as vendor management systems for hiring and managing temporary and contract personnel), performance and learning management systems and workforce planning tools on one integrated platform will eventually become standard best practice as buyers demand products that can handle all of their staffing and talent management needs. Hiring managers and recruiters will demand more and improved candidate screening, ranking, sorting and assessment tools. More large organizations will choose to outsource all or large components of HR to specialty organizations such as business process outsourcers (BPOs) or human resource outsourcers (HROs) for efficiencies and cost savings, and in order to focus internal HR expertise on strategic and consultative roles.

For reasons explained in subsequent chapters, the concepts of talent relationship management, internationalization, wider HR technologies platform integration, screening and assessment, "total workforce management" and strategic outsourcing will shape emerging best practices this decade. Talent relationship management is discussed in detail in Chapter 7, talent management solutions integration in Chapter 4, screening and assessment in Chapter 5 and outsourcing in Chapter 10.

Organizations seeking an edge should:

- Above all, focus on employee retention by providing all career opportunities and HR information resources to existing staff through intranets and employee portals and by integrating systems, such as performance management that help employers know who to retain and learning and career management tools that help employees achieve their development and career objectives. Make it easier for talented employees to fulfill their career aspirations inside the organization than outside.

- Allow candidates to monitor the progress of their applications as they make their way through the hiring process. This will reduce calls to hiring managers and recruiters and will communicate the organization's respect for candidates' desire to know that their applications are being considered.

- Respect candidates' time and privacy. Allow them to view and apply for positions anonymously. Request no more information than necessary. This is especially challenging for internal applicants from whom extensive information is needed for planning purposes but for whom privacy (with respect to applications for internal transfer) may be even more important. Balance this with rules that restrict hiring managers' access to information that they do not need. More importantly, develop a culture inside the organization that respects employees' right to fulfill their career objectives inside the organization and does not tarnish or punish them in any way for attempting to do so. While it is reasonable for employers to require a certain tenure in a position before the employee looks elsewhere (e.g., twelve to eighteen months), it is dangerous to unreasonably (explicitly or implicitly) restrict their ability to move within the organization.

- Streamline the profile/resume-building process for candidates by using data extraction tools that parse information from their existing resumes into electronic profile fields. These tools can be built into the corporate career site such that candidates cut and paste or upload their resumes to pre-populate the fields of the online profile rather than having to key all of that information in themselves.

- Push vendors for more control (configuration options) over their solutions after they have been implemented so that the system can change with the shifting priorities of the organization. Organizations should also demand easier administrative tools to make the changes. In the same vein, look for solutions that are scalable and flexible. Buy only what you need now but be sure to choose a vendor that can scale to your growing needs. For example, if you need a solution to manage the flood of resumes you are receiving now, choose a vendor that excels in this area, but make sure to select one that offers the additional tools you will need as your talent management process becomes more demanding and sophisticated. After you have solved the candidate management problem, you may turn to talent relationship management, workforce planning or retention as priorities. If your vendor cannot supply those tools or integrate third-party tools, you will need to replace them and start over.

- Use Web mining software, build alumni networks (of ex-employees), integrate employee referral programs and conduct Web research to source new candidates.

- Reduce the time and costs of hiring by using prescreening questionnaires, skills/competency-based screening and online assessments. As discussed in the next chapter, the corporate career site is the first line of defense in candidate screening. A site that describes the organization, its culture and benefits, and its job openings well helps candidates screen themselves. Also utilize screening software (as described in Chapter 5) that eliminates candidates based on answers to questions and by systematically comparing their skills, competencies and preferences to the requirements of positions.

- Use online testing and assessment software to help convert screened candidates into shortlists of candidates and finally into interview lists.

- Process and analyze the data generated by talent management solutions to gain insights into the workforce, such as the supply of talent, workforce trends, and the best sources for candidates.

- Institute disciplined workforce planning processes through analysis of the invaluable data generated and stored by talent management solutions. Look for vendors that are tying workforce analytics and planning tools into their e-recruit solutions.

- Align recruitment goals with learning and performance management. Plan to integrate these technologies with e-recruitment technologies (including applicant/candidate management systems) and workforce/succession planning tools in order to see the workforce from end-to-end and leverage the power of one seamless platform for talent management.

- Develop an e-recruitment strategy that connects employment branding with e-recruitment functionality. In other words, do not launch an initiative to market your organization to young workers as a modern employer of choice if you have not installed leading-edge tools for those candidates to learn about your organization and apply for positions within it. Young workers will react incredulously to any employer that attempts to reach them, and then subjects them to an antiquated hiring process.

- If applicable, develop a global e-recruitment strategy that shares one flexible and adaptable solution. Multinational organizations too often saddle themselves with disparate recruiting technologies throughout their subsidiaries in various countries. Develop a global recruiting strategy using one solution that is flexible enough to handle different processes in different countries, yet capable of being managed centrally and rolling all data into one database.

- Choose an e-recruit vendor that has built or plans to build its solution on the Web services architecture so that integration with other systems is simplified. Ensure that vendors are evolving their platforms in step with HR-XML standards.

- Choose a solution that allows hiring managers to recruit for and administer temporary, hourly, contract and permanent staff from one system. This will increase the ROI in the system and streamline the process of acquiring and managing all talent. As with integrated workforce planning and learning and performance management, few vendors will offer integrated solutions in the immediate future, but their blueprints should be in place.

- Consider outsourcing the transactional and administrative elements of HR processes to niche outsourcers or HR BPOs (see Chapter 10).

- Consider making online application via the corporate career center the *only* means to apply for work in your organization. In 2003, about 45 percent of the Fortune 500 did so because it eliminates the expense and inefficiency of running multiple application processes to reach candidates that are, in many cases, unlikely to pass initial screening.[1] By continuing to allow paper and faxed resume applications after going to the expense of implementing talent management systems, organizations perpetuate inefficiencies and might well increase their total costs of recruitment. Today, with ubiquitous Internet access at homes, schools, libraries, cafes, airports and elsewhere, few candidates can make a legitimate claim to needing alternatives.

---

[1] Alice Snell, iLogos Research, "Process Savings Through Careers Site Best Practices" (2002).

The Selection Process

Web-enabled talent management and e-recruitment has evolved quickly. Vendors have rushed in to provide solutions that often offer very little by way of differentiation. Organizations should look to suppliers that have proven track records in their specific industry and in satisfying clients of similar size and with similar needs. Vendors should be able to satisfy the implementation, change management, integration, data security, financial viability and customer service questions you have.

In the selection process for talent management technologies, large organizations should expect to spend six to twelve months and tens of thousands of dollars (on requests for information [RFIs] and requests for proposals [RFP], consultants, trade show attendance, research, etc.) depending on the type of solution(s) they desire. First, the organization must examine and document its current processes thoroughly in order to know what it wants to keep and what it wants to change. Otherwise, bad processes will simply become automated bad processes.

A project team comprised of a project manager, a domain expert (someone with knowledge and experience of the technology sought), HR managers, recruiters, and hiring managers should be formed and a senior-level project sponsor identified. Simulated process reengineering (on paper) should take place where the organization believes it can use technology to save time and money, and the organization should develop its wish list independent of what it believes the technology can deliver. A discovery period, including an RFI to determine what is available and how well it relates to the organization's expectations, should follow. This might require two to three months to create, distribute and analyze the results.

The analysis of the RFI should include at least a cursory review of the organization's options. Though it is highly unlikely that a "build" over "buy" decision will be warranted, elimination of this possibility should be documented. In very rare cases, an organization will find that its unique needs cannot be met by the market and it may have to consider the option of building from scratch or heavily customizing a vendor's software. This might occur in a highly regulated or unionized environment, for example, where explicit policies are in place that might require union negotiations or even legislation to change.

More relevant to most organizations, however, is the option of licensing and installing a solution versus outsourcing its hosting and maintenance to an application service provider (ASP). ASPs are suppliers who offer the option of leasing or licensing their software but who charge monthly or annual fees to host and maintain it on their own or a partner's premises. The ASP option appeals to organizations that desire fast implementation and/or that want to unburden their IT departments and/or that want to pay as they go rather than purchase a perpetual software license all at once.

The RFP stage will take at least as much time as the RFI stage. The RFP itself must be carefully constructed so that the best vendor on price, fit, functionality and business components (viability, customer care, etc.) is selected. The project team will need to consider privacy impact because the solution collects personal information. This is typically done during a formal privacy impact analysis that looks at the data flow to determine who sees it and the reasons why. The team will also need to look at accessibility for disabled users.

The project should develop a change management plan that includes communications, training and orientation. If, as is often the best option, the organization plans to outsource to an ASP, the project team must concern itself with service level agreements (SLAs) to govern the relationship with the vendor, an exit agreement, which describes the process and obligations of supplier and customer should the relationship terminate early, and code-in-escrow and data transfer agreements to protect itself should the vendor go out of business. Expertise will also be needed to evaluate the ASP vendor's hosting facilities, disaster recovery plans, security (network, physical and personnel) and other related concerns before SLAs, exit agreements and escrow arrangements are made. The SLA, exit and code-in-escrow agreements protect the organization against unforeseen problems and should be carefully constructed. The SLA should contain measurable metrics and targets so that it can be easily monitored and enforced.

After evaluating responses to the RFP, a shortlist of three to four vendors should be constructed (in fairness to the vendors and the project team, this list should be as short as possible).

These vendors should be invited on-site to perform scripted "live" demonstrations that display the ability of their systems to perform as required. The script should include ease-of-use criteria and proof that the solution can be easily adapted to the changing needs of the organization. The supplier should also demonstrate that the solution is responsive (loads pages and performs functions quickly) and able to handle load volumes. Also, it should show that it can provide the core functionality identified as mandatory in the RFP, such as candidate features, searching, screening, etc. Rated functionality should be separated from mandatory requirements, and a scoring key developed. The demo session or a separate one should cover questions about the vendors' financial viability, customer service standards, flexible SLAs (for ASPs) and problem-escalation processes (who to contact for technical and customer service issues). Ideally, vendors should send their senior management to the Q&A session to ensure that all questions can be answered and all concerns addressed.

Shortlisted vendors should be asked for references and for audited financial statements. The organization's chief financial officer or a qualified analyst should examine the financial statements to determine the soundness of each vendor's financial position. Many vendors in the TMS space are not yet profitable and have been funded by venture capitalists. This is not in itself a reason for disqualifying the vendor, but the buyer might wish to interview key investors to gauge their commitment to a money-losing operation.

Customer References

Buyers should ask for and check at least five references from organizations as similar as possible to their own. Standard questions should be developed as a guide for each reference and in order to track and score the results effectively. Where practical, a reference client should be visited so that the system can be observed in a business environment (though this may be quite difficult to arrange). Buyers should make efforts to speak about the solution with a range of users, especially line hiring managers, recruiters, in-house trainers and tool administrators. If the system is to be installed on the premises (not outsourced to an ASP), the reference company's IT department should be queried as to maintenance, performance, scalability and upgrading and any compatibility issues with existing platforms and architecture. In practical terms, few organizations may be willing to allow site visits, but reference customers should at least be available for extensive telephone interviews. Organizations should also review the latest research, product reviews and customer surveys. Look for information offered by research organizations and the vendors themselves, and for teleconferences with other users and potential buyers hosted by research organizations, consulting firms and others.

Buyers should not necessarily limit their investigation of potential vendors' customers to the reference clients supplied. Where doubt or questions remain after supplied references are checked, buyers should determine who some of their potential vendors' other customers are or were, and interview several of them as well. In the case of ex-customers, this effort should also be used to determine what prompted them to leave. Many non-reference customers are willing to participate in short telephone interviews at the very least.

Vendor Visits

After ranking the vendors and determining a winner, and before a contract is signed, the project manager should visit the highest scoring vendor's business, and, where applicable, hosting facilities. If an ASP has been selected, a qualified technical/network specialist should visit the vendor's hosting facility to perform due diligence on the privacy, security, performance and disaster recovery elements discussed above. The project manager will want to investigate evidence of a solid, professional and structured implementation capacity. This must include documented processes, a project management office that audits previous implementations and one that learns continuously from its successes and mistakes. The project manager should look for the same structure and discipline in the product development team; usually an interview with the chief technology officer (CTO) or equivalent, or the vice president of product development can address these concerns.

Depending on the review of the vendor's financial statements, the project manager might wish to interview the chief financial officer (CFO) or vice president of finance. The manager should come away with a general sense of efficiency, solid management and order at the facility.

If these visits verify the information provided by the vendor in its RFP response, product demonstrations and Q&A, the organization can be confident in the vendor's ability to execute its end of the project. Provided the project team has a good relationship and rapport with the vendor and feels that the technology is the best fit for the organization, it should commit to the purchase and contract with the vendor.

After Selection

In short, best practice involves extensive preparation and careful selection of the right technologies and technology partners for the organization. Once the solutions are in place, effective change management, including training, is critical. In many cases, it will be impractical to train all users of the system in the traditional sense. For most TMS components, hiring managers, for example, may use the systems only once or twice per year. To train several hundred or thousand hiring managers before the launch of a technology is not only time-consuming and expensive, it may be wasteful because they might forget what they learned by the time they need to use the solution for the first time. A creative mix of product orientation, train-the-trainer, classroom training, just-in-time training (delivered by regular users in-house), Web-based tutorials and online help, combined with the selection of solutions with highly intuitive user interfaces, including e-mail integration of certain tasks like requisition approval and interview scheduling, is necessary.

After implementation, success relies on having the in-house capacity to leverage the solutions and align their use to corporate objectives. Vendor relationship management is also important, especially where the decision has been taken to outsource to an ASP, HRO or HR BPO.

Conclusions

The debate as to whether talent management systems are necessary has passed. Today and in future, organizations must concern themselves with choosing, implementing and leveraging solutions that give them the greatest advantage. In subsequent chapters, we will look at each of the key technologies in detail, starting with the corporate career site.

CHAPTER 3

卍

Corporate Career Site Best Practices

At present, it is safe to say that nearly all North American mid-size and larger employers are utilizing the Internet and/or corporate career sites for recruiting. Independent research done by HR.com in early 2003 indicated that 88 percent of organizations with between 250 and 25,000 employees in North America had distinct corporate career sites (exhibiting wide ranges in sophistication).[1] iLogos Research, which monitors the use of online recruiting tools, reports that in 2003, 94 percent of Fortune 500 companies used corporate Web sites for recruiting. This compares to 91 percent in the previous year.[2]

It is not just corporate North America that has taken to the Internet for recruiting. The U.S. and Canadian governments were among the earliest adopters. In Canada, the Electronic Labour Exchange and the National Graduate Register predated nearly all commercial job boards. In the U.S., USAJOBS lists thousands of government vacancies. The U.S. federal government has recently hired Monster Worldwide to revamp its site and presumably

---

[1] One hundred companies with 250 to 25,000 employees were reviewed. About 10 percent of corporate career sites were judged "rudimentary," meaning they either offer job postings or scant information about working at the company and an e-mail or mailing address to send resumes.

[2] See www.ilogos.com.

Figure 3.1: Corporate Career Site?

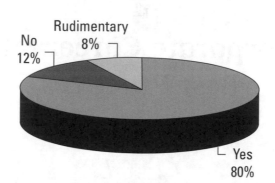

Of the one hundred organizations with 250 to 25,000 employees reviewed by HR.com at random, the vast majority (80 percent) operate interactive corporate career sites. Eight percent offer career sites with job listings but do not allow online applications and 12 percent do not operate a corporate career site at all.

make it as user-friendly and feature-rich as Monster.com. Moreover, Monster Worldwide will provide government managers with better tools to search and otherwise leverage its database of resumes.

In academia, a segment of the economy that often trails in adopting business technologies, colleges like many companies have gone so far as to require that all applications be submitted via their Web sites. Some campuses of the University of California, for example, state that professors and others who are not willing or capable of going online to apply are not of interest to them. The University of Kentucky requires all candidates for non-academic positions to apply online and may soon require the same for academic positions as well. Across the board, at least 45 percent of Fortune 500 companies have adopted the best practice of requiring all candidates to apply online.

The main reasons are clear. Internet recruiting is faster, less expensive and reaches a much larger audience than traditional methods. A high percentage of job seekers use the Internet in their search for work. A 2002 Society for Human Resource Management poll put the figure at over 90 percent. Other recent surveys have findings in the 50 percent to 80 percent range with young people (eighteen- to thirty-year olds) and upper-income groups in the higher ranges. Seniors and lower-income groups tend to be at the bottom of the range. Pew Research, published May 2003, reveals that 61 percent or 122 million Americans regularly go online and 43 percent of them use the Internet to search for jobs. Over 5 million people search for jobs on the Internet each day.[3]

Further evidence of the ascendancy of online job seeking and recruiting comes also from numbers published by the Newspaper Association of America. According to statistics generated over the past several years, it is clear that job boards are fast gaining in overall recruitment advertising market share and are doing so at the expense of newspaper classifieds. According to Forrester Research, Monster.com (the industry's largest player) more than doubled its income from job postings in 2001 while newspapers reported a 17 percent decline. In 2000, employment classified advertising in U.S. newspapers was worth US$8.7 billion. That plummeted to about US$4.3 billion for 2002 and probably less than US$4 billion for 2003.[4] This loss of more than 50 percent in two years cannot be attributed exclusively to a slowing economy. The Newspaper Association of America's preliminary results for real estate and automotive classified advertising (the only two other distinct categories it tracks), for example, show growth of 4.5 percent and 5.5 percent in 2002, respectively.

By any measure it is safe to say that on any given day, many millions of North Americans are looking for information about jobs online and that the Internet has become the premier communications medium for the talent market in North America, if not the entire industrialized world. But, by as late as 1998, only a minority of large organizations and very few small to mid-size companies owned a corporate career site. Many companies ventured into e-recruitment by placing their postings on public job boards like Monster.com and HotJobs. Candidates would use the job boards to find positions and then apply through mail, fax and e-mail. As employers' sophistication grew around the use of the Internet, they began to develop corporate career sites to complement their use of public job boards, to build the organization's employment brand (attractiveness in the eyes of job seekers) and

---

[3]Pew Internet & American Life Project, March–May 2003.

[4]Based on the Newspaper Association of America's preliminary statistics for 2002 and 2003. See www.naa.org.

to provide a candidate-sourcing tool as the public-facing portion of their recruitment and talent management systems.

Even more than the effective use of public job boards, corporate career sites are now considered the first plank in an e-recruitment strategy. The career site lets employers drive traffic to one place (from all print ads and public job boards) where they can brand the organization, sell job seekers on the organization's merits, advertise positions and collect candidate information.

Figure 3.2: Online Applications—Preference Versus Requirement

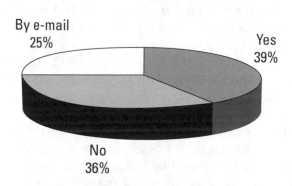

Candidates Can Apply Online

By e-mail
25%

Yes
39%

No
36%

Online Profile Application

Yes
48%

No
52%

Of 100 small- to large organizations, the majority (64 percent) allow online applications (if e-mail is included) and a slight minority (48 percent) facilitate online profile building—the ability for job seekers to create candidate profiles.

Of 100 small to large organizations, the majority (64 percent) allow online applications (if e-mail is included) and a slight minority

(48 percent) facilitate online profile building—the ability for job seekers to create candidate profiles.

Branding

The corporate career site usually becomes, for large organizations, one of its most visited set of Web pages. As the number one or two site by traffic in the company, the corporate career site should be featured prominently on the company home page (one click away) and on every secondary page. It is best practice to include a "careers" link in the top or bottom navigation bar so that the career site is only one click away from every publicly accessible page on the site.

The corporate career site should have consistent branding and graphics, intuitive navigation and a privacy statement (see Chapter 8). The use of meta or search tags, as well as registering the site with major search engines, will assist potential candidates in finding the site in general Internet searches.[5] Every print ad should contain the URL and a statement to the effect that more detailed information can be found on the site.

Development of an employment brand (the main theme or message about the organization that it is trying to convey to job seekers) is the topic of another book entirely, but once the development of the brand has occurred, the corporate career site must reflect that strategy and must complement other branding initiatives. Large, well-branded organizations might receive ten thousand or more resumes per day and face the difficulty of screening, sorting and managing the volume.

Small and obscure companies, on the other hand, may face a separate challenge even in weak employment markets. If an organization is not well known, job seekers may not visit it directly to look for jobs. One way to counter this problem is to post positions on the largest job boards and direct interested candidates to the corporate career site to apply. In time, this will facilitate the building of talent pools (the topic of Chapter 7). Another way is to join a career network that bypasses public job boards by joining corporate career sites together in large networks.

---

[5]Meta tagging involves the use of keywords to describe a site or page. Some search engines use the tags to build their indexes. See http://whatis.techtarget.com.

Profile: Direct Employers—The E-Recruiting Association

The not-for-profit E-Recruiting Association offers annual memberships for US$12,500. To date, over 120 organizations from mid-size to Fortune 500 companies have joined. Membership includes unlimited use of the Direct Employers career network, unlimited use of NACElink, a college career network and access to iLogos recruitment research.

Direct Employers (www.directemployers.com) upholds the principles of best practices by working to drive all candidate traffic back to the corporate career site. At twenty-four-hour intervals, the service indexes all of the jobs listed on its clients' sites. Job seekers who visit Direct Employers perform searches and receive results similar to that shown in the next figure.

Rather than displaying the postings directly, a separate window pops up when candidates click on a job link. This window takes candidates to the client's corporate career site where the position is displayed. There are several benefits to this approach. Candidates tend to stay and conduct more searches (three to five on average, according to Direct Employer research). More importantly, candidates cannot blast employers with thoughtless applications (a negative side effect of e-recruiting). They must follow each organization's application process and complete whatever profile they require. E-Recruiting Association Director of Business Development, Chad Sowash, says this results in fewer applications but much more suitable candidates.

Membership also includes access to NACElink, a joint initiative of the National Association of College Employers (NACE) and the E-Recruiting Association. NACElink has over one hundred U.S. colleges in its network of schools that employers can post to. It provides privileged access to job postings for current students and alumni in cooperation with college career centers.

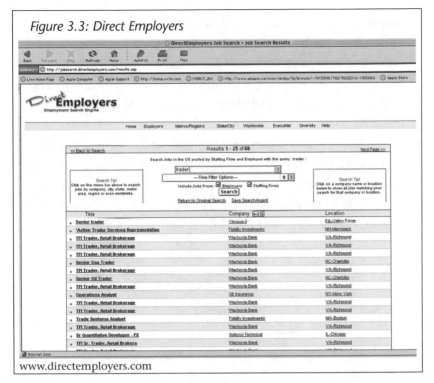

Figure 3.3: Direct Employers

www.directemployers.com

Another means of gaining targeted reach for online job advertising, and to access strategic information on the best places to post is to use a "broker" service like TruStar Solutions (see profile below).

Profile: TruStar Solutions—Providing Internet-Based Broker Services

TruStar Solutions was founded in 1997 as International Internet Recruiting Consultants (IIRC). Its mission is to aid online job advertisers (employers) as an "advocate" in distributing their job postings easily across multiple job boards and to the boards best suited to their needs.

It differs from other online job distribution tools in a few important ways. First, employers pay nothing. TruStar consults with clients to determine where they should post, and they negotiate concessionary rates from job boards. TruStar receives its pay from the boards in the form of commissions. There are an estimated thirty-five thousand job boards in existence, making the choices for employers somewhat overwhelming.[6] TruStar monitors several thousand of them and can help its clients target the right ones.

TruStar will also collect and analyze clients' recruitment data and produce custom reports. In order to prove its worth, it is willing to compare its results (measurements around the quality of candidates received) against its clients' previous recruitment methods and results, and demonstrate the improvement.

Figure 3.4: TruStar

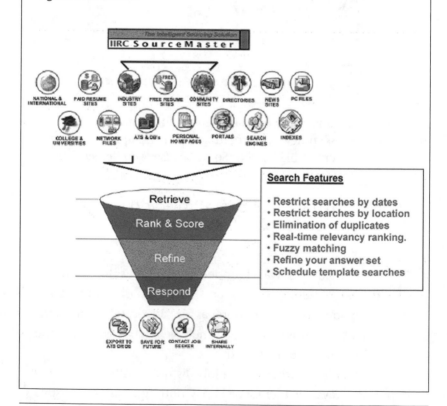

[6] This is TruStar Solution's estimate. See also *CareerXRoads*, an annual report on the leading job boards across numerous categories, for more information.

Finally, TruStar can broker clients' use of third-party screening and assessment tools, background checking, resume processing, and other suppliers in the e-recruit supply chain. For example, if a client tells TruStar that they require a tool or combination of tools, TruStar will help select the ones best suited to the client's needs and provide consolidated billing and vendor management services.

TruStar's SourceMaster service helps to source candidates from a wide and deep pool. It also filters the results into manageable folders. A client starts by knowing what type(s) of candidates it is seeking. TruStar determines the best job boards, Internet sites and indexes to use. TruStar collects the results (candidate applications) and puts them through a filter that eliminates clearly unqualified candidates. It then scores and ranks those remaining. TruStar coordinates the client's response to all applicants and can deliver the entire list or just the top-ranked candidates to its client.

Utility and Information

A corporate career site should allow candidates to browse and search for positions by location, job category and time of posting (such as all jobs posted in the past forty-eight hours), especially if the site advertises a high volume of postings. Only a minority of job seekers find keyword searches—in which a term such as "project manager" can be entered—useful. However, this option is standard with most software and can be bypassed by job seekers if they wish.

Figure 3.5: Job Search Functionality

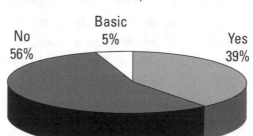

Only 39 percent of the small, mid-size and large companies reviewed offer true job search functionality in which candidates can use flexible search options to find positions of interest on corporate career sites. This functionality is nearly universal on Fortune 500 sites.

Hyperion, a 2,200 employee business software company, gives job seekers an uncluttered search, the option to view all jobs, and access to the company's "Hot Openings."

Figure 3.6: Hyperion

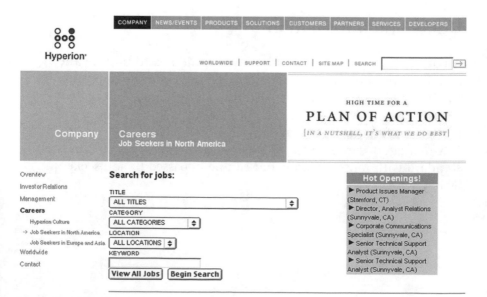

http://careers.hodes.com/hyperion

Internal and external candidates should be able to build, store and edit online resumes or candidate profiles and apply for positions online. Serious candidates are generally willing to spend the required time to apply for jobs they are interested in, but that time should be reasonable, perhaps no more than fifteen minutes according to various usability research. Best practices speed the process of applying online by allowing candidates to upload and/or cut and paste their resumes to reduce data entry.

Leading-edge sites will extract name and address, education, previous employment and other information from the resume automatically to speed the process of online profile building. This is done with the use of embedded data parsing engines—tools that automatically extract information from unstructured documents, like resumes, and place that information into fields, such as those used in online candidate profiles. Designers should *not* assume that candidates know how to use these tools without instruction; useful help tools are necessary. Finally, candidates' ability to store more than one version of their resume/profile and cover letter is a good option because it enables job seekers to apply for different types of positions with information that highlights their qualifications for different jobs.

Self-Selection, Screening and Sorting

The corporate career site gives employers unlimited space to offer information about the organization. The site should be used to convey compelling information about the organization and its values. This is sometimes described as the employment value proposition or EVP. Career sites should provide detailed and current information about working conditions, including corporate culture, and varied information about culture and lifestyle if the company operates in diverse locations. To assist candidates in self-screening and selection, positions should include clear job descriptions (described in Chapter 5). They should also include salary ranges and current benefits information where possible.

Fast-food retailer Jack in the Box has over twenty thousand employees. Most are entry-level, high-turnover workers doing temporary or seasonal work. Jack's EVP tackles the image issue head on. Links to additional information about working at Jack in the Box round out this site's excellent use of the Internet as a medium for unlimited information (see Figure 3.7 on next page).

Figure 3.7: Jack in the Box

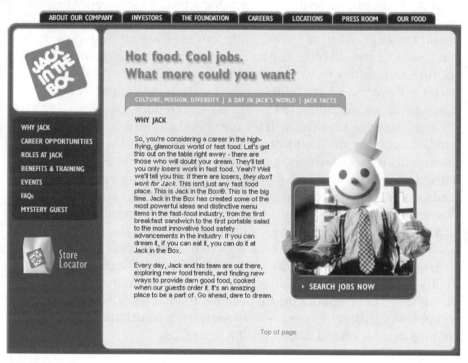

http://careers.jackinthebox.com/whyjack.asp

Organizations should provide product information, information on company locations and information on what working conditions are *really* like. Several progressive companies are using their corporate career sites to walk potential applicants through online self-assessments. Done well, these tools can provide real insight for candidates to help them determine whether they are suitable for the job—before they decide to apply.

Games, simulations, deep and detailed information, honest descriptions of jobs, the good and the bad, what it takes to succeed, even the types of personalities best suited to the position can aid job seekers in determining whether they should apply for a position. For example, a visitor to a well-designed career site will be able to quickly understand the organization's appeal to job seekers. He or she will find a list of the benefits afforded employees and will be able to browse or search detailed job listings without any form of registration. Advanced sites might offer some form of quiz, particularly for entry-level or new-graduate job seekers, that determines their interests and steers them toward the listings that best match. They might be able to access employee testimonials. Position listings will contain questionnaires particular to the job advertised. These will tell potential applicants more about the position and, from the employer's perspective, answers to the questions can be used to eliminate, score and rank all applicants.

Employers should include information about training and development, opportunities for advancement inside the organization and their views on work/life balance. Organizations should know what differentiates them from other employers. For instance, in the public sector, it may be the scope of career possibilities combined with the chance to "make a difference." In some companies it may be competitive compensation or benefits combined with opportunities for advancement or training. This message should be central to the employment brand communicated throughout the site.

RTI International in South Carolina employs just over two thousand people, including hundreds of highly sought-after scientists and technicians. Its EVP appeals to candidates who are looking to make a difference in people's lives.

Figure 3.8: RTI

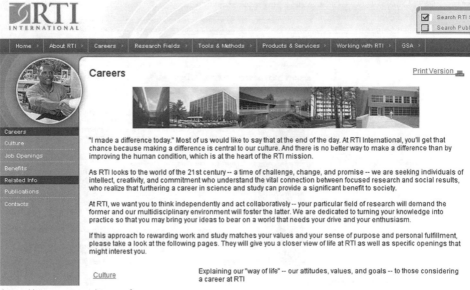

http://www.rti:org/page.cfm

Employee Testimonials

A growing number of employers are adding employee testimonials to their career sites. Testimonials can be very powerful when they contain meaningful content and have the ring of truth. Credible employees who are high achievers are normally featured. They should be encouraged to be honest about the company and their jobs. For example, if it takes extremely hard work and dedication to succeed to higher levels in the company, that message should be stated clearly. However, it should be tempered with other honest messages about work/life balance (i.e., what employees do outside of work), training opportunities and employees' ability to choose less aggressive career paths while still being appreciated. Honest testimonials can be difficult to obtain and make public, but may give candidates the best possible picture of life inside the organization.

Figure 3.9: Jordan's Furniture

Careers

Careers	The J-Team
■ The J-Team	Here at Jordan's Furniture we create 'Raving Fans' out of our employees. We provide internal
□ Find Jobs	growth opportunities to our J-Team members, establishing a career path. We offer an extensive benefits plan and unique features like employee "Fun Days" opportunities to win
□ Apply Now	concert tickets and a great team environment. Jordan's is known for its exceptional atmosphere and if we're smiling, shouldn't you be too?

Rug Gallery

Sleep Lab / Mattresses

Design Center

What Employees Are Saying

Click on a picture below to find out more about that employee and the role they play in making Jordan's Furniture a great place to work. Hear what makes Jordan's Furniture an exciting career choice for them.

J-Team Events
Jordan's holds appreciation events to thank employees for their hard work and loyalty. They got us where we are today!

Bermuda Trip:
We filled 4 full-size planes, taking the entire J-Team to the beautiful island of Bermuda for one day. Barry and Eliot thanked all employees for their hard work, and treated them to a sunny, 90-degree day of beach bbq, live music, water games, and dancing.

Fleet Center Party:
Barry and Eliot treated the J-Team to a fun-filled party including indoor fireworks, dancers from New York, floor-to-ceiling music videos, a deejay and a delicious buffet.

Mama Mia:
Each J-Team member received 2 tickets to the show. Then, Barry and Eliot hosted a 70s disco party with a high-energy live band and a delicious buffet. That night, Jordan's kicked off an employee drive on behalf of the American Red Cross Disaster Relief Fund. With matching funds, Barry & Eliot and the J-Team raised $60,000 for the relief efforts.

http://www.jordans.com/careers/landing.asp

King & Spaulding (www.kslaw.com/recruiting), for example, is a law firm with over seven hundred attorneys in Atlanta, Houston, New York, and Washington, D.C. It has a track record of recruiting some of the best legal talent in the United States. King & Spaulding has posted video clips with soundtracks on its corporate career site to introduce prospective recruits to lawyers who work there. Simple narratives and e-mail links to employees can work just as well. Jordan's Furniture (www.jordansfurniture.com/careers/landing.asp), which employs just over one thousand people in Massachusetts, lets job seekers interact via e-mail with a cross-section of employees on its corporate career site. It also highlights events that Jordan's has sponsored for staff.

Some organizations, like Dell Computer, have constructed interactive exercises that guide potential candidates in finding suitable jobs in their companies. Most often, due to time and expense, these types of tools are developed for specific, hard-to-fill positions, or to give college graduates a sense of what certain entry-level positions might entail.

The Dell corporate career site provides an example of a candidate self-selection tool. Tools like this, and more sophisticated ones, will be seen more in future as employers try to encourage appropriate applications by offering candidates more information and encouraging them to screen themselves out of jobs they are either not strongly interested in or are unqualified for. Self-selection tools can be used to direct candidates to divisions or specific jobs that may appeal to their interests or match their skills. More sophisticated versions may incorporate psychometric testing and precise skills and aptitude matching.

Figure 3.10: Dell

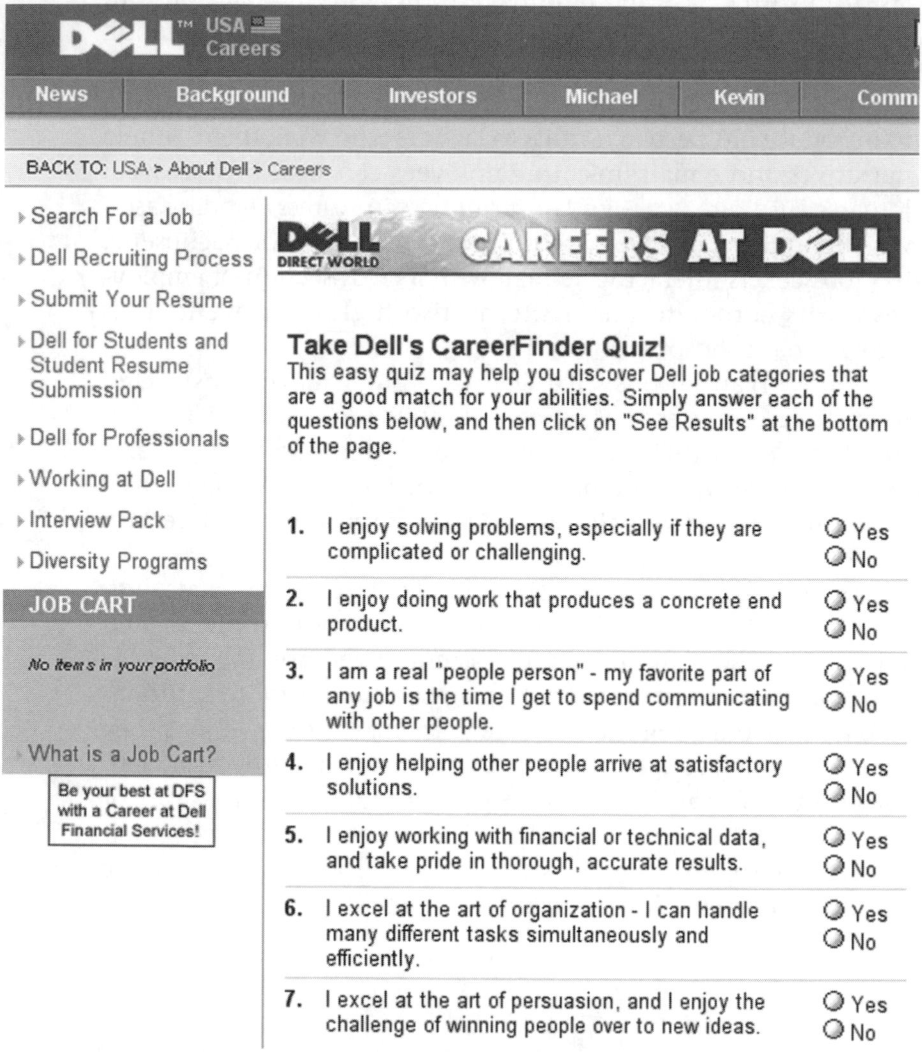

http://dellapp.us.dell.com/careers/needhelp/survey/index.asp

Intranet Career Sites

Internal career sites are normally separate sites that are similar to external sites but may contain enhanced information and additional functionality, such as full employee-referral tools that allow staff to recommend friends and colleagues for jobs in the organization. For internal candidates, organizations should post all positions and internal assignment opportunities. Additional information about positions that may be meaningful to internal candidates (the name of the manager it reports to, salary/bonus bands, the unit, etc.) should be considered.

Many talent management systems support workflows in which positions are posted internally for a period of time before automatically becoming visible to external candidates (to ensure that staff get the first crack at openings). These solutions also offer the option to post slightly different job ads for internal and external candidates. For example, the name of the hiring manager and short descriptions of some of the projects or functions the unit is responsible for may be useful and meaningful to internal candidates.

Candidate Experience, Diversity and Relationship Management

Candidates have different needs and expectations of career Web sites. As a rule of thumb, employers can expect that some of the best potential candidates, passive job seekers (those who are usually fully employed and not actively seeking work), for example, are the ones most likely to leave career sites quickly if the site is not user friendly (i.e., streamlined and engaging) or asks too much of them by way of information or data entry on the first visit.

Corporate career sites should attempt to collect information gradually, starting with the e-mail address of all candidates who visit the site. While many visitors may be happy to submit resumes or complete online profiles, others may not be. A good practice is to offer well-written, descriptive job profiles and other information on the initial pages of the site and make it easy for visitors to view job postings. Unless they are applying for specific jobs, visitors should not be required to complete online profiles or upload their resumes in order to gain access to the postings. Instead, they should be invited to leave their e-mail address and describe the type of position(s) they are interested in so that they can receive automatic e-mails from the employer whenever a matching position is posted. This is a good way to collect e-mail addresses without requiring the completion of a profile from mildly interested and first-time visitors. Registration for the job agent is often the first step in building a relationship (see Chapter 7) with "passive" talent.[7]

Though space on the Web may seem unlimited, no one wants to wade through reams of information. It should be presented in a "Web-friendly" manner. Interactive exercises, streaming video and other potentially bandwidth-intensive features should be paired with low-bandwidth alternatives for users with slower connections or older computers. In order to make sites as accessible as possible to those with disabilities, organizations should familiarize themselves with the W3C (World Wide Web Consortium) and the U.S. Government Section 508 accessibility standards (see www.section508.gov and Chapter 8) when designing their corporate career site(s).

When candidates apply for positions online, the employer should always acknowledge them. At a minimum, candidates should receive personalized, automatic e-mail confirmation that their application has been received. Ideally, this will include their name, the position they applied for and an estimated amount of time it may take to receive a response. Automated feedback (via the corporate career site or e-mail) to the candidate through each major step of the hiring process (for example, if they have been screened in, screened out, invited to interview or rejected for interview) is a best practice supported by several talent management solutions. For reasons described in Chapter 7, however, this feedback has been adopted by very few organizations to date. Proper use of these tools can bolster talent relationship-building and alleviate candidates' concerns about their applications dropping into black holes never to be heard of again. The practice will also reduce calls and e-mails to HR staff from candidates seeking information on the status of their applications.

Employers should also use corporate career sites to promote diversity initiatives that target minority candidates. A strong diversity program demonstrates the tolerance and openness that many talented job seekers, especially youth, are looking for.

---

[7] Passive talent refers to casual job seekers who are fully employed, a group that most recruiters

Gap Inc., whose Web site is shown below, is a well-known clothing retailer that targets youth. The Gap markets its diversity efforts and programs through a separate page off its career site.

Figure 3.11: Gap

http://www.gapinc.com/careers/working_here/diversity.htm

Viral Marketing

Refer-a-friend functionality—the ability for candidates to send e-mail to their friends or colleagues with the details of a position they think might be of interest—and job alerts/agents—the ability for candidates to describe ideal positions and receive automatic e-mails when matches occur—are established best practices that contribute to effective talent relationship building as described in Chapter 7.

Tools such as candidate job baskets that job seekers use to store or hold positions of interest for future consideration are nice, inexpensive features for candidates. These features allow candidates to apply to many or all of the positions in their job baskets with one click, so to speak. They are popular with job seekers but not necessarily best practice from the employer point of view, as they may encourage less thoughtful applications. In situations where employers feel they are being deluged with applications, these features should be disabled.

Though few career sites flag urgent or hot jobs (e.g., with a flashing symbol, bold font or in a separate highlighted section of the site), doing so is clearly an effective tool for employers to draw attention to certain positions. In a similar vein, some systems support wireless-enabled messaging so that recruiters can be instantly alerted when candidates that match the criteria they have defined as "hot" enter the database or apply for positions. An emerging leading-edge best practice is the use of integrated chat software and/or short messaging service (SMS) to candidates' cell phones and pagers, etc., to communicate with candidates in real time. Chat software may be a particularly promising add-on to career sites. Whether it is a group Q&A at a scheduled time or a facility for candidates to engage with corporate representatives on an individual basis, chat tools embedded into the corporate career site can add a layer of true interactivity to the site.

Specialized Recruitment Sub-Sites

Many organizations follow the best practice of providing a separate section off their career site aimed at recruiting senior college students and recent graduates. This can be further subdivided by sections for undergraduates and those with MBAs and other advanced degrees. Some companies, such as Capital One, have built separate sections to attract military personnel. Others, MetLife for example, have built interactive exercises to determine aptitude for sales positions. Sub-career-sites are useful in delivering specialized messages to targeted groups. Minus the clutter of the general purpose career site, they can offer different profile templates, tailored information, a look and feel that is more suitable to the particular audience and a means to establish specialized talent pools and talent relationship management initiatives.

The Applied Physics Laboratory (APL) at Johns Hopkins University employs dozens of new graduates each year. The APL offers an information-rich section for new graduates off its main career site. It includes static information about the Maryland area, on topics such as housing and recreation, for example. It also provides e-mail links to recent graduates who are currently working at APL so prospective employees can send questions to them.

Figure 3.12: APL

http://www.jhuapl.edu/employment/

Corporate career sites should reflect the fact that, depending on the company's lines of business, nearly half of all visitors will be experienced workers seeking mid- to senior-level positions. The corporate career site should be geared to all levels of job seekers, even to the executive level. Separate sub-sites can also be used to attract candidates by their level of experience, whether they are entry-level, mid-career, management or executive.

Progressive organizations are also starting to add separate marketing initiatives to re-recruit alumni—certain individuals who have worked for the organization in the past—depending on their skills and the circumstances of their departure. This usually consists of a separate career site with a specific and targeted marketing campaign. The career site for alumni should include features that let them connect with each other and with friends still in the company. It is critical that alumni be able to refer their friends and colleagues to positions as well. In this manner, ex-employees, who understand the organization's culture and needs, can be leveraged as "ambassadors." Alumni may be more inclined to refer excellent prospects to their current employers, but in cases where the match and fit are better, or a particular position is in question, they can often be counted on for excellent referrals. Certain alumni, essentially those that the organization would hire back under the right conditions, should be tracked and communicated with. The alumni network sub-career site, combined with a campaign to invite alumni to the site, will seed the beginnings of a special pool of company ambassadors and potential hires, valuable because its members are known quantities and individuals who are virtually job-ready if they can be enticed to return.

Burson-Marsteller, a mid-size public relations firm, has developed a separate section for alumni off its career site. It invites ex-employees to register for the site to facilitate networking, and, no doubt, to track them and invite some to consider positions within the company.

Though not yet an established best practice, leading sites are beginning to allow candidates to apply for positions anonymously. Early indications suggest that this is particularly appealing to experienced candidates and facilitates a healthy amount of job shopping inside organizations. Sometimes the best candidates are the ones who are most concerned about their privacy. This may be especially true inside the organization. A thriving internal talent market might be easier to build if staff can apply for positions with some measure of anonymity, at least until interest is expressed from the hiring manager. Organizations should be aware, however, that abuse of this option can result in unwieldy numbers of "fake" profiles and the subsequent waste of recruiters' and hiring managers' time.

Figure 3.13: Burson-Marsteller

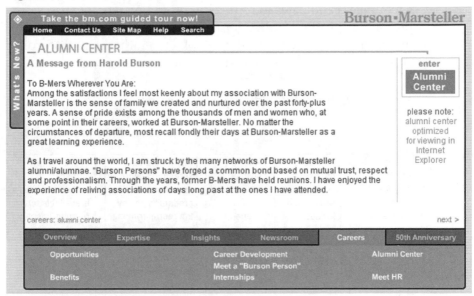

http://www.burson-marsteller.com/careers/alum_cen.html

Navigation and Ease of Use

Corporate career sites should be as intuitive as possible, with easy navigation and page-sensitive help screens. Use of organizational jargon and acronyms should be carefully edited out and replaced with labels and terms that can be easily understood by those unfamiliar with the organization. This is especially important in classifying jobs into categories, since category searches are the option preferred by the majority of job seekers. A simple but effective ease-of-use feature is to provide icons on each page that tell the candidates where they are in the process (of building their online resume/profile, for example) and how much they have remaining. Candidates should also be able to save their work and return to it later for completion.

The diagram below charts the typical paths of candidates on a corporate career site. Note that candidates should never be lost inadvertently just because there may be no position of interest at the time they enter the site or because they are screened out of the selection process for a specific position. Instead, candidates should be given the choice of applying for a position and/or leaving their profile in a searchable talent pool. This process encourages candidates to return (by providing reusable password-protected profiles, job agents, direct requests from hiring managers who search the talent pool, etc.) rather than discarding all but the ultimately successful candidate.

Figure 3.14: Typical Workflow for Applicants

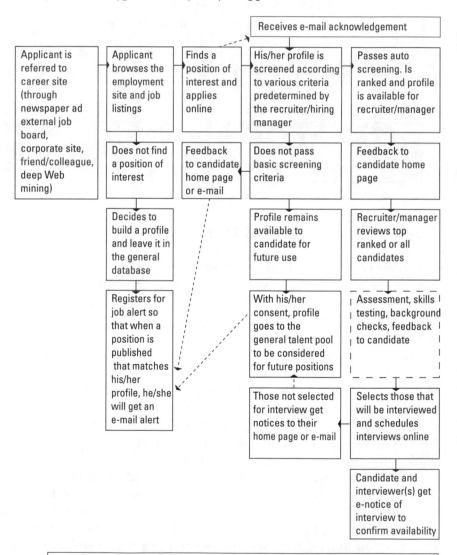

Note: Leading-edge best practices in the candidate user experience also involves elements of talent relationship management that are explained in Chapter 7.

Organizations should avoid the mistake of proceeding with employment branding strategies before implementing career site best practices. Money and time spent on advertising a positive message about the company can be completely or severely undermined if candidates have a negative experience when attempting to use the site to conduct company research and/or apply online. Similarly, a site that incorporates best practice features and functionality in the absence of a defined employment brand will also fail to leverage its investment fully.

Global Recruiting

Though this topic is described in greater detail in Chapter 4, it is applicable to the corporate career site discussion. The career site is the front end of any talent management system and the only part regularly seen by candidates. Multinational organizations and those that want to expand their recruiting nets should offer job opportunities in multiple languages. Of the one hundred organizations examined for this chapter, only five offered job information in more than just the English language. Four of these were Canadian organizations with French components and one was a U.S. company that offered some listings in Spanish.

Organizations should look at vendors that offer multiple-language capabilities or have technology architectures that support adding broad language capability (multibyte and 32-bit architectures) and other "internationalization" features. The cultural and regulatory differences at play throughout Europe, for example, can present substantial challenges to organizations that attempt to implement a unified global recruiting strategy.

Corporate Career Sites: A Final Note

Of great importance for any organization that chooses to use the Internet in its recruiting strategy are automated screening tools that eliminate, sort and rank applicants. While these are often driven by the "back-end" talent management system rather than as stand-alone features of the corporate career site, companies that do not own TMS software should nonetheless strive to reduce the number of applications a recruiter or hiring manager has to sift through by using automated screening tools. One such tool is an online questionnaire that can act somewhat as a pre-interview.

By attaching a short questionnaire to each job posting, organizations can require candidates to answer critical questions up front. Their answers can be used to eliminate them from consideration automatically, and/or rank and sort them depending on how well they answered the questions. The next chapter, and Chapter 5 on screening, sorting and ranking candidates, discusses this and other tools in greater detail.

Starbucks uses prescreening questionnaires. The completion of a questionnaire that has been tailored by the organization for each job posting is mandatory in order for a candidate to submit an application for most positions in the company.

Figure 3.15: Starbucks

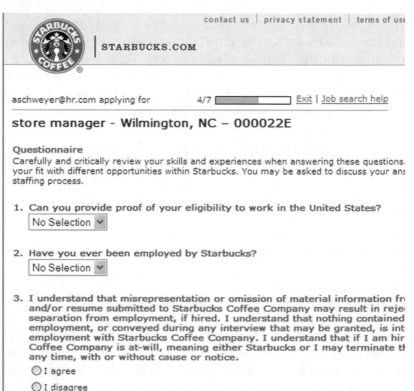

www.starbucks.com/aboutus/jobcenter.asp

Organizations should not neglect to monitor the success and use of their corporate career site after its launch. Site traffic should be watched and users occasionally polled as to their opinions of the site. Where applicable, new hires can be asked to rate their experiences using the site. A cross section of employees in the company can be assembled as a focus group before the site is launched, before major changes are made and/or to advise on what changes should be made. A simple approach can be to add a survey on the site itself in which users can comment on the effectiveness of the site and make suggestions.

Finally, smaller organizations that cannot afford the time or do not have the in-house expertise to build and maintain a corporate career site should consider third party vendors. There are several companies that offer Web-based templates that allow users to build career sites quickly and without having HTML or other expertise. Users can choose colors, fields, backgrounds and links. They can also upload their corporate logo. Vendors can host their clients' sites and provide them with Web interfaces to add jobs and make other changes. See the profile below for information on one such company.

Profile: MyWebJobs

MyWebJobs is a relatively recent entrant to the e-recruitment space and occupies a very narrow niche at its front end. For any small organization that wants to build a corporate career site, but does not have the expertise or time to develop one, MyWebJobs.com may be the answer.

Founder and CEO Doug Berg says the idea came to him when he was with Techies.com, a large, niche job board for technical recruiting. Berg recalls how Techies customers would often ask him if they could get their career site built for them. Usually they were HR professionals who had limited access to their technology group or corporate servers, and they wanted an easy, hosted solution that they could manage from within HR.

MyWebJobs is certainly not the first or only vendor to offer hosted, remote-controlled corporate career sites. Its service is, however, accessible, simple, inexpensive and hassle-free. It is also surprisingly robust. New users can build and launch a career site directly from the MyWebJobs.com site. They can choose from a variety of templates, easily post their jobs, and start collecting resumes—either by e-mail or, in the unlikely event they have an applicant/candidate tracking system, by referring applicants to their profile-building tools.

MyWebJobs.com creates dynamic search options for candidates based on the categories, locations, salary and requirements of positions posted. A sleek HTML editor lets users cut and paste job descriptions. Valid HTML is generated automatically. Customers can link their career sites to corporate HR information, such as benefits and company culture, residing on the corporate Web site. A partnership with eQuest (a job posting distribution company) enables automated job distribution to thousands of public job boards.

Fees are billed monthly and range from US$25 to US$100. For a nominal extra charge, clients can add job alert/agents. So far, MyWebJobs has signed more than one hundred customers. They are mainly small staffing firms, independent recruiters, small companies, colleges and volunteer organizations.

Figure 3.16: MyWebJobs

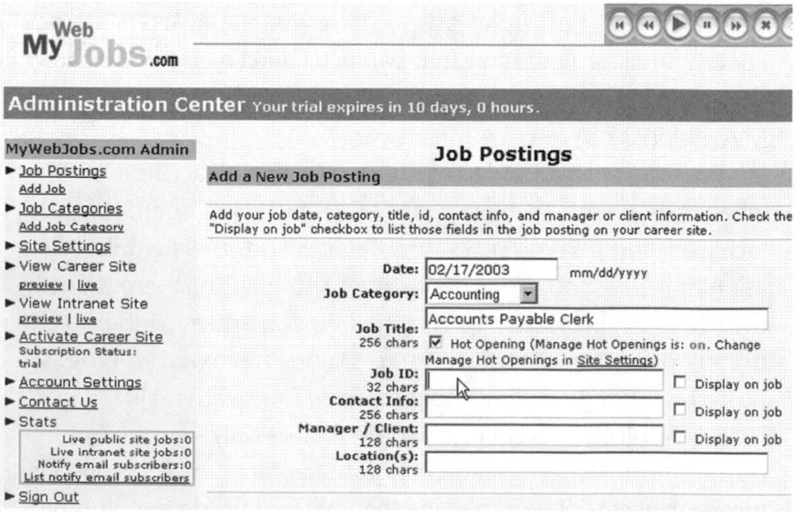

http://www.mywebjobs.com/demo/add_jobs.htm

Conclusions

The corporate career site represents the all-important candidate-facing portion of an e-recruit or talent management system. It must be easy to use and easy to find. It should contain detailed and rich information about the organization, including full job descriptions and culture and benefits information. Corporate career sites should be consistent with the organization's brand and should advertise its EVP—the benefits and advantages that make it a compelling place to work. Career sites should be developed as the front pieces to back-end database-driven solutions that facilitate other components of e-recruitment and talent management.

CHAPTER 4

卍

Talent Management Solutions: Overview

S oon after the emergence of job boards and corporate career sites, e-recruitment software vendors began to offer client/server and Web-based back-end software to help organizations manage the applications they received both online and off (i.e., mailed and faxed resumes). Those solutions were best known as applicant tracking systems (ATSs). Today, most large and progressive organizations tie their corporate career sites to a database-driven solution that can integrate numerous tools and third-party software components to facilitate effective workforce management.

Best practice, even for small and mid-sized organizations, is to integrate the corporate career site with a TMS that not only manages resumes and tracks applicants, but also delivers strategic advantages that enable users to hire faster, cheaper and better. The term TMS, in this sense, is in many ways synonymous with "hiring management system," "recruitment management system" and "candidate management system," but with several important distinctions.

As mentioned above, TMS ancestors include ATS. Most of the original ATS vendors have expanded their offerings such that the term is no longer sufficient to describe the range of their solutions. Moreover, the trend toward integration of a variety of e-recruitment and workforce management software with other tools in the talent "supply chain" to form end-to-end solutions requires a much broader term to describe it adequately.

As organizations move toward online recruitment, the largest single problem in applicant management is resume processing. Fortunately, the digitization and indexing of resumes is solved for applications that are received online. By encouraging candidates to apply via the corporate career site using application templates, organizations receive structured, digital resumes or profiles directly into a searchable database. Because resumes may arrive from a variety of sources, many solutions automatically check for duplicates and combine them into one record. This isn't to say that talent management systems do not or should not process mailed and faxed documents. In fact, many organizations maintain policies that allow for different methods of application. Solutions to capture and structure data from paper, fax and e-mails is discussed later in this chapter.

The Three Types of TMS Vendors

With well over one hundred vendors offering some or all TMS components, the industry is complex. Buyers must do their homework to discover the differences between the offerings in order to find the best fit for their organization. The problem can be simplified somewhat by looking at the vendors in several broad categories. First, there is the top category of suppliers who offer TMS as their only line of business, and are typically first to innovate with new features, services and functionality. Today, the top pure-play solutions providers include Recruitsoft, BrassRing, Hire.com, Recruitmax, Deploy, Yahoo! Resumix, VirtualEdge, Peopleclick, Unicru, Alexus and Kenexa. These vendors offer the best pure TMS solutions. They are particularly attractive when considering experience, focus, technology, upgrade schedules, project management and customer service. Thousands of organizations, from as few as several hundred employees to as large as several hundred thousand, use the suppliers above.

However, while tier-one solutions offer best-in-class technology, they come with a corresponding price tag often ranging from a few hundred thousand dollars per year to well over one million. And, while a few tier-one players are profitable, many are still losing money—even some with customer bases of more than one hundred (which is considered a healthy number of customers in this industry). Only a few are likely to go out of business or be acquired soon, but customers can and should protect themselves with solid SLAs and code-in-escrow guarantees that secure a copy of the latest software code at a third-party location as some assurance against the vendor going out of business (discussed in greater detail in Chapter 11). Finally, the top vendors have proven they can integrate their solutions with ERPs, but the process is often expensive and time consuming compared with TMS solutions offered by the ERPs themselves (though buyers should not assume that ERP e-recruitment solutions are delivered fully integrated).

Nevertheless, buyers representing large organizations with heavy recruiting requirements and a need for the best in technology and service should put tier-one solutions at the top of their lists. Eligible organizations include all of those that require proven solutions, high service levels and have a vision that includes strategic talent management. Strategic talent management might include such things as total workforce acquisition capabilities (hourly, salaried and contingent), workforce and succession planning, performance and learning management, career planning, and employee retention initiatives. While few of the suppliers can offer all of this in one package, they have the capability to integrate other systems and many have made public their intentions to offer end-to-end talent management systems.

The premier ERP solutions providers, PeopleSoft, SAP and Oracle, have also developed TMS within their HR suites. All tend to offer advanced features but have, to date, lagged behind the tier-one solutions in offering leading-edge functionality, tools, implementation processes, and R&D-related innovation. This may change. Oracle has launched an impressive system called iRecruitment and has attracted a number of marquee clients. SAP is latest to the market with mySAP HR E-Recruiting, and PeopleSoft is slowly but surely improving its TMS, called eRecruit, which is now boasting dozens of satisfied and reference-providing clients. On price, ERP TMS solutions may have greater flexibility to bundle their TMS products with other human capital management (HCM) or ERP tools, but buyers can expect to pay about the same in the end as for tier-one "best of breed" solutions.

ERP-supplied TMSs sometimes eliminate integration concerns (when integrating to the supplier's own ERP), which is perhaps the buyer's biggest advantage. Upon implementation, the TMS is a seamless part of the enterprise HCM suite, including payroll, Human Resource Management System(HRMS), learning and whatever other modules are licensed (however, as noted previously, this should not be assumed. Sap's e-recruitment solution, for example, requires a full integration effort even to integrate within SAP's own HRMS). Many tier-one solutions can also be integrated to the same degree but usually with considerably more time and expense. Another ERP advantage is chief financial officer (CFO) and chief information officer (CIO) preference for having one solution provider, maintaining one relationship and leveraging in-house knowledge of that vendor's technology.

Major ERPs are more financially stable than any of the tier-one solutions providers, but they are also pulled in many different directions. For example, ERP vendors have been known to assign a talented team to the development of a business component such as e-recruiting, only to disassemble it for other projects once the module is "complete." ERP vendors typically build and maintain a broad suite of integrated software, hence the name enterprise resource planning software. Recruiting and talent management is only one small element of their business, as can be seen by visiting their Web sites and trying to find information on those products. Moreover, their broader solutions are complex and expensive to purchase, operate and maintain. Many large organizations have spent tens of millions of dollars on full ERP rollouts including software purchase, implementation, maintenance and upgrades.

While ERPs can be seen as delivering more stability than other providers, established ERPs can be the target of takeovers, as with Oracle's 2003 bid for PeopleSoft and PeopleSoft's more friendly acquisition of JD Edwards the same year. While there is some risk that a tier-one solutions provider might go out of business or be acquired, there is also a small risk that an ERP could be acquired or lose interest in TMS, both leading to problems for its users.

ERP TMS solutions are best suited to large organizations with fairly strong recruiting needs that are less concerned with leading-edge practices and more focused on integration and single-platform issues. For example, a process-oriented organization like government might already be using an ERP across the enterprise. It is concerned that its recruiting solution be robust but equally viable. Instead of implementing the best-featured solution available, it might be as well served by purchasing its ERP vendor's e-recruitment toolset. It is unlikely that it will save costs doing so, nor will it necessarily have a more integrated system. It will, however, maintain just one vendor relationship and can be better assured that its provider will remain in business. As long as it is prepared to wait for the latest feature sets, the ERP option might be its best course of action.

Tier-two pure-play solutions are those players with less-known brands and, generally, less functionality that is aimed squarely at solving the resume management, applicant sourcing and applicant tracking challenges (applicant tracking systems, in other words). Tier-two players usually offer the necessary core functionality for the tasks above, and charge considerably less for their products—in many cases, under US$50,000 per year and almost always less than US$150,000. Most target organizations with 250 to 10,000 employees. Some tier-one point solutions providers have "light" versions of their software that compete with tier-two players. Tier-two players include Webhire, WetFeet, Workstream, iCIMS, Brainhunter and many others.

The primary risk with tier-two vendors is their stability. Indeed, several point solutions providers, including former tier ones, have exited the marketplace (Personic and Icarian, for example), leaving their customers scrambling for a replacement and, in some cases, without their data. Because tier-two players tend to be newer (with exceptions like Webhire), have fewer customers and smaller revenue streams, and face stiffer competition, they are generally more at risk than either tier-one or ERP suppliers.

Nonetheless, several tier-two players offer technology and services that are comparable to tier-one and ERP provider offerings—and they tend to provide it at more competitive prices than either. Webhire, iCIMS and Hodes iQ are examples of tier-two suppliers that offer core functionality (for sourcing, selecting, screening, tracking and measuring applicants) that compares well with their tier-one competition. Others, like HRsmart and Integrated Performance Systems (IPS), offer tools like integrated performance management and succession planning that are unavailable from all but a very few tier-one competitors. Many also provide guarantees (code in escrow and SLAs, for example) that can alleviate, though not eliminate, client concerns as to their stability. Small, mid-size and even some large organizations with aggressive recruiting strategies should shop around in this segment of the market. Buyers should look for solid customer lists (one hundred or more), good references, financial statements, results from audits of hosting facilities, flexible SLAs, code-in-escrow agreements and a professional services team capable of solid implementation and follow-through. The temptation to save money by purchasing in this end of the market is compelling and often a wise course of action, but due diligence is necessary. Organizations may find that a tier-two provider is capable of handling today's problems but they should also be sure that it can scale up to greater demands should they arise, that it has plans to develop its software in line with the buyer's future needs and that it can address all data, physical and network security concerns.

Finally, large job boards such as Monster (MOHQ) and HotJobs (SoftShoe) have come out with their own integrated solutions for resume and applicant management. Both are solid products that leverage the power of the world's largest job boards, with obvious benefits. They provide simple applicant tracking tools and relatively sophisticated features for screening, database mining and online job requisition building. They are almost always less expensive, even than the tier-two point solutions, and sometimes they are included in the fee a user pays to post jobs on the board, potentially putting these solutions within the grasp of organizations with only a few hundred dollars to spend at a time. Job board ATS solutions, while very lightly featured, offer some advantages that no other providers can claim. Buyers that are loyal and heavy users of the corresponding job board are obvious potential customers. Large companies that recruit extensively may use a job board ATS to complement a tier-one or ERP TMS solution. In rare cases, they may even use the job board solution exclusively, though this approach has clear limitations in robustness and scalability and lacks most of the extended elements of talent management discussed above.

TMS: The Basics

Basic talent management solutions let employers create, publish and store job requisitions. They should also allow for the collection, search, screening and sorting of candidate profiles. They should let companies organize profiles for easy retrieval and track them through the process from application to hire (when they are handed off to HRMS). TMS should be as easy to use as Web-based banking solutions, or sites like Amazon and eBay that let customers order or buy and sell goods online. Otherwise, TMS solutions will be difficult to implement across an organization with all types of users. Separate interfaces for power users (solution administrators), heavy users (recruiters), light users (hiring managers) and rare users (managers who approve requisitions only, for example) are necessary to leverage the full power of the solution and facilitate user adoption of the system. In a large organization with several thousand light and rare users, training may not be a practical option. Hiring managers, for example, might use the solution once or twice per year. If it is so complicated as to require training, it is probable that hiring managers will forget most of what they have learned in the space of time between uses of the system.

Common features in the best TMS include personalized access to users depending on their role in the hiring process. Client administrators should be able to configure an individual's user interface to display only the tools and features he or she is authorized to use. Recruiters, for example, might log in and see a welcome screen on which their outstanding tasks are listed in priority order. They might also see a list of their outstanding requisitions and the status of each. They may have access to requisition building screens, search tools, statistics, key performance indicators and the resume database, for example. There will likely be communications tools that let them collaborate with colleagues, hiring managers and external partners such as ad agencies and outside staffing firms, and alerts that warn them of logjams in the workflow and/or targets that are at risk. These alerts can be triggered by users to monitor the system automatically for events (or non-events) that are critical to the user's ability to perform their role efficiently.

Senior managers, on the other hand, may never have to access the system. Even though they might need to approve requisitions, review shortlisted candidates, participate in interviews and help rank interviewed candidates, they are often able to do so through e-mails that can be generated by the system. Their responses will automatically flow back to the system to update the appropriate records.

Several TMS solutions providers, offer functional and well-designed user interfaces. The screens below show what a recruiter or hiring manager would see in a well-designed interface. It tells them, at a glance, what requisitions they are working on and what is happening within each. Note that nearly everything is hyperlinked so that users can get more detail on any particular item with one click. Note also the help tools available, tips for users, and icons. The best solutions offer user interfaces that are deliberately designed to eliminate the need for formal user training—at least for casual users.

Figure 4.1: Hiring Manager Desktop

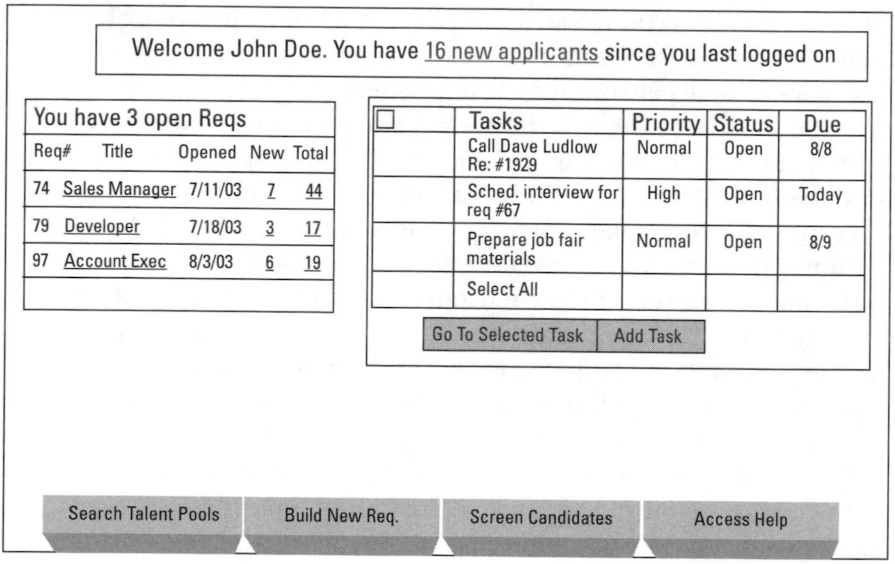

Welcome John Doe. You have 16 new applicants since you last logged on

You have 3 open Reqs

Req#	Title	Opened	New	Total
74	Sales Manager	7/11/03	7	44
79	Developer	7/18/03	3	17
97	Account Exec	8/3/03	6	19

Tasks	Priority	Status	Due
Call Dave Ludlow Re: #1929	Normal	Open	8/8
Sched. interview for req #67	High	Open	Today
Prepare job fair materials	Normal	Open	8/9
Select All			

Go To Selected Task | Add Task

Search Talent Pools | Build New Req. | Screen Candidates | Access Help

Organizations and vendors have discovered that TMS solutions can enable the supply chain of talent. This effectively moves the recruitment process from a reactionary exercise (cycle begins with an open requisition) to a proactive one in which partially prequalified talent pools can be created in anticipation of future hiring needs. The supply-chain approach is realized when technology is used to create synergies and information exchange between all of the collaborators (recruiters, hiring managers, candidates, recruitment ad media, external vendors and others) in the recruitment value chain. It is analogous to what has long been in place among goods manufacturers, their raw materials suppliers and subcontractors, and those they supply finished product to. In order to execute production and delivery most effectively, the supply chain must deliver materials and goods with the expected attributes (quality, price, etc.) as they are needed and based on forecasted demand. In the workplace, the demand for talent and skills can also be predicted. Talent management systems can aid in this forecasting and can act as the glue around which each of the suppliers and facilitators play their roles in delivering the right talent to the right place at the right time.

The Supply Chain Analogy

End-to-end e-recruitment cannot be better explained than by using the popular business concept called supply chain management (SCM). SCM normally refers to the process beginning with the order for merchandise through to its final delivery. In the HR recruiting world (a major component of talent management), the supply chain starts with an open position and ends with the hire. The diagram below illustrates how the main elements of basic and leading-edge best practices impact on the recruitment supply chain.

The diagram illustrates possible workflow in an organization that has adopted end-to-end e-recruitment. In the diagram, the solid path or line represents the best practice in which you have a partially prequalified talent pool from which to draw enough candidates to make posting the job unnecessary in at least some cases. When a job posting is necessary, it goes through approval(s) and is posted to the intranet, the corporate career site and possibly to print and public job boards. All external candidates are pushed through the corporate career site to apply. Those who apply by mail (ideally none or very few) are "processed" by a partner (organizations usually outsource this work) who scans and puts the resume through OCR software, verifies the resumes and seamlessly uploads them to the TMS. Screened-in applicants proceed along the chain. Screened-out applicants who meet minimum criteria for the general database are routed there.

Figure 4.2: The Supply Chain Analogy

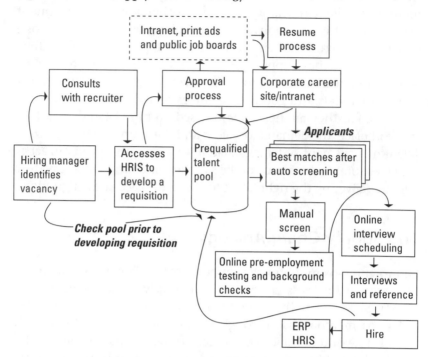

*Ideally, requisitions are constructed using clearly defined and objective criteria that can be measured scientifically against the information elicited from the candidate. This information is normally stored in the HRMS after job analysis.

Profiles of candidates who do not meet even the basic threshold set by the organization are eliminated altogether.

Note that the cycle does not end with a candidate being hired; rather, the cycle is continuous. New hires remain in the talent pool and are treated, like prequalified potential candidates, as a strategic resource to be further developed, marketed to and, in this case, retained if they prove to be valuable employees. Another diagram might show cycles involving the treatment of high-performing staff who leave the organization. In these cases, the ex-employee will be interviewed and invited to remain in the organization's alumni talent pool for the same purposes described above. The concept of corporate HR departments creating and managing prequalified pools of external, internal and even alumni talent is new and has not been adopted for use beyond a handful of organizations that have been practicing this method for only a few years. However, it is not a new concept entirely. Recruiters have long understood the value of networks in doing their work. Recruiters mainly nurture relationships with employed individuals in anticipation of matching them to future jobs on behalf of their clients. They understand the inherent inefficiencies involved in starting each new talent search from scratch. Recruiters know that they could not compete without their networks, which are, in effect, prequalified talent pools.

Back-end TMSs should perform a variety of basic best practice functions. In addition to integrated Web mining, screening, ERP, and background checking, which will be discussed later, organizations should look for candidate sourcing features (various methods to market jobs to potential candidates wherever they may be) that support broad distribution of job postings. It is rare to find a TMS that does not allow users to post to their intranet and corporate career sites, print media, agencies and hundreds or thousands of fee and free job boards from one interface, with just a few mouse clicks.

Job distribution features should support the timed release of postings. Positions should reside on the intranet exclusively for a period of time before automatically posting to the corporate career site and external job boards or media. Consolidated billing and reports demonstrating the results (candidates referred) from each of the sites posted to are must-have features. The best job distribution tools for online postings, when integrated with a TMS, can report not only which job boards supplied the most candidates, but also which supplied the best candidates. Here, "best" means those candidates who were selected for an interview and those who were offered positions.

Talent management systems should be equipped with powerful search engines that allow users to drill into their resume database with precision. Keyword, Boolean-based searching, while effective, is not as useful as next generation tools that enable searches on the same fields as candidates use to create their resumes. Even more advanced are search engines that allow entire job descriptions and/or model resumes to be used as search terms. Organizations should look for artificial intelligence in a search engine—the best of which, like Engenium's HireReasoning (see Chapter 6), use advanced pattern recognition to "learn" and improve over time as the resume/profile database grows. Advanced search tools are also indispensable in sorting through the electronic equivalent of piles of applications to find only the most appropriate candidates. Finding the proverbial needle in a haystack becomes more and more possible in direct correlation to the strength of the search tools in a TMS.

Below is a rendering of an advanced candidate search interface. Note the multitude of options both in terms of search criteria and methods of search. This layout does not represent every potential search option, but highlights the essential basic search and some elements of an advanced searching interface. A flexible search tool will allow searching by candidates name, by keywords, skills, education, location and many more parameters—the tool should be configurable to allow searches on any field in the candidate profile. It might also allow for conceptual or artificial intelligence based searching that enables the user to turn an entire job requisition or resume into a search parameter and lets users type in natural language search strings such as "operating room nurses in Detroit" for ease of use.

Figure 4.3: Advanced Search

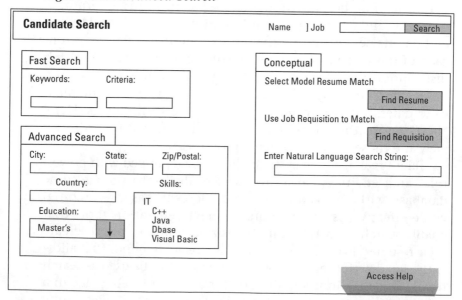

Of critical importance are a solution's tools to help recruiters and hiring managers screen, sort and rank candidates. Significant productivity improvements are possible by automating the process of eliminating inappropriate and/or unqualified candidates. This is typically done in several ways. Beyond the construction of an informative corporate career site and detailed job descriptions (see previous chapter), TMSs should offer the ability to create unique prescreening questionnaires for each job posting that eliminate or rank candidates based on their answers. A TMS should also support the use of skills and competency-based screening such that recruiters and hiring managers can advertise the attributes and experience levels they require within the job posting. Candidates can respond to these requirements by self-assessment and the solution can evaluate and rank them appropriately for recruiters. Also, as described above, a powerful search engine is needed to drill into the resume database with precision when looking for specific types of candidates.

Figure 4.4 below provides an example of a system that archives pre-screening questionnaires so that an organization can create a library approved for recruiter and hiring manager use. Developers and subject matter experts typically create sets of questions based

Figure 4.4: Pre-screening Questionnaire Libraries

Publish Job Requisition		

Attach Questionnaire		
Document Name	Description	Organization
Select Sr. Project Mgr	5 Questions	IT
Select Admin Assistant	Generic	HR
Select Account Executive	Replaces 2002 version	Marketing
Select Bookeeper Level 1	Generic	HR

on attributes, skills and experience that reliably predict success in any particular job or job family. Alternatively, or in combination, questionnaires can be used to simply screen out candidates that are clearly not qualified or eligible for the position (e.g., do not have authority to work in the country, are underage, do not hold the required license, etc.). These questions are stored in the system and emerge as an option whenever a recruiter or hiring manager initiates a job requisition for a related position.

Beyond the basics, organizations should explore the viability of using psychometric testing and online skills, knowledge or abilities tests to reduce shortlisted candidates even further—potentially down to the three or five candidates who will be invited to interview. Automated screening and assessment must be monitored and integrated with human screening and selection processes, but the practice of manually screening hundreds or thousands of applicants for each position is inefficient, inconsistent, inaccurate, non-transparent and potentially unfair compared to the automated processes available now. Screening and assessment tools are discussed more thoroughly in the next chapter.

TMS vendors offer various levels of screening through their questionnaire and search functionality. Candidates can be assessed in stages through integrated screening questionnaires, assessments and skills matching in the resume database. In Figure 4.5 below, the hiring manager or recruiter sees a ranked list of candidates that match against a skills search. Note that each candidates' name is hyperlinked for easy retrieval of their resume and that each of the headings in the table will resort the candidates if they are clicked on. Initially, all candidates are ranked against how well they matched to the search criteria, including the questionnaire.

Figure 4.5: Ranked and Sorted Search Results

47 Candidates Met Your Criteria							
▲ = External ▼ = Internal							

Name	Type	Location	Source	Date Received	Activity	Rank	Show?
Nancy Drew	▲	Dallas	Monster	8/4/03	Yes	79%	
Walter Waloshuk	▼	Toronto	Intranet	3/16/03	No	77%	
Bill Harlow	▼	Boston	Intranet	5/22/03	No	77%	
Patsy Cline	▲	Toledo	Career Site	7/9/03	No	76%	
Nancy Drew	▲	Dallas	Monster	8/4/03	Yes	75%	
Tom Hardy	▼	Toronto	Intranet	3/16/03	No	75%	
Bill Harlow	▼	Boston	Intranet	5/22/03	No	72%	
Patsy Cline	▲	Toledo	Career Site	7/9/03	No	67%	
Norma Kraay	▲	Dallas	Monster	8/4/03	Yes	65%	
Tom Hardy	▼	Toronto	Intranet	3/16/03	No	61%	
Bill Harlow	▼	Boston	Intranet	5/22/03	No	57%	
Feita Kraay	▲	Toledo	Career Site	7/9/03	No	53%	

Refine Search	Access Help

Global-Ready TMS

Organizations with offices in several countries may require a solution that can operate in different languages, cultures and even currencies. Moreover, systems used for international or global recruiting must respect local data privacy laws and customs. Many vendors, such as PeopleSoft, Recruitsoft, Hire.com, BrassRing and Peopleclick have numerous customers based in a variety of countries throughout North America, Europe, South America and the Asia/Pacific region. Vendors without existing international clients may still be worth considering if their solutions are written in such a way as to facilitate translation, internationalization and multiple configurations. Buyers should look for customer lists that include multinationals using the solution in multiple countries, for vendors with plans to establish international offices and for a software architecture that supports 32-bit or double-byte character sets.

Many of the ERP and tier-one TMS providers let customers build front ends for job seekers in numerous languages. What is more unique are solutions in which the entire back end, the portion not seen by job seekers, is also fully translated, making use by hiring managers, recruiters and administrators much more comfortable. MrTed and VirtualEdge are two providers that offer this capacity.

Recruitsoft offers one of the industry's most global-ready solutions. With clients in more than sixty countries, and offices in North America, Europe and Asia, it caters to multinational organizations needing one solution that can be customized for local use worldwide. Global recruiting goes far beyond language requirements however. It includes the ability to offer different corporate career sites with different applicant and user workflows, yet capture all of the relevant data in one central database for analysis. In short, it means catering to local legal, language and currency requirements as well as cultural preferences in multiple countries while maintaining just one solution centrally.

Figure 4.6: Language Options for User Interface

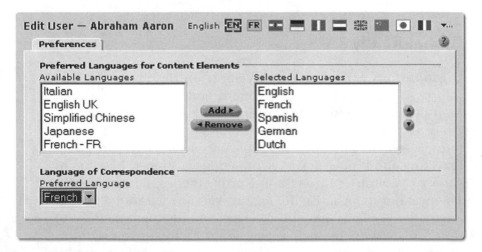

Resume Processing

As referred to several times previously, an historic challenge facing recruiters has been the handling of unstructured resumes.

There are an infinite variety of ways to present information on a resume. Some candidates lead with objectives, others highlight their education, while some present their work experience up front. Skills-based resumes de-emphasize education and work chronologies in favor of listing the skills and competencies acquired throughout the job seekers' academic, work and personal lives. As a result, when recruiters and hiring managers receive a stack of resumes, they have no easy way to quickly compare them. Instead, they must find the information they are looking for in each by reviewing the entire document.

Structured profiles, on the other hand, are a form of resume that forces candidates to place their information in a standardized template. While this stifles creativity to a degree, it enables recipients to find the information they need fast because they know where it will be in the document. On paper, this speeds the sorting process significantly, hence the preference some organizations have for the paper-based application form. In TMSs, standard profiles enable the collection of skills, experience and education in a structured format that enables automated screening, searching and sorting as well as easy manual comparison of applicants.

Resume processing is important in TMSs because it can convert otherwise unstructured resumes into structured profiles. Unless an organization is planning to institute a Web-only application policy, it should look for a TMS that offers integrated resume processing options. For e-mailed resumes, most vendors offer methods to automatically receive and structure incoming resumes, then attach them to specific jobs and deposit them in the general resume database/talent pool. Paper resumes must be scanned and digitized, then processed into the database. Many vendors offer integrated services and will do this for their customers at an additional cost of between US$1–$3 per resume (depending on whether it is mailed, faxed or e-mailed), declining with volume.

Organizations should look for resume processing solutions that are fully integrated with their TMS. This is accomplished by using either the TMS vendor's own solution or a preferred partner's solution. Both it and the TMS vendor should use open architectures and support XML APIs for true integration.

Resumes can be obtained from any source. If they are mailed or faxed, they need to be scanned, run through OCR software and cleaned up manually before they can be put through extraction. Resumes collected from spiders (tools that automatically search Internet resume databases and the Internet itself) and job boards can arrive in HTML, Word, WordPerfect, Rich Text Format (RTF), Portable Document Format (PDF) and text. Most extractors will recognize and work with all of these formats. Resumes are processed and converted to structured documents—in some cases, the extractor will process them into HR-XML (Human Resource Extensible Markup Language or the XML used by large vendors like Peopleclick, Recruitsoft and Monster.

For corporate career sites, extraction software can come at the beginning of the process so that candidates need not complete a template to build a profile or online resume. If they cut and paste their existing resumes into the extractor, their online resume/profile is built for them (to varying degrees), leaving them with the much smaller task of reviewing and fixing any extraction mistakes or omissions.

This means that resumes received from the corporate career site can enter the database in a structured format along with those from other sources. For resumes received by e-mail, most vendors offer a tool that reads the e-mail, separates the attachment or appended resume, processes/extracts it into XML and, based on the subject line in the e-mail, places it in the correct job folder within the database and/or into the general database itself. Organizations should ensure that their processing solution is capable of automatically communicating back to candidates who have e-mailed their resumes in application to jobs. Using the candidates' e-mail addresses, an automatically generated e-mail is returned to the candidates, thanking them for their application and providing them a usercode, password and URL that they can link to if they want to access the profile constructed for them from the resume they e-mailed. This method directs applicants to the preferred application method—the corporate career site.

The figure below illustrates the process necessary to convert paper resumes to structured profiles, and the advantages of collecting candidate data directly via the corporate career site. Note: the best practice use of extraction software for job seekers is assumed, as is the best practice of processing data in XML.

Figure 4.7: Resume Processing

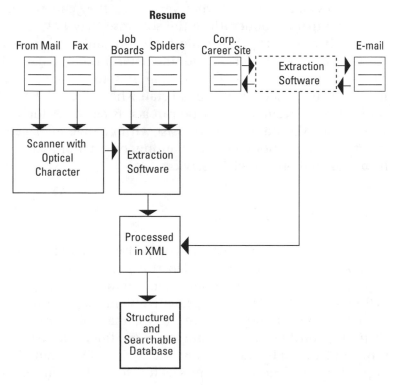

TMS and the Intranet

Talent management systems can support retention efforts when made available internally through the corporate intranet. They can integrate employee referral plans (Chapter 6) and aid enormously in understanding the corporate skills and competency inventory. They can also aid in performing skills gap analysis, workforce analysis and workforce planning (Chapter 7). For example, some hiring management systems, like Hire.com, BrassRing, Oracle and others, facilitate the development of an internal database of workforce information. Among other things, this type of database can enable a planned and orderly filling of positions with both internal and external candidates, rather than an urgent and reactionary response as key positions become vacant.

Organizations should ensure that they fully understand the capabilities and features of whatever system they choose. Far too often, companies underutilize the software they have paid for because it can be expensive and time-consuming to train staff adequately, or even to read and understand the manuals. First, choose a user-friendly system, develop in-house trainers who are trained by the vendor, and appoint staff who will get to know the application thoroughly and who can act as resources for others. The vendor should be able to assist with change management issues through various levels of training, orientation, self-service help tools and other tools or services.

ROI

With tight budgets and plenty of competition for scarce resources within most organizations, HR departments are forced to make a strong bottom-line case for new spending on technologies. The ROI presented by talent management systems depends on a variety of factors. In organizations using manual processes and spending considerable amounts on recruitment advertising in print and through headhunters, the ROI in TMSs can be very impressive. For those that are seeking to replace an outdated "home-grown" solution with a tier-one TMS, the ROI should also be very strong. Organizations that fall prey to the trap of automating poor processes may actually encounter negative ROI because they might find themselves supporting parallel recruitment procedures. The quote below is excerpted from a conversation with a state government project manager who led the implementation of a TMS. It is used because it speaks to the type of ROI that is often overlooked, that of time savings for corporate users, improved relationships with candidates and the likelihood that better hires are made as a result.

> *In the first six months that we have been in operation, we have placed fifty-one recruitments [requisitions] into our automated system. These fifty-one recruitments have generated over twelve thousand applications that have been reviewed by our automated system. This has resulted in a savings of 112,773 minutes (1,880 hours) of our staff*

time (opening mail, sorting the applications, manually reviewing the applications, manually reviewing and scoring qualification exams and data entering the information into our mainframe for name certification).

The biggest savings however, is in the amount of time applicants save when applying for jobs. Our new streamlined testing process is vastly faster and easier for the candidate than the old exam processes we used. For example, some job classes required the candidates to drive to one of our test sites (ten sites located around the state), take a four-hour qualification exam, and then drive home. This routinely required the applicant to take at least six hours of their life to test as we scheduled them to appear. Our new process lets them apply when they want to—from home, office or anywhere with Internet access—and apply online. The average time to apply is approximately thirty minutes. Quite a change from six hours. Not all exams were as extensive, but almost every exam shows some savings to the customer. Our figures show that twelve thousand applicants have saved a staggering 497,602 minutes (8,293 hours) of their time. We've received quite a few compliments for that change.

TMS Project Leader,
Washington State Government

Clearly, organizations and the candidates they hope to attract stand to gain a great deal in time and cost savings through e-recruitment. However, to realize these gains, organizations must encourage candidates to visit the corporate career site to browse, search for and apply to jobs, and to use this over all other methods. Simply opening another channel for sourcing, while maintaining budgets for traditional recruitment advertising and staffing, will result in more expenditure rather than less. Organizations should examine their current recruitment processes to understand where technology can offer improvements. The Web has surpassed newspapers in its ability to reach more, more specific, and more diverse candidates, for example, and it is also a far more cost-effective medium. Talent management systems have proven their ability to manage applications and screen candidates automatically as well. This is another clear winner in

terms of saving money and time. Saving job requisitions, enforc-
ing pay scales and streamlining the contingent workforce
spending are other examples that can demonstrate clear hard
cost savings.

The more an organization is willing to leverage its TMS solution, the more ROI will be achieved. For example, about 45
percent of Fortune 500 companies have adopted Web-only application policies already, according to iLogos Research.[1] This is a
reasonable step toward a rational and efficient process, especially
now when virtually every job seeker (with the possible exception
of those in the remotest of places) has some sort of access to the
Internet either at home, the office, libraries, Internet cafes or
other public Internet access sites. As per the previous chapter,
some organizations have gone so far as to say that they are not
interested in candidates who cannot demonstrate the minimal
resourcefulness necessary to find and use their corporate career
site. The practice of accepting applications online only can also
aid considerably in instituting and tracking an affirmative
action/EEO plan (see Chapter 8: Legal, Ethical and Fairness
Concerns in E-Recruitment).

Nevertheless, an organization not yet ready to make the leap to
a Web-only application policy should at least promote the corporate career site as its preferred method of application. The figures
below roughly outline the costs and benefits associated with the
three methods by which individuals can normally apply to jobs in
organizations. Note the tremendous list of advantages for online,
Web-based applications compared to e-mail and traditional applications. Also note that counter to the normal course of things, the
option offering the most advantages also presents the lowest costs.

Figure 4.8 illustrates two things. First, the organization that
encourages online applications via its corporate career site provides
the candidate with an exponentially richer, more valuable experience. Candidates can take advantage of numerous tools to make
their job-hunting easier, less time-consuming and more fruitful.
They can access deep information about the job and the organization, and they can better track and manage their job search
depending on the tools the organization offers them on the corporate career site (see last chapter). All of this adds up to better

---

[1]See www.ilogos.com/en/expertviews/trendwatch/trendWatch_073.html.

Figure 4.8: Best Practice ROI

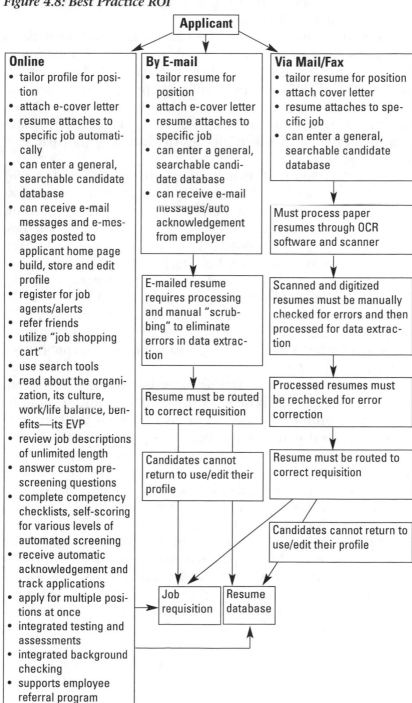

employment branding for the organization and the likelihood of attracting better candidates.

Second, organizations that take advantage of all the benefits offered by fully automated e-recruitment often garner enormous time and cost savings. "Back office" management of applications results in more efficient processing of applications in general, and faster, more accurate and more objective screening and sorting, which results in the identification of the best candidates more quickly. Further, it promotes the values of transparency, equity and fairness.

Organizations that switch from print-based employment advertising to Web-based advertising can realistically expect cost savings in sourcing of between 85 percent and 95 percent. Indeed, the use of print advertising of job vacancies in the U.S. has been in steep decline since 1999, while the use of the Web has been growing at an incredible pace. Today, the Web is by far the largest venue for job postings in North America. Clearly, there is an advantage to routing all applications through the corporate career site. Not shown in Figure 4.8 is the commonly cited statistic estimating the costs of processing resumes made online—at about 5 percent of the cost of processing applications made by mail or fax.

By using effective TMS technologies there is less need for concern of volume when posting positions. The requisition can be distributed online as widely as desired through the corporate career site and external job boards. Applicants will be pre-screened instantly against the standard criteria and job-specific requirements set by the recruiter or hiring manager. This, in combination with descriptive job postings and information-rich career sites, will ensure that only the most qualified candidates need be processed through human screening.

Automating the recruitment workflow helps standardize the consistency of the hiring process. This should result in better quality hires. It enables decentralized execution of tasks among thousands of users while sustaining high quality because central control over the standards and overall process is maintained.

Automation of the recruiting process enables organizations to build prequalified pools of potential new hires that can be tapped into the instant a vacancy arises (see Chapter 7 for more detail). By mastering what is usually referred to as talent relationship management (TRM), organizations reduce average time to hire, become more competitive employers and avoid the lost productivity and momentum that arises when a key position lies vacant. TRM means building rapport, interest and trust with individuals before they apply, after they apply, through the hiring process, after they have been hired and even after they leave the organization.

Conclusions

Talent management systems encompass a broad range of tools that do three essential things. First, they streamline processes for hiring managers, recruiters and administrators, saving time and money in the process. Second, they improve the experience for job applicants and candidates, enhancing the organization's brand and securing for it a better quality of applicant. Finally, TMSs provide a means to manage the workforce strategically—to build, reorganize and develop talent so that it is always in the right place at the right time with the right skills.

CHAPTER 5

꼬

Screening, Sorting and Ranking Applicants

In survey after survey of HR professionals, hiring managers and recruiters, applicant overload ranks among the main concerns. Since the 2001 market meltdown, as the unemployment rate has increased, organizations are receiving much greater numbers of inappropriate and clearly unqualified candidates. While this problem persists, and even when it eases, technologies that assist in screening, ranking and sorting candidates will permeate the HR technologies landscape.

The Internet has extended organizations' ability to reach many more job seekers. The result is often a flood of applications, which creates more work in screening and sorting. Large, well-known companies like Microsoft and Lockheed Martin receive between six hundred thousand and one million resumes per year. Even smaller companies that post on the big job boards like Monster and HotJobs can expect to receive hundreds, even thousands of applications per job posting.

Despite this, due to unawareness or fear of unproven technologies, organizations have been slow to adopt automated screening, sorting and assessment tools. Today, most organizations that use these tools do so to eliminate just the basic layer of clearly unqualified candidates—those that lack a certification necessary for the position, for example.

This initial pass/fail type of screening is very useful and practical. It involves the use of prescreening questionnaires specific to the position advertised. Candidates are required to answer the five to ten questions that typically form a questionnaire and the solution automatically sorts applicants according to how they answered the questions. Many organizations find that they can eliminate between 25 percent and 50 percent of applicants this way, automatically, and in real time (as they apply). Another benefit of using technology to separate qualified from unqualified applicants is the ability to process, screen, filter, sort and rank candidates without getting tired or bored. This means that thousands of applicants can be screened in real time and systematically according to the criteria entered by the hiring manager without the possibility of human inconsistency skewing the results.

In general, using screening technologies to separate minimally qualified candidates from those who clearly fail to meet basic criteria cuts selection costs dramatically, by 50 percent to 95 percent according to credible research.[1] The ROI in basic prescreening tools is compelling. After minimal up-front effort, the time and costs associated with the classic separation of applicants into two piles, one for those who clearly cannot be considered and another for those who require further screening, can be accomplished instantly. If a position has six hundred applicants, for example, and it takes an HR assistant earning US$40,000 per year forty-five seconds to accurately review and sort each of them, the cost savings are almost US$200 from just one function associated with one job requisition.

Almost all TMS vendors offer prescreening capacity as part of their toolset. Normally, this allows hiring managers to "knock out" candidates who provide negative responses to mandatory requirements. More sophisticated prescreening questionnaire tools also allow for weighing and ranking responses to questions. Depending on the technology used, the hiring manager or recruiter logs into the system to access a ranked and sorted list of candidates that can be further sorted and searched upon. The list tells her or him how closely the list of applicants match the criteria set out in the questionnaire. By clicking on a candidate's name, the full resume or profile, as well as the candidate's specific answer to each question, can be seen. Again, depending on the solution, the manager or recruiter may be

---

[1] According to an Aberdeen Research report by Dr. Katherine Jones entitled "Enterprise Talent Management: Sourcing, Staffing, Hiring 2002."

able to reset the weights originally assigned to individual screening questions and adjust the candidate list accordingly.

Adding to the administrative burden of screening resumes is the need to store applications for a period of time in case hiring practices are challenged by an applicant or the government. The difficulty for employers in the United States is that there exists no clear and legal definition of an applicant. This makes it difficult for employers to know whether they are in full compliance with regulations concerning the treatment of applicants and the storage of their information. In 2001, the U.S. Office of Management and Budget (OMB) gave the Office of Federal Contract Compliance Programs (OFCCP) and U.S. Equal Employment Opportunity Commission (EEOC) a mandate to create a clear definition, but as yet they have not done so. The consensus interpretation of the rules to date suggest that each employer should create its own defensible definition of an applicant, document it and enforce the application procedure that goes with it.

For example, at Company A, an applicant is someone who follows the organization's application procedures. This means they must complete a short profile on the company Web site, attach their resume, answer any mandatory questions that are attached to the position and submit it. At Company B, no such definition or procedure has been defined and communicated. In theory, Company B must treat every person who expresses an interest in any position in any manner, even orally, as an applicant. The only guidelines that exist state that an applicant is a "person who has indicated an interest in being considered for hiring, promotion, or other employment opportunities."[2] Without a defensible company definition in place, the fallback may be this more rigid, if somewhat vague, definition. For example, does it mean that anyone who sends an unsolicited resume to an organization must be treated as an applicant? If so, the implications for organizations that do not operate a talent management or applicant tracking system might be overwhelming in terms of record-keeping.

In the scenario above, Company A, which owns and has deployed recruitment technologies, is in a much better position to handle applicants and defend itself against challenges from candidates or regulators. It receives applications from one source only and

---

[2] See OFCCP (Office of Federal Contract Compliance Programs) Web site: www.dol.gov/esa/ofccp.

the bulk of the processing is left up to the technology. If its systems are tuned appropriately, 25 percent to 50 percent of applications will be deemed unfit upon initial automated screening. In accordance with employment laws, those applications will be stored by the system for easy retrieval for a determined period of time. Meanwhile, Company B spends days and weeks sorting and screening unstructured resumes and then must devote space in filing cabinets to the storage of thousands of resumes.

Company B finds itself in an ongoing quandary when it comes to screening and assessing the "good" pile of resumes. Company A has reduced its candidates virtually instantaneously with 100 percent accuracy using its automated prescreening toolset. It can now apply advanced automated screening, such as skills profiling and online testing to reduce its "good" pile to a shortlist suitable for final manual screening. Company B must pass its "good" pile on to people with more expertise to reduce the list to ever smaller piles until an interview list is finally arrived at.

While it is true that no computer algorithm can produce the best and final match for a job, when properly calibrated by experts to the requirements sought, software is better suited than humans in conducting initial screening against clear-cut and unambiguous requirements, as well as systematic and objective skills, education and candidate preference information. The best practice of using technology to screen applicants enables recruiters and hiring managers to focus on fewer—but higher quality—candidates.

Before even prescreening questionnaires, the most basic screening tool is the job advertisement itself. A well-constructed job posting starts the selection process correctly by giving candidates a means of self-screening. The first line of defense against a tidal wave of applications is arming candidates with enough information to self-assess their suitability for an advertised position. Following that comes the use of prescreening questionnaires and, finally, more sophisticated automated screening in back-end technologies that filter, sort and rank candidates.

Self-Selection through Online Job Advertising

As above, the job description is the first line of defense in screening candidates. Postings should spell out firm requirements and provide details to allow effective candidate self-screening. It is a fallacy that Internet job postings need to be brief—they don't. Full sentences should be used and abbreviations and jargon avoided. As described briefly in Chapter 3, organizations should take care to lead candidates through their corporate career sites to the divisions and positions that best match up to their qualifications and interests.

This can be accomplished in a number of ways. First, candidates should be able to search all available postings without registering on the corporate career site. However, before allowing online applications, it is wise to require some information from the candidate, usually an electronic profile. The profile is much like a resume. It collects candidate information in a structured manner, including classic "tombstone" information (name, contact info, etc.) and most other items found on resumes such as career, education and objectives information. Upon completion of the profile, candidates can be allowed to apply for the position that initially caught their eye and they can be encouraged to sign up for automated job agents that e-mail, at desired intervals, advertised positions that match up to their interests and qualifications. Candidates are notified of any suitable positions by e-mail.

Effective online job advertising can be summed up and remembered using a simple acronym developed by HR.com for training purposes—ADS: *attract*, define, sell (see figure below). The first part of the ad should attempt to attract candidates. The job ad is the first and often only thing candidates see. Remember that the job title (especially on public job boards) will often appear in a list with ten or more other job titles. So, instead of calling a position "Project Manager," try something more descriptive such as "PeopleSoft Implementation Project Manager—Fortune 500 Company" or "Project Manager—Cutting-Edge ERP Implementation Assignment."

The job description forms the *describe* section of the ad. It should encourage candidate self-screening. The purpose of the describe section is to discourage unqualified candidates and encourage qualified ones. At a minimum, do the following:

- Give as much information as is possible and practical.
- State the minimum qualifications prominently and clearly.
- Describe qualifications that will be used to rank applicants.
- Include required hard skills (programming skills, for example) and level of proficiency/experience.

- List experience desired in the industry if any, or in general.
- List educational requirements.
- Describe necessary soft skills (teamwork, for example).
- Describe the working conditions as realistically as possible (solo or team work; flexible hours or set times; long hours; regular weekend and night work; shifts; travel requirements; high level of structure; or flexible or ambiguous work, among other things).

Finally, *sell* the remaining candidates. Hopefully, your *describe* section will have eliminated many or most of the unqualified candidates. Advertise the good points. For example:

- Is the salary in the top quartile for the position and industry?
- Are benefits a strong point?
- Are there excellent developmental and/or career opportunities?
- Does the company have strong work/life benefits (casual dress code, telecommuting, sabbaticals, or better-than-average vacation allotments, for example)?
- Is it in a great location? Are the facilities exceptional?
- Does it enjoy a strong, recognizable brand (e.g., IBM, Microsoft, Fidelity)?

Figure 5.1: Creating Effective Online Job Ads

- Are there interesting/intriguing projects in the works or in the pipeline that the successful candidate might be working on?
- Were previous incumbents promoted or recruited to higher positions (i.e., possibility of strong advancement potential)?
- Is the corporate culture attractive and/or well known (e.g., SAS, Southwest Airlines, etc.)? Has it been recognized as a top employer (e.g., in Fortune, Forbes, Bay Area Top 200, etc.)?

Prescreening Questionnaires

If too many applications from unqualified candidates are being received, features that allow applicants to apply for several positions with one click (for example, job carts with multiple apply features) should be eliminated. Some employers, in addition to attaching a comprehensive "statement of qualifications" to each posting, require that all candidates answer prescreening questions (as described previously) before submitting their applications. If the answers do not equal a "pass," the candidate receives a polite rejection e-mail almost instantaneously.

Most talent management solutions let recruiters build and/or select questionnaires for each specific job advertisement (Figure 5.2). Typically, questions can be set to "knock out" to eliminate candidates who answer questions incorrectly. Questions may also rank the candidates. Some questions or answers are weighted or awarded more heavily than others. Candidates will not be eliminated based on their answers to these questions but will be ranked versus other candidates. In Figure 5.2 on page 116, candidates that select "No" in question one or "No, I require a visa" in question three might be eliminated or knocked-out. Candidates that answer "Business/ Commerce" in question 2 might get three points while those that answer "healthcare" might get one point depending on the requirements of the job. Not shown is the recruiters ability to add drop down and free text type response options.

Information about type and years of experience, willingness to travel or relocate, eligibility to work in the country, education and salary requirements is useful information against which to screen out unsuitable candidates online using job- or job-class-specific questionnaires. For example, a hospital that is seeking nurses might

Figure 5.2: Prescreening Questionnaire

Build questionnaire for Project
Manager

1. Do you have hands on experience with Microsoft Project Version 4 or higher?
   - ◯ No
   - ◯ Yes, 6 months or less
   - ◯ Yes, 1 year
   - ◯ Yes, 2 or more years

2. What was your major area of study in college/university?
   - ◯ Business/Commerce
   - ◯ IT/Computer Science
   - ◯ Engineeringr
   - ◯ Healthcare

3. Are you legally entitled to work in the United States?
   - ◯ No, I require a visa
   - ◯ Yes, I am a citizen
   - ◯ Yes, I have a green card or work visa

| Add Question | Access Help |

ask candidates whether they possess a professional designation. A construction company might ask applicants for an electrician position whether they are certified. Prescreening is easy to implement and can save time because it eliminates the manual procedure of sorting eligible and ineligible resumes into two piles. Beyond that, it can provide a rough ranking of candidates within the "consider further" pile. Implementing this level of screening is a quick win for most organizations that have implemented e-recruitment tools.

As discussed previously, this basic level of screening can remove 25 percent to 50 percent (or more) of applications automatically and without any manual intervention. No talent management system should be purchased without it.

Profiling Candidates' Skills, Competencies, Education and Experience

In addition to answering custom questionnaires attached to job postings, all candidates, both internal and external, should complete skills, education and competency profiles. Details from profiles can be quickly and accurately compared to requisitions and against other candidates' profiles by the software's search engine. This exercise also produces a greater ability to redeploy human capital internally because the organization obtains a skills inventory and can match employees to requirements swiftly and systematically. Beyond skills, competencies and education, candidates might also be asked to indicate their preferences vis-à-vis working style, supervision, preferred task types and work environment.

Concerns that some job seekers, particularly the more qualified ones, may be unwilling to complete skills questionnaires have proven to be unfounded in a number of studies. When candidates, both internal and external, are satisfied that their time investment pays off with better, more efficient matches to positions and faster response to applications, most will spend a reasonable amount of time (perhaps fifteen to twenty minutes or more) necessary to apply for positions they are interested in.

Clearly, organizations that employ recruiters or clerical staff to perform the first level of screening should replace this inefficient process completely through the use of the techniques described above. It makes little sense to utilize e-recruitment technologies (such as job boards, corporate career sites and Web mining, for example) if the almost inevitable increase in applicants means recruiters, hiring managers or their assistants are going to spend even more of their time sifting through the hundreds of thousands of resumes or profiles of unqualified candidates.

Advanced Automated Screening and Sorting

Beyond basic prescreening, sophisticated screening is often performed by HR consultants, recruiters and hiring managers. This stage usually involves reducing the applicants screened in during the initial stage to a manageable group that may be considered for interviews, background checks, skills testing and assessments. It is more difficult to automate this level of screening because it is the type that attempts to predict candidate success in the job. However, if an organization is willing to invest the time to examine each of its positions (commonly referred to as job analysis) or at least job families, current technologies can be used to further filter applicants to specific positions (also see Legal, Ethical and Fairness Concerns in E-Recruitment in Chapter 8). The following steps are necessary:

1. Positions (ideally) or job families must be examined so that success criteria can be defined. What skills, experience, knowledge, competencies, work values/preferences and personality traits are important and necessary to be successful in the position? At the very least, create a competency profile for each critical position and others for "classes of similar positions." Note that some vendors of assessment technology (such as ePredix, Kenexa and SHL) have many years worth of data. They have validated their assessment tools against thousands of jobs that are common to many employers. Engaging this type of partner can save considerable time. In many cases, job analysis can be avoided (for certain positions) altogether and the work significantly reduced for others.

2. Questions must be formulated that will draw information from candidates that can be used to fairly evaluate them against the criteria. For example, if a position has been determined to need a person with strong consensus-building skills, a solid question might be, "During negotiations, are you inclined to compromise, or do you focus on achieving agreements that give you or your client the clear advantage?" Note that the candidate cannot guess at what constitutes a correct answer. For some positions, a compromising personality might be better; for others, an adversarial approach may be desirable.

3. The software must be able to compare candidates against the criteria and each other objectively, transparently and fairly. This can happen if an organization undertakes a comprehensive job analysis and/or selects a qualified partner that has done so for similar positions. It can't happen if recruiters and hiring managers are allowed to make up ad hoc screening criteria for each

position. It can happen if all applicants are required to answer the same questions and are matched against the same criteria. It can't happen if some candidates apply online and are subject to the screening, while others apply by mail and fax and are put through a similar but different process involving manual screening. Advanced resume processing as described in the previous chapter can address this problem.

Proper implementation of sophisticated (sometimes referred to as "scientific") online screening tools can result in faster time to hire and in candidates that are better matched to positions and the organization itself. As above, this type of screening may require up-front research to define corporate-wide standard skills associated with dozens or hundreds of job descriptions. Fortunately, increasing numbers of vendors offer standard assessment tools that have been validated against hundreds or more positions. While standard validations for common positions eliminate much of the skills/competency analysis work, each organization should ensure that off-the-shelf competency profiles actually do match up to specific positions within the organization. This can be done in much less time than a complete job analysis since it requires validation and fine-tuning rather than building a set of job profiles from scratch.

"Off-the-Shelf" Skill Libraries

Some TMS vendors, such as Workopolis CorporateWorks, Kenexa and Alexus have partnered with expert consultants and psychometric testing firms to build libraries of job descriptions with skills and competencies attached. Using these libraries, organizations can rely on the defensible (empirically proven) work of experts to eliminate candidates based on their own self-assessed skills and competency levels, and perhaps on their responses to questions set up to test their personality fit with the position and company. Again, organizations using off-the-shelf, third-party assessments and tests are responsible for ensuring that the questions used are all calibrated to the positions within that organization. In other words, that they are all valid predictors of on-the-job success and not superfluous in any way.

Not all third-party online assessment and testing tools will integrate with all talent management systems. Some TMS vendors have built advanced online screening, testing and assessment tools into their products, while others use their open standards, Web services platforms or XML to integrate partners' products. Buyers should question vendors about their ability to allow recruiters and hiring managers to control the purchase and assignment of tests and assessments within the TMS (i.e., whether tests and assessments can be truly integrated). They should also find out if a seamless transfer of the results back to the candidate's profile can occur. Organizations that plan to utilize online testing and assessments extensively do not want to have to manually key the results into their TMS.

Consolidated billing and vendor management, such that the TMS vendor manages the relationship with the third-party testing/assessment supplier, are other levels of integration that some TMS suppliers offer.

Some TMS' incorporate hundreds of defined skill sets that can be tailored to an organization's preferences. This enables recruiters and hiring managers to select from approved and validated checklists that can be used in job postings to assess candidates. Screening and sorting is then done automatically and candidates are ranked according to their self-assessments. In the example used in figure 5.3 on the next page, the manager or recruiter has chosen a competency/skills checklist for HR Generalist. By selecting the skills and competencies they wish to use in the requisition, they will create another means by which to assess and screen candidates quickly and accurately.

Assessments and Online Testing

Among the best screening mechanisms related to on-the-job success and quality of hire are testing and assessment tools. Today, numerous companies (though still a small minority overall) offer TMS-integrated, online testing and assessment tools. Typically, shortlisted candidates who have passed previous levels of automated and/or human screening are invited, via e-mail, to complete an online test to assess technical or other skills and personality or aptitudes. Several e-recruitment solutions vendors have incorporated testing services like Brainbench, ePredix, Prove

Figure 5.3: Skills Checklist

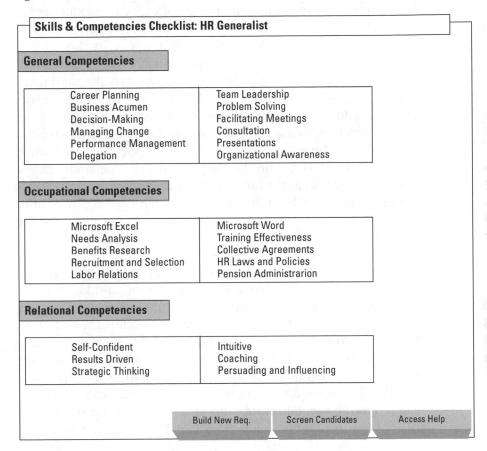

It! and Test.com into their products. Some online test services can also generate candidate-specific interview guides (with suggested questions and scoring) designed to probe candidates' strengths and weaknesses as determined by the tests and to inform the training and development plan following the hire. Good interview preparation software is an ingredient in TMS that many organizations overlook. Because interviewing is possibly the worst selection tool in most organizations as it relates to quality of hire (many interviewers have been shown to make decisions based on superficial factors within twenty seconds of meeting a candidate, for example), an integrated interview package can produce excellent ROI, especially if it helps move the organization toward structured, behavioral interviewing techniques.

Results of online tests can be automatically passed back to the applicant's record where algorithms score and rank the candidates. Brainbench, for instance, uses XML APIs so that it can integrate with most HR solutions. Online testing and assessment providers have, for the most part, validated their tests scientifically against a bank of common job types and have data to support the correlation between test results and on-the-job performance. A separate exercise to validate the tests against the specific positions you are using them against is necessary, but this need not be a terribly lengthy or onerous process, depending on the amount of validity the vendor can demonstrate (which is often, but not always, a factor of how long it has been in business).

Online testing may be best suited to evaluating technical or hard skills. Once you have analyzed a position and know that a candidate requires certain skills and competencies to be successful, it may be possible to purchase, rent or develop a scientifically sound test to measure your candidates' abilities with respect to those requirements. For example, a process to hire C++ programmers can be streamlined by requiring the final twenty-five or so candidates to take a challenging online test that can be used to gauge specific programming skills as well as the candidates' ability to solve problems. Such tests can be purchased from any number of providers, many or which will be able to demonstrate validity through results from thousands of test takers.

Tests can be administered online, but the results will be more valid if they are monitored. Nevertheless, a leading online test provider, Brainbench, asserts that many of its clients run its technical and other tests online, without monitoring or proctoring, and achieve good results.[3] It reports that during the interview, it is fairly easy to ascertain whether the candidate took the test themselves, either by requiring candidates to write a similar but different test onsite after the oral interview or by asking a series of technical questions during the interview. Common practice is to inform candidates that they will be required to take a similar

---

[3] Author interview with Bobbi Michalowsky of Brainbench, April 15, 2002.

test onsite should they be selected for an interview. Personality-type tests eliminate advantages in cheating but may be more likely to place an employer on tenuous legal grounds (this is discussed more fully in Chapter 8).

Background Checking

Verifying a candidate's references, education/credentials, work experience, credit rating and legal background (including drug screening) is not a new best practice. Employers have been doing so for many years. Integration of these types of background checking within the e-recruitment and TM supply chain is a recent best practice that streamlines processes and reduces time to hire.

Background checking is, after all, an information-based service perfectly suited for online delivery. Leading vendors of end-to-end talent management systems have formed partnerships with service providers such as HireRight and ADP's Screening and Selection Services. Once you establish an account with the company, you can build whatever levels of background checking you like into your e-recruitment workflow. For example, a security company may require a criminal background check, a driving record check and a drug test. A bank might want a criminal and credit check, whereas a hospital might also check academic credentials for nurses and physicians before extending an offer or as a condition of offer.

The candidate's details are sent to the vendor electronically. The vendor usually takes responsibility for obtaining the candidate's consent and performs the checks. Generally, the results are returned to the candidate's record in the TMS within twenty-four to forty-eight hours for hiring manager perusal. Employers are billed by transaction depending on the number and type of reports/checks per candidate. As with testing and assessment providers, some TMS providers will manage the background check relationship for their customers so that integration is completely seamless. Employers receive one consolidated monthly bill from their TMS provider for background checks and whatever other third-party services they use, including resume processing and testing.

It is also possible to partially automate the process of reference checking. It is arguable that, done well, reference checks may provide the very best predictor of fit, aptitude and future success on the job. At least one company, SkillSurvey, has developed a cost-effective means of integrating survey software with e-mail for the purpose of soliciting and analyzing reference checks. SkillSurvey recommends clients use its eReference product between the first and second interviews. It is priced at less than US$20 per reference check so that employers can afford to use it as a screening tool for shortlisted candidates. Clients send a form to candidates who enter the names and e-mails of their references. The references receive a questionnaire (see Figure 5.4 below) by e-mail and can usually complete it in less than ten minutes. Respondents' answers are rolled up into an aggregate report. The reference providers remain anonymous. SkillSurvey claims that it gets a 70 percent response rate from reference providers and the vast majority of them reply within thirty-six hours.

Clients receive the results rolled up into a report that lists the names of the candidates and the individual and aggregate scores they received from references. The report lets recruiters compare candidates against each other more easily. Reports provide insight into candidates' abilities and competencies as well as their aptitudes and behaviors. The tool also provides an interview guide that suggests questions designed to probe gaps in candidates' competencies and abilities. For those hired, eReference comments on areas of opportunity for improvement through coaching. These suggestions might include developing a candidate's leadership skills, for example, and are based on the responses of the reference providers.

SkillSurvey (see Figure 5.4) has developed a library of over one thousand competency-based reference check elements grouped by job type. Clients can use these to configure online questionnaires that are e-mailed to reference providers. Reference providers are anonymous to the employer, which SkillSurvey says improves both the response rate and the candor of respondents.

Automated reference checking is a new and relatively untested concept, but there is every reason to believe that survey software and e-mail can speed the process and result in better response rates. To repeat, anonymity for the reference provider probably means more accurate and honest assessments of candidates.

Figure 5.4: Online Reference Check

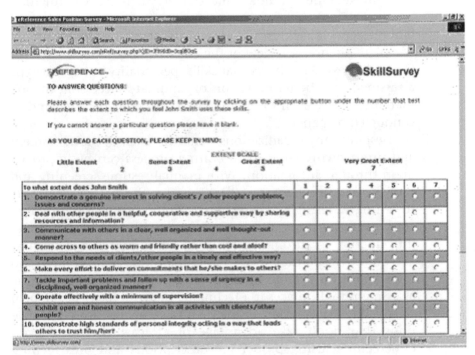

www.skillsurvey.com, choose "eReference/Competency Based Selection Products," choose "Sample Surveys & Reports," choose "sales or manager survey," then choose "Sample Survey."

Conclusions

All candidate selection should involve screening, ranking, filtering and assessing. Traditional methods use tools like the resume and interview to make comparisons between candidates. Where large volumes of applicants are concerned, manual prescreening usually means that assessors can realistically spend fifteen seconds or less per resume. Interviews have proven to be only marginally better. Studies show that typical interviewers make decisions in the first twenty seconds or so, based largely on the candidate's appearance and mannerisms. Getting to the root of what makes one candidate more likely to be successful than another is hard to do in an interview. Offline tests, simulations and reference checks, for example, are needed to paint a more complete picture. A review of the extensive literature on screening and assessment shows that skills, personality/culture-fit-type assessments are better indicators of candidate success on the job than interviews, even when interviews are behavior-based and/or conducted by panels.

Despite many organizations' concerns, each of the assessment and interviewing steps in the hiring process can be improved upon through automation. With manual resume screening and traditional interviewing as benchmarks, the use of electronic screening, filtering and assessment should not be a frightening concept for most organizations. It is very likely that the proper introduction of automated tools will bring more rigor, fairness and objectivity to the process rather than less. That promise, and the trend toward more field-proven and fraud-resistant online assessment tools, makes it a technique that will likely be adopted widely, if not universally, in the years to come. For now, organizations that don't take advantage of at least the base levels of screening, using proper job descriptions and prescreening questionnaires, are simply wasting resources.

Online testing and assessment is a topic that should be explored further. For more information, visit www.rocket-hire.com. The site is run by Dr. Charles Handler, a well-known and respected author and consultant in the field. Also visit Development Dimensions International at www.ddiworld.com for white papers and research on the topics of selection and assessment.

CHAPTER 6

拉

Searching and Candidate Sourcing

Closely related to the processes of screening, sorting and ranking covered in the previous chapter, the ability to search for candidates in a resume/profile database is one of the most important advantages to e-recruitment and automated talent management. Candidate searches can take place on public resume databases and on an organization's own resume database or talent pool. Recruiters can also search narrowly against applicants to specific job postings or as wide as the Internet itself. Normally, a TMS will ship with search tools that enable searches of clients' own talent pools and job posting results. Through subscriptions to public Internet resume sites like Monster.com, organizations gain access to millions of additional resumes that can be searched and candidates imported into their own private talent pools. Many TMS vendors have integrated external resume databases into their offerings and will manage the relationship for their clients. Similarly, some have partnered to provide broad and powerful search tools, like AIRS Oxygen, that give their clients the ability to search the entire Web for resumes and other relevant documents belonging to potential candidates.

AIRS, a Vermont-based recruiting technology and service company, developed the first and still the best-known tools with which to conduct direct and automated resume searches over the Internet itself. Millions of resumes, profiles and other documents describing individuals reside on the Web. Using AIRS Oxygen, it is possible to find candidates and move them into private talent pools where they can be communicated with and invited to consider job openings. For employers that need to expand their search, the Internet represents the greatest possible numbers of candidates, including those who are actively seeking work and those who aren't.

Figure 6.1: AIRS Deep Web Search

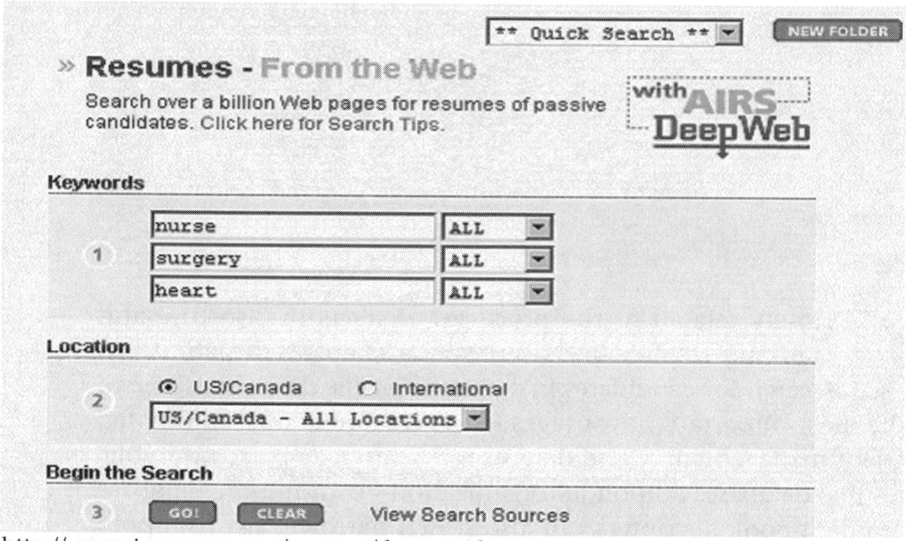

http://www.airsoxygen.com/spartner/demo.guid

   More commonly, organizations search their own talent pools. Due to the trend toward structured profiles over unstructured resumes, most talent management systems allow fast and accurate field-based searches that give users the ability to search by any combination of the fields used by candidates when they complete their online profiles. Field searching eliminates some problems associated with keyword searching. For instance, poor results due to user or candidate spelling mistakes are greatly reduced. More importantly, recruiters and hiring managers can create highly specific, complex searches without the need to understand and create search strings with Boolean operators. For example, if a recruiter is looking for candidates with project management experience in a hospital environment and skills in Microsoft Project, estimating, and team leadership, combined with a degree in computer science, he/she can select the appropriate fields to search on knowing that candidates will have completed their profiles using the same set of fields. If the database were filled with unstructured resumes and the recruiter had only a keyword search tool, he/she would have to come up with a highly sophisticated Boolean search string to match the field search described above—a skill very few recruiters and even fewer hiring managers possess.

Most TMS' offer users an intuitive interface from which to build search terms and search parameters. They typically allow for keyword searching that can either be used on its own or incorporated into the field search. Users can save searches for future use or configure searches to run at regular intervals automatically and alert the user when matches are made.

Figure 6.2: Combined Field and Keyword Search

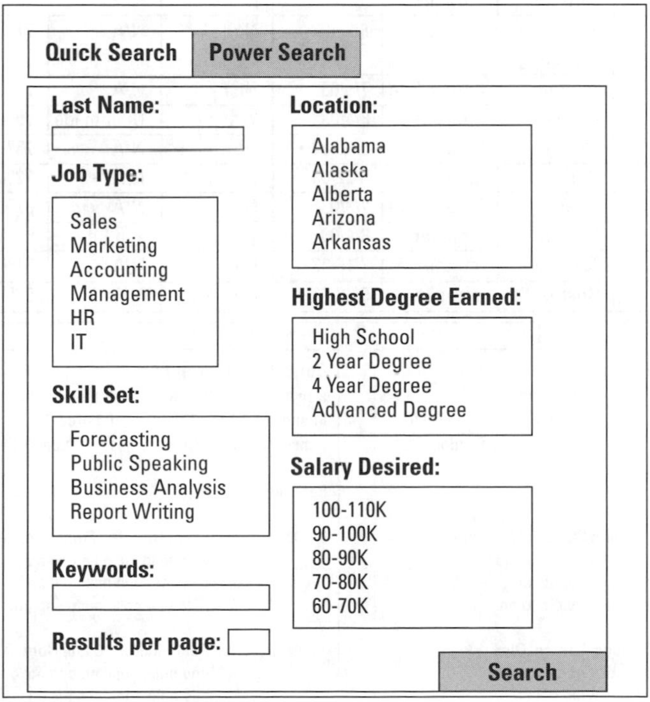

Results of the search (below) are listed according to how well they matched the user's criteria. Full profiles can be viewed by clicking on any of the links. Note the various symbols beside each of the names. Many TMS solutions use icons to tell users where candidates came from (internal versus external) and their status (Are they being considered for other positions? What stage they are at in the hiring process?). Some TMS' enable the user to call up specific resumes side-by-side for comparison as shown in Figure 6.3.

Figure 6.3: Search Results

| 17 Candidates Met Your Criteria | | | | | | | | ▲ = External ▼ = Internal | |

Name	Type	Location	Source	Date Received	Activity	Stage	Rank	Show?
Nancy Drew	▲	Canton	Monster	8/4/03	Yes	2nd Int.	79%	
Tom Hardy	▼	Toronto	Intranet	3/16/03	No	N/A	77%	
Paul Coulombe	▼	San Francisco	Intranet	5/22/03	No	N/A	77%	
Patsy Cline	▲	Toledo	Career Site	7/9/03	No	N/A	76%	
Bill Blass	▲	Dallas	Monster	8/4/03	Yes	Offer made	75%	
Tom Hardy	▼	Toronto	Intranet	3/16/03	No	N/A	75%	
Bill Harlow	▼	Boston	Intranet	5/22/03	No	N/A	72%	
Patsy Cline	▲	Toledo	Career Site	7/9/03	No	N/A	67%	
Nancy Drew	▲	Dallas	Monster	8/4/03	Yes	2nd Int.	65%	
Farah Mather	▼	Toronto	Intranet	3/16/03	No	N/A	61%	
Bill Harlow	▼	Boston	Intranet	5/22/03	No	N/A	57%	

Candidate Information

Name: Nancy Drew	State/Province: Ohio
Phone: (564) 895-9022	Desired Salary: $50-60,000
e-mail: ndrew@hotmail.com	Education: B.A. Economics

Resume:

12/9/01-present: Holistics Corp: St. Louis, Missouri
ono nollo pollo no ono nollo p
ollo nolo ono nollo pol on
nolo ono pollo nollo ono pol

11/2/99-present: HPauly Shoes: Canton, Ohio
ono nollo pollo no ono nollo p
ollo nolo ono nollo pol on
nolo ono pollo nollo ono pol

Education
5/9/95-11/3/99:   Ohio State University
Economics with minor in commerce
Graduated Summa Cum Laude

Candidate Information

Name: Paul Coulombe	State/Province: California
Phone: (415) 902-2877	Desired Salary: $55-60,000
e-mail: harlow123@bay.com	Education: BBA-Finance

Resume:

3/4/00-present: Great Owl: San Francisco, CA
ono nollo pollo no ono nollo p
ollo nolo ono nollo pol on
nolo ono pollo nollo ono pol

1/6/97-present: Peace Corps.: Chad, North Africa
ono nollo pollo no ono nollo p
ollo nolo ono nollo pol on
nolo ono pollo nollo ono pol

Education
2/9/92-1/29/97:   UC Berkeley
Bachelor or Business Administration
Spent one year in Paris at the Sorbonne

Refine Search   Access Help

Beyond field and keyword searching are leading-edge concept- and pattern-recognition-based search tools. Burning Glass, Engenium and zREP pioneered concept-type searching in HR. Simply stated, this refers to a search that does not require the exactness of keyword and field searching; rather it is capable, through pattern recognition, of understanding the various meanings of a word or phrase and can apply that knowledge to return surprisingly accurate search results. This type of search is sometimes referred to as incorporating artificial intelligence (AI).

Some concept search engines claim the ability to process vast amounts of unstructured data (the more the better) and learn from it so that more and more patterns can be recognized and remembered. These tools offer search capability more powerful and scalable than anything seen before. The more the software knows about the industry—be it IT, health care or law, for example—the better it can sift through resumes and find accurate matches. At its best, it can even locate and alert the recruiter to clues revealing what it would take to convince candidates to join (based on their career path to date), what their career path might be in the future, and how to keep them in the organization.

At present, Engenium (see vendor profile below) has emerged as the strongest competitor, at least where applicability to human resources is concerned. Its HireReasoning software adds an additional dimension (as described previously) to typical search engines. A growing number of prominent and progressive TMS vendors (Recruitmax, Bernard Hodes, PeopleCapital and VirtualEdge) have integrated HireReasoning into their products. Others, like Deploy Solutions, Kenexa, Unicru and Yahoo! Resumix, for example, offer proprietary search engines that utilize their own advanced, concept-based search technologies.

Additional advanced search techniques include the ability to use job requisitions or descriptions and resumes or profiles as search parameters. In other words, users can simply cut and paste a job description into the search window, press the search button and be presented with a matching set of candidates. The utility in this is obvious; not only do hiring managers and recruiters save time, they are spared the work of defining search terms. Instead they use what is often the best measure—the job requisition itself, or a model resume from a high-performing employee. The ability to use job requisitions/descriptions, resumes/profiles and other full documents as search parameters is a best practice that only a few vendors provide.

Profile: Engenium's HireReasoning (Semetric) Search Tool

Engenium is a privately owned company based in Dallas, Texas that is one of a handful of pioneers in the AI-based searching business for human capital management. Engenium started operations in 1999, entering the knowledge management business and specializing in news and financial information for various corporations.

After working on information management solutions for various clients, Engenium saw a need for searching beyond keyword, taxonomy-driven (search engines that use an extensive database of definitions into which information is classified) and field-based matching. The resulting product is called Semetric— one of the first tools to look at information, words and phrases and "learn" the relationships between them.

Engenium has targeted the human resources industry for Semetric. Its HR product, HireReasoning, has been installed in various talent management systems to date and with much success.

How It Works

Keyword searches on resume databases, job postings and other bodies of information work most often and most effectively with well-formed Boolean search expressions. A resume database is usually indexed on a regular basis so that all the words in each resume can be recognized in a search. A typical Boolean expression, (e.g., Java AND programming OR programmer) should return accurate results but, for reasons explained in the next paragraph, is likely to miss a significant number of good candidates depending on the size of the resume database.

A complex Boolean search will often require a paragraph or more of terms, including operators like AND, OR and NEAR, and multiple nested expressions within parenthesis. Very few people know how to create these search strings. Even if they do, or the search tool adds Boolean expressions for them, the results will probably still miss good candidates because the search is literal and fails to consider applicants that don't match perfectly to the search terms.

HireReasoning will find the same candidates as those found by a good Boolean, keyword search. However, it will also find candidates who failed to mention explicit words like Java and instead mentioned expertise in JDK, J++, JCK, applets, related positions with Sun Microsystems, and other such experience.

The other advantage of Semetric and HireReasoning is their scalability. Engenium's search tools actually grow better as more resumes are added. Where other systems might slow down on keyword searches involving ten thousand or more records, HireReasoning's performance remains constant and the search results get better because the "brain"—HireReasoning's AI algorithms—learn more and become more sharply tuned as additional data is entered. This is possible due to the nature of the tool. As it gathers more information about a subject, say health care, it builds more connections between words and recognizes more patterns. It begins to understand, for example, that a nurse who works alongside an anesthesiologist is an operating room nurse, even if he/she doesn't say so implicitly on the resume.

Pattern Recognition Versus Field Searching

Fielded searches are 100 percent accurate because they find terms that have been entered into the database through templates. The problem is they are limited to the fields that make up the template and, by definition, they require structured documents. For instance, if you are looking for candidates from Denver, you will find them as long as you have captured city information in a field within your resume template. What if you are looking for operating room nurses with bachelor's degrees and at least five years' experience? A detailed field search might find them but the more you go down this route, the longer your resume template becomes and the less likely candidates are to complete it. Moreover, as with a Boolean search, the engine cannot return results that do not precisely match your search criteria. A search for "computer programmer," for example, will ignore candidates who called themselves "software engineer."

Engenium is designed to provide the accuracy of field searching with the power and convenience of concept searching. You can require a limited number of fields in HireReasoning and allow the applicant to cut and paste the rest of their resume. HireReasoning will accept the fielded information and perform a concept search on the rest. The results are highly accurate returns without requiring applicants to spend inordinate amounts of time giving you their information. And setting up the search is easier for the recruiter. They can identify the fielded information (search terms) they are looking for and dump the rest of the job description or a model resume into a text box. HireReasoning considers all of it and returns ranked results.

Combine HireReasoning with Internet search and extraction tools and you can mine resumes from the Web, extract them into the fields you deem necessary and deposit the rest in whatever structure you wish. As described above, HireReasoning will actually get better as you add more resumes and data.

Artificial intelligence (or concept) searching presently comes in a few flavors. There are technologies that can best be described as "pseudo AI" in that they perform concept searches by maintaining a back-end list of keywords, abbreviations and jargon that are associated with related terms. For example, these tools will find software engineers when you search for computer programmers because those terms have been mapped to each other in the taxonomy. Semetric is one of a few technologies that offers true AI. There are no taxonomies, rather the effectiveness of the system relies on algorithms in the software itself that were designed to create relationships between words, abbreviations and phrases dynamically and without human intervention—pattern recognition, in other words.

The Semetric advantage is its scalability and ease of maintenance. It improves as the resume database grows, while other systems have to maintain expanding lists and taxonomies to remain effective. Taxonomists, the experts who create and maintain the back-end lists, are expensive, so it is reasonable to expect cost savings in the long run with a fully automated system like HireReasoning.

The information presented so far in this vendor profile may appear to run counter to some of the advice provided earlier in the book. Though HireReasoning can manage unstructured documents, most customers use it in combination with job seekers' fully structured and partially structured profiles. Despite the ability of HireReasoning to make sense of unstructured resumes, it remains best practice to require applicants to complete skills profiles because profiles are important in many other aspects of talent management, such as workforce planning, succession planning, performance management, etc. HireReasoning adds another important dimension to a search but does not eliminate the need to profile employees and job seekers.

The Tests

Using Engenium's built-in spidering tools, fifty thousand random resumes in various formats were pulled off the Internet. Semetric reads resumes at a rate of three thousand per minute and learns from them based on pattern recognition and relationships between words and phrases. For example, if a portion of the fifty thousand resumes were from programmers with Java experience, the tool would learn to associate with Java words like Java Bean, J++, Sun, JDK and others. This helps it find results in which search terms may not explicitly contain a word or phrase.

The tests involved a variety of searches including several by cutting and pasting job descriptions and others with a few key words. In every case, the tool pulled out highly appropriate and ranked results. Some of the resumes were surprising; there were excellent candidates who would have been missed altogether in a keyword search. They were the ones with extensive related experience but who used words and acronyms to describe their positions that all but the most experienced recruiters would not have thought of.

This is important because a recruiter, especially in a fast-changing field, may not be able to keep up with all the new terms and changes in the jargon. Semetric can do this provided there is a regular stream of resumes coming in from which it can learn.

The only drawbacks to the results from the searches were HireReasoning's inability to screen out overqualified candidates. The tool has difficulty eliminating these candidates because it finds all of the appropriate terms and patterns it is looking for in their resumes. Over time, however, you might be able to train the tool to eliminate or rank these resumes lower by using HireReasoning's "Find resumes like this" tool in which you use an entire model resume as a search term. This feature lets you sort resumes based on the ones you like best, in effect training the system to your preferences.

Engenium can install HireReasoning and have it working in about forty-eight hours. Its unique toolset lets it convert data in over three hundred different formats at a rate of about three thousand records per minute. Engenium claims that it can migrate data from virtually any system in any format with the help of its Java-based API.

HireReasoning can ship with a "default brain" that does not need to be trained. For example, if you hire in a defined industry—health care, for example—Engenium can train the brain for your industry before it is delivered by feeding data (resumes, white papers and other documents) to it. Engenium is willing to demonstrate the tools with your data before you commit to any purchase.

Engenium's claim that it can integrate with virtually any format and install its tools in your existing setup within forty-eight hours is impressive. What is better is its willingness to prove this and then demonstrate the results before you've even agreed to purchase anything. Expect to pay up to $100,000 for a perpetual license if you are purchasing HireReasoning separately.

Of course, search tools can also be used by job seekers to find jobs on career sites, and by recruiters and hiring managers to retrieve archived requisitions for reuse and interview notes in candidate selection. TMS vendors normally incorporate these simple tools into their offerings. Some also allow users to configure their job listing search tools for candidates so that more or fewer search options are made available depending on the volume of postings on the site.

Advanced and power search capabilities, however, are mainly applicable to candidate resume/profile searching. Excellent search tools can enhance the screening and sorting tools discussed in the previous chapter, and the workforce planning tools discussed in the next chapter. By accurately mining its talent pool, an organization can find individuals with the precise skills, experience and other characteristics it is looking for. This can work whether the search is being conducted for workforce planning purposes, to market opportunities to a specific segment of the talent pool, or to find candidates for a specific vacancy.

Most buyers, especially those that intend to build talent pools and emphasize proactive versus reactive recruiting, should put search capabilities near the top of their lists. There is little point in developing talent pools of tens or hundreds of thousands of candidates if they cannot be mined effectively.

Candidate Mining on the Web

Web-based robots (Web bots or spiders) for recruitment are automated tools that continuously scan the Internet for resumes that match a recruiter's preset criteria. As with employee referral plans, many TMS providers have integrated third-party vendors' candidate mining software into their toolsets. Candidate resume mining is useful in that it frees recruiters from the need to constantly monitor sites on the Web for passive and active "hidden" or "not-in-play" talent.[1] An organization that has identified Web sites that often yield good leads can program the Web bot to monitor those sites continuously and deliver promising leads to recruiters automatically.

Web bots can also search both fee and free resume databases and other free or subscription-based sources on the Web, like Monster.com's and others (they can be programmed with passwords for the fee sites). Web bots generally do a much better job of finding resumes and related information than could be found using Google or other general Internet search engines, and they do so without human involvement except to define the search criteria.

Vendors like Eliyon (see vendor profile below), infoGIST and AIRS provide candidate mining software and services. infoGIST and AIRS partner with HRMS and talent management system vendors to incorporate their solutions into the recruitment supply chain.[2]

Profile: Eliyon Technologies

Eliyon uses spidering technology that crawls the Web, finding press releases, articles, bios, event listings and research. It then pieces it all together into profiles of individuals. It currently has more than two hundred customers subscribing to its services on daily, monthly or annual terms. Users range from individual recruiters, staffing firms, corporate HR departments and sales departments (for lead generation). Microsoft and AOL are among the larger customers.

Eliyon finds that HR departments that have scaled back their use of external recruiters like the system because it generates "uncoached" leads and circumvents the "enhancements" found

---

[1]Companies have reported reduced costs per hire of 60 percent using Web bots. See "Internet Recruiting" by the Corporate Leadership Council, March 2001.

[2]See www.infogist.com and www.airsdirectory.com.

on many resumes. In other words, because Eliyon builds profiles from various documents on the Web, a more objective picture of the potential candidate is created. The candidate is not involved; in fact, there is no reason for a person to know that an Eliyon profile even exists for them.

Eliyon has more than 12 million profiles (although many are duplicates) in its database. It has been crawling and spidering the dot-com domain since 1999 and has recently begun pointing new crawlers at the dot-ca (Canada), dot-au (Australia) and dot-uk (United Kingdom) domains. Do not expect foreign languages to be offered anytime soon, as the technicalities of adding any new language is a multiyear process and Eliyon is only beginning to show the promise of profitability.

The Tests

Eliyon was first tested in a search for writers. If John Doe is a freelance reporter for Salon, *Wired* and *Fast Company*, his title of "reporter" will always be the same, but because the companies are different Eliyon does not combine his records. So if you are looking for a freelance writer, you will probably get dozens of duplicate profiles, possibly one for each article that writer has published on the Web.

That said, if you search for a "writer" from *The New Yorker* for instance, the results are terrific. Eliyon is not intended to be a tool for name searching. Google and other search engines are better for that purpose and are free. Eliyon's value-add is in piecing together profiles of passive (and unaware) candidates from a variety of Web sources.

A general search on "nurse" came up with more than ten thousand hits. After narrowing the search parameters to "operating room nurse" Eliyon produced sixteen names. At the top of the list was a bookkeeper who had recently died, but had, in the past, been an operating room nurse. The search was narrowed again to exclude past employment and returned a "practice administrator" at an eye center; this person had been an operating room nurse in her previous employment also.

In all, of the fifteen or so "candidates" returned from the operating room nurse search, perhaps three were worthy of consideration and one of them had an e-mail link. The others had either moved up the career ladder or had left nursing long ago. One was a decorated Port Authority police officer. Still, in a tight labor market for nurses, three decent leads is nothing to be sniffed at.

A search on Google for "operating room nurse" AND resume got 7,740 hits (one was a Web site called Operatingroomnurse.com). While this sounds good, none of the visible links were to actual resumes. A recruiter would have had to spend considerable time sifting through the links to get three decent leads. Eliyon also offers a networking tool. After opening the profile of one of the nursing candidates (from Cedars-Sinai Medical Center) returned in the search, the networking link returns dozens of the nurse's colleagues at Cedars-Sinai and many other health practitioners from Toronto's Mount Sinai Hospital to the New England Sinai Hospital.

Moving to technical positions, the tests simulated a recruiter looking to fill a wireless application protocol (WAP) developer position. On the search term "WAP," Eliyon returned 188 results. This time the candidates were much better. There were heads of WAP projects, WAP Forum board members, WAP engineers, even the co-founder of the WAP Developer Expert Group. A "networking" search on this person revealed the names of dozens of other members of the WAP Forum. Almost all of these results included e-mail addresses and a good portion could be called real leads—neither under nor overqualified.

Finally, Eliyon is most impressive in recruiting for very senior positions. Because it relies on there being press releases and various other mentions of a person on the Web, CEOs, VPs, presidents and others usually return the most complete profiles. In general, for senior-level people, the profiles are of excellent quality and almost always include detailed bios, e-mail links, current and past employment, and education.

Eliyon subscriptions can be purchased for about US$12,000 per year.

Automated Employee Referral Plans

Employee referrals are the original form of recruitment, and, according to many polls and surveys, still the most valuable.[3] Employee referral plans, however, are new to e-recruitment. Many talent management solutions providers offer employee referral plan modules within their solutions to provide seamless integration with the recruitment supply chain. For those that do not, employee referral plan solutions can be outsourced to third-party providers or licensed as stand-alone products from TMS vendors and integrated with HRMS or other talent management solutions.

No longer a leading-edge best practice, integrating an employee referral plan in a talent management solution is a logical step and a solid strategy. Employees should be able to search for positions, refer friends and colleagues, track the progress of their referrals online, and expect that should their candidate be hired, information will pass seamlessly to payroll and/or to others in the workflow to process the reward.

Integrated and automated employee referral plans simply means that hiring managers or others can flag all or some positions as eligible for the referral program. Normally a reward of some kind is set for successful referrals. Employees can see the eligible jobs and the rewards associated with them. Using the interface provided they can forward the job to their friend or colleague, inviting them to apply, or in some cases they can directly apply for the job on behalf of their friend or colleague.

The employee can track the status of the people he/she has referred from their user interface on the TMS. If their referral hasn't applied, they can be sent a reminder. If they have applied and been

---

[3]Dr. John Sullivan, "The Most Effective Recruiting Tool: Employee Referral Systems" (October 30, 1998). Kevin Wheeler, "Periodic Potpourri: The First Set of Results" (April 24, 2002).

rejected, the employee should see brief reasons. If and when their referral is offered the position and accepts, the employee should see that this has occurred and that the reward is being processed in payroll where applicable.

Figure 6.4: Employee Referral Plan Success

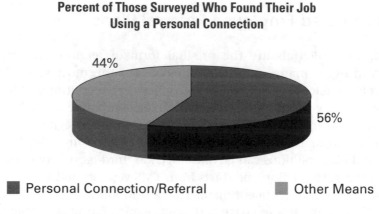

Percent of Those Surveyed Who Found Their Job Using a Personal Connection

44%

56%

■ Personal Connection/Referral   ■ Other Means

Source: Business Wire/"The Tipping Point" (Malcolm Gladwell)

As discussed in previous chapters, alumni (select ex-employees) should have access to and be encouraged to use the employee referral plan tools to refer candidates. Previous employees can be tapped as ambassadors who promote the organization to friends and colleagues or perhaps even return themselves. Vendors such as SelectMinds can assist in creating an alumni network as part of your talent relationship database.[4]

Intranets

Best practice in e-recruitment includes the provision of a separate channel and interface that displays internal opportunities for staff. The corporate intranet provides the vehicle on which to host an internal corporate career site. This is a simple extra feature, not a parallel system. The internal career site is a virtual

---

[4] See www.selectminds.com.

separate portion of the TMS. It gives organizations the ability to post jobs internally for a period of time before releasing them to external candidates should that be necessary. Staff are recognized by the TMS when they log in and are given permission to view the information on the intranet, which might include enhanced information about jobs that might not be appropriate for external candidates. Temporary and career development opportunities can also be posted on the intranet, as can various HR bulletins and marketing messages (e.g., for the employer referral plan).

It is uncommon for a TMS vendor to not offer an intranet version of the corporate career site as a standard or optional feature. Most integrate the internal career site so that postings can be distributed both internally and externally with one click.

An extension to job postings and bulletins offered by some employers is a staffed and/or virtual career advice center where employees can obtain information about advancement or lateral opportunities. Some employers hire counselors to provide career advice and guidance. Some give access to online aptitude and interest tests for self-assessment and career planning. Large organizations should provide a virtual library that staff can access for advice on resume writing, interviewing, job research, internal career advancement, and training or learning opportunities.

The Internet has given rise to several other candidate sourcing innovations. Among them are candidate exchanges on which employers can state their needs and recruiters can bid on candidates. Exchanges can also work between employers and independent contractors directly (these are covered in Chapter 9).

Profile: B2B Exchanges, ResourceOcean

Another innovation in e-recruitment is the B2B exchange concept for attracting candidates through professional recruiters. Companies like ResourceOcean, RecruitersCafe and Bridgepath (Bullhorn) are examples.

With ResourceOcean, employers can post jobs they are having trouble filling to an eBay-like site. Recruiters then access the site with a password and can bid on filling the positions. The employer puts in a "reserve bid" of, for instance, 20 percent. That means that the most they are willing to pay as a headhunter's fee is 20 percent of the successful candidate's starting salary. The employer also posts the details of the job and what they desire in an ideal candidate. Recruiters post resumes along with their bids and can ask for 20 percent or anything less. Employers judge the bids based on the quality of the candidates and the percentage bid by the referring recruiter.

Employers assume very little risk. They can post their jobs free, perhaps get their money back if their new hire does not work out (ResourceOcean offers this type of guarantee, which is unique in the industry) and can take advantage of auction dynamics. Auctions with enough participants tend to favor the seller (the employer in this case). This is because a room (real or virtual) filled with rational people who know what something is worth and will not bid more usually has a few irrational, emotional, desperate, or poorly informed bidders who can cause the price of something to go far beyond (or, in this case, below) its worth. A recruiter exchange, especially in a poor business cycle, will probably heighten this dynamic so that employers will see bids asking for much smaller percentages than what recruiters typically demand. This is partly because the work is available on the site and recruiters have to spend less time and money pursuing it.

ResourceOcean claims that it has already reduced the average winning bid by 20 to 30 percent over typical recruiter fees. Furthermore, according to ResourceOcean there is little risk that recruiters will not participate, especially in a weak economy. Moreover, recruiters can place their own ads for positions they cannot fill, reasoning that a split fee is better than none at all. Recruiters pay US$1,000 per year on top of 10 percent of their placement fee payable to ResourceOcean when they place a candidate.

The toolset includes a Web-based administrative module so that employers can build their postings, monitor the responses and track their open and closed positions over time.

Conclusions

Search and sourcing tools are numerous and varied. The key points to remember, however, are that search tools come in three basic flavors. The most common type of search is the keyword, Boolean variety. While useful, it is less accurate and more difficult to use than the more advanced options common today. The second type, field-based searching, is important because it is both easy to use and accurate. Because most TMS-driven corporate career sites require candidates to complete profiles, a recruiter's search options can match to the same fields that are used by candidates to apply for jobs and deposit their profiles into talent pools and resume databases. Finally, AI-type searching based on pattern recognition is an option to consider because it is the most powerful instrument in a recruiter's search toolkit and is even easier to use than field-based searching. Moreover, AI tools allow organizations to collect some unstructured data knowing that they can search through it quickly and accurately.

Among the variety of candidate sourcing tools at a recruiter's disposal, print advertising and staffing agencies are traditional and expensive options. In the context of technology and TMS, corporate career sites (as discussed in Chapter 3), resume and profile databases, public job boards, Internet spiders, tools like AIRS and Eliyon and even auction sites like ResourceOcean are available and inexpensive. Automated employee referral plans and, most important of all, the intranet career site, round out the key technologies available to draw candidates from near and far.

CHAPTER 7

卍

Talent Relationship Management and Workforce Planning

T he first part of this chapter describes the best practice of building relationships with high-quality external candidates,
alumni and high-performing staff, mostly through automated
processes. The second part of this chapter discusses workforce analysis and planning using technology to turn recruitment and other
data into insightful information about the workforce and how it can
be optimized.

At its heart, TRM involves the development of pools of applicants who have not been placed but are considered good prospects
for future openings or are high-performing staff that must be
shown career paths inside the organization and have their career
aspirations facilitated to the greatest extent possible in order to
retain them. TRM also means proactively seeking candidates and
treating them like customers. Anonymous applications, prequalifi-
cation of applicants, "candidate experience" and marketing to the
candidate pool are discussed.

The concept of creating and nurturing distinct talent pools is
catching on. Organizations spend time and money implementing talent management systems, partly to facilitate the collection
of resumes. Many times this happens in surprisingly short order.
It is not unusual for organizations to receive hundreds or thousands of applicants for each online job posting. TMS and

e-recruitment, including the sourcing techniques discussed in the previous chapter, greatly extend an organization's reach. TMS-integrated tools distribute job postings to dozens of job boards. Integration with tools like AIRS Oxygen, Eliyon and other Internet search tools let recruiters scour millions of resumes on the Web. Automated employee referral programs and "e-mail-a-friend" tools use the principles of viral marketing to spread word of jobs in the organization further. This results in what is often a nearly overwhelming response.

Leading-edge best practice involves screening these applicants automatically and depositing those with potential into a separate section of the talent pool or resume database. All of these candidates should have expressed some interest in the organization, either by applying to an advertised job, submitting their resume directly into the talent pool or consenting to be included (i.e., if the candidate was found in a "deep Web search" or referred by a third party).

Many of the resumes a company receives will be discarded because the candidate is assessed as having no potential value to the organization. Others will have that potential, but there will be no current positions available. These potential employees are an important resource. If managed well, this pool of candidates can be drawn upon when a position opens in the organization. Most of these potential employees will already be working. It is therefore necessary to keep them interested in the idea of working for your organization using the techniques described in this chapter.

Creating relationships with a large pool of potential candidates may sound extremely labor intensive. Why spend hours building personal relationships with candidates you may never meet, let alone hire? The reality is much different, fortunately, as most mass talent relationship management can be accomplished in an automated fashion. For instance, the technology should automatically sort candidates by skill sets and interest. If, for instance, the organization has a partially prequalified pool of fifteen hundred programmers, its IT director need only load the quarterly newsletter into the system and e-mail it to everyone who agreed to receive company information. In this efficient manner, candidates are reminded of the organization and they might also take the time to read about its recent achievements. These same candidates will have been encouraged to register for job alerts so they may receive appropriate programmer job postings each time one is advertised.

Select individuals might even be invited to company events if a more personal approach is desired.

Other tools like e-mail acknowledgement of applications, easy-to-use corporate career sites, automatic feedback to candidates through each step of the recruiting process, the ability to apply to positions anonymously (leaving a masked e-mail only), requiring only the minimum information necessary from the candidate (allowing the candidate to release more information as the relationship grows) and stated and demonstrated respect for the privacy of candidates' personal data are measures that communicate a positive message to the candidate and help build a trusting relationship. Occasional automated reminders to visit the corporate career site, and hiring managers who use their job requisitions to search the talent database and then invite (by personalized batch e-mail) matching candidates to apply are others. None of these techniques require additional resources, yet they build ongoing positive relationships with job seekers, keeping them "warm" as prospects when appropriate positions come available.

The challenge is in using the tools to develop meaningful and lasting relationships with potential recruits, internal staff and alumni so that recruiters know more about them and can fill positions with the right candidates faster. It bears repeating that rather than using an expensive TMS to simply store and track resumes, organizations must leverage their investment in TMS to build communities of partially prequalified people who may, at a future date, be interested in joining the organization. A separate talent pool of existing employees is even more critical (for reasons discussed below).

Over time, efforts to communicate with candidates in the talent database can be measured for effectiveness against the response rate to various types of e-mails. Candidate self-service to access publicly available corporate reports, planning exercises and other additional information is also a requirement for effective relationship building. Employee portals and self-service options that provide staff access to benefits information, their leave balances, payroll, internal career opportunities, career planning, mentoring, and training and development also contribute to internal TRM and retention.

At its most basic, TRM can be accomplished using the search tools described in Chapter 6. Using the TMS talent pool search feature, recruiters and hiring managers can mine the resume database or talent pools for the types of candidates they are looking for. The resulting list becomes a group of high-potential candidates that can be marketed to, invited to apply to a particular job or invited for an interview, for example. Most TMSs allow for the ad hoc creation of candidate folders. Promising candidates can be assigned to folders and communications tracked between them and the organization. Candidate folders are, in effect, separate, specific talent pools that can be kept for positions, categories of positions or even locations, among other things.

As in customer relationship management, it is helpful if the software tracks each interaction the candidate has with the organization. This is especially helpful to recruiters and hiring managers when the time comes to speak to the candidate personally, either to answer questions directly or to interview.

The ultimate outcome of TRM is improvement to the organization's employment branding (a measure of job seekers' views and opinions of an employer) and, more to the point, a reduction of the costs of having empty seats and the costs of sourcing candidates. Theoretically, if the relationship with a set of pre-qualified candidates is developed well, those candidates will be ready to be interviewed the moment a position comes available so that the organization need not even advertise the position.

Figure 7.1 opposite contrasts the traditional method of reactionary recruiting (recruiting only in response to a vacancy) versus that associated with TRM.

Figure 7.1 is a simplistic view of a paradigm shift. The development of a talent database is not as simple as reversing the first two steps of the traditional approach. The "building of the candidate pipeline" stage is an ongoing process, not geared to any specific job posting, and involves regular though largely automated communication with potential candidates. The pipeline may combine all or some of the sourcing tools discussed in the last chapter. What is important is that it continues to refer candidates who can be automatically assessed and either rejected or classified into the appropriate talent pool for relationship-building purposes.

TRM is only now truly emerging as a best practice. It starts with the way both internal and external candidates are treated when they apply for positions in organizations and it continues throughout the life cycle of a candidate resume or profile in the system. And it doesn't stop there. TRM also means building the relationship after hiring a person, during that person's time on staff and, in some cases, even after the person has left. For these reasons, TRM

Figure 7.1: Traditional Versus TRM Approach to Recruiting (Simplified)

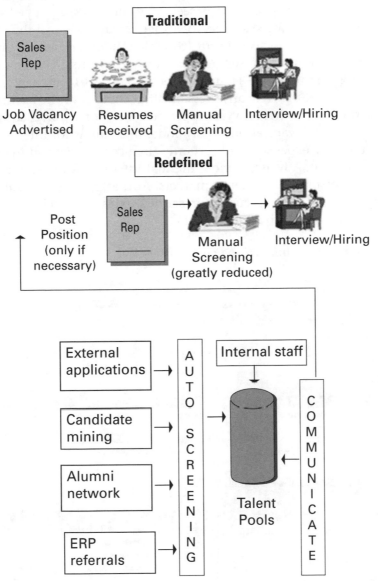

can be seen as a constant in the use of talent management systems and a process that is related to workforce planning.

Few solutions handle TRM specifically in all of its components. For instance, very few vendors ship their solutions with tools that assist organizations in properly and automatically tracking all communications with candidates. Auto connect/online chat buttons, such as those frequently seen on e-commerce-equipped sites, that would allow job seekers to engage recruiters in real-time text conversations are also absent (though Yahoo! has partially integrated its Yahoo! Messenger chat service into its TMS: Resumix Hiring Gateway—see Figure 7.2 below. Access to managers for group "meet the company" sessions that could easily be facilitated via the Internet have not yet appeared on corporate career sites. Of course, the organization's cost model must allow for interactive, potentially expensive and certainly time-consuming features like online chat. Advanced, more manual-intensive features like this may blossom in tight labor markets. At that point, organizations may have to go to customer service extremes, such as those described above, to attract talent.

Figure 7.2: Resumix Hiring Gateway

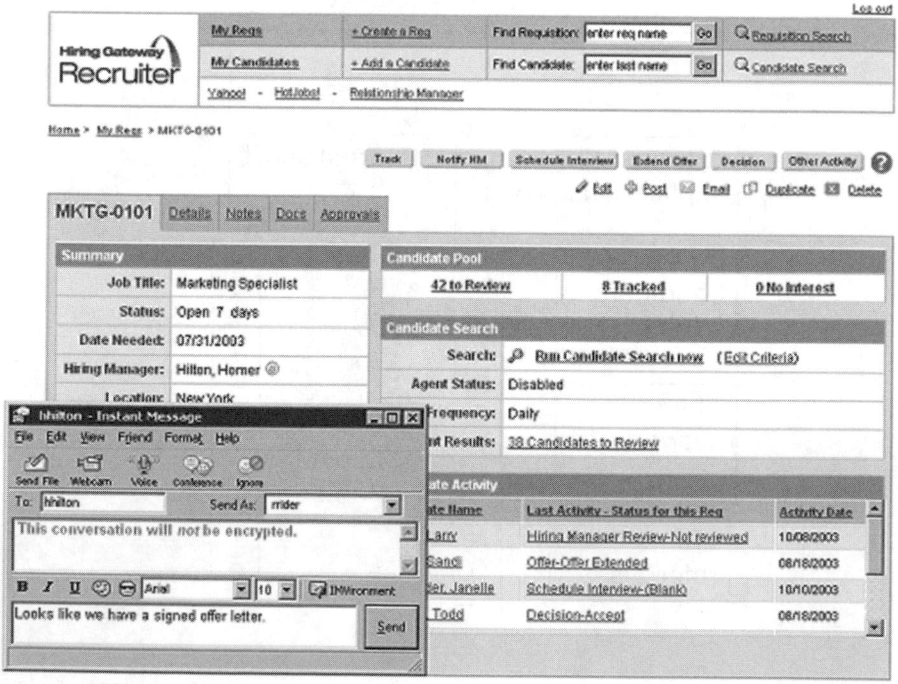

Hiring Gateway lets recruiters open a chat, or instant messenger, session with candidates in a separate window.

The importance of building candidate relationships is evidenced in part by a decision of BrassRing, a tier-one TMS vendor, to entirely restructure itself around the concept of TRM. It is now beginning to offer advanced software to handle automated TRM, as well as outsourced services to perform advanced TRM and recruitment initiatives with trained personnel. This direction signals a shift into the mainstream for the concept of TRM and will almost certainly result in more creative ways to engage talent with technology in a manner that leads to shorter cycle times in filling vacancies with better hires.

Nevertheless, the time for advanced and more labor-intensive TRM may not arrive on a large scale until severe labor shortages reoccur. Still, even for screening purposes, it can be cost and time effective to use the corporate Web site for initial human contact with candidates of interest. If this is done in online, scheduled group information sessions, say one hour per week, the results can more than justify the expense. There are many anecdotes about the recruiter whose phone rings or pager beeps after hours with a message from the TMS alerting him/her that a hot new candidate has just applied for a hard-to-fill position on the corporate Web site. The recruiter immediately calls the startled (and impressed) candidate to discuss the position and arrange an interview. Scenes like this occurred with regularity during the intense competition for skilled IT workers during the dot-com era and are happening now for other hard-to-fill positions. This is old news from a technology point of view, however, it represents a level of TRM that becomes commonplace wherever competition for talent is intense.

Together, TRM and the concept of talent pool creation pay off in another important way. As more organizations return to an understanding of the value workforce planning offers, internal and external talent pools that inventory skills, competencies, interests and potential are invaluable. Before an organization can build a qualified talent pool to justify the expense of relationship-building, though, it must sort through the flood of applicants that online sourcing inevitably produces. Knowing which candidates are deserving of greater attention can only come from intelligence gathered in the process of workforce planning.

Workforce Planning

Workforce planning encompasses skills and competency tracking, succession planning, analysis of workforce metrics and broad initiatives to align corporate objectives to the current and future workforce. It is far broader than the space possible in this chapter and is a topic worthy of its own book. In the context of TMS, however, and in relation to talent relationship management, workforce analysis and planning is a process that must not be overlooked.

For the purposes of illuminating best practices in e-recruitment and talent management, workforce planning has to be addressed. It is the key component that makes everything else the organization does in talent management strategic—or planned and considered, in other words. The relationship is symbiotic. Data derived from TMS, including recruitment and candidate sourcing data, training and development outcomes, performance management, retention efforts and redeployment within the organization, is critical data for workforce planning efforts.

If an organization is to conduct talent management strategically, it must create a cycle by which all of its efforts send data to the workforce analytics and planning components of the TMS. In this way, all efforts can be assessed, analyzed and reported on to ensure that desired outcomes are being achieved in relation to broader, strategic workforce growth, reduction or optimization efforts. For example, if the corporate objective includes opening a new engineering division in order to build a product for a new market, the workforce plan must provide direction to subsequent talent management activities. It should immediately be capable of telling senior management which employees with the necessary expertise are already on staff and where they are located. It should be able to create a list of staff who are almost qualified and may have indicated a desire to move into the position(s) in question. It should give senior managers a picture of where in the external talent pools the required talent is concentrated and be able to predict the time and costs associated with hiring external candidates, redeploying existing staff and developing the required skills in others. With this information, the organization will know where best to locate the new team, how much it will cost to staff it and how long it will take to be operational. Human resources will be able to predict the most efficient means of staffing the operation—through a combination of external recruitment (full-time and/or contract), internal redeployment and training/development.

All e-recruitment plans, traditional sourcing, retention efforts and training should be preceded by workforce analysis and planning. To do otherwise is to recruit, retain and train with only one eye open. Mistakes are bound to occur, including hiring that is mismatched to corporate requirements, retention of the wrong people and development of staff in the wrong directions.

During corporate planning and strategy formulation, HR executives should be closely involved to ensure that corporate strategy is realistic given the organization's current talent pool and skill sets, and what both are capable of developing into in the time required. HR can bring this information to the table only if it has an intimate knowledge of the organization's talent, its deficits and surpluses where particular skills and competencies are concerned, its sourcing capacity, its ability to develop skills and competencies among existing staff, and what talent is available outside and inside the organization.

To illustrate how talent management processes and technology can paint this picture, it is useful to recall diagrams and processes introduced in previous chapters. As a benefit of Internet recruiting, the organization may have already developed rudimentary talent pools. Care must be taken to ensure that the talent pools are organized into prequalified external and internal (existing staff) segments. The pools should also be structured so that they are easy to "slice and dice" in order to determine where the talent resides and what precise skills, competencies, aptitudes, interests and overall capacity is available. This will enable ongoing analysis of the workforce in relation to corporate objectives so that the talent pools can be further refined according to the current and future needs of the organization—an ongoing cycle, in other words.

Workforce planning starts with existing staff. Once a TMS with workforce planning capacity has been purchased, all staff should be encouraged to complete profiles. In order to be useful, profiles should include fields that capture experience, skills, competencies, education and the employee's career interests (often a narrative component sometimes combined with a multiple-select list of positions in the organization). In the beginning, the profile will be a self-assessment (meaning the employee will judge his or her own skill set). However, over time it will include all training and development completed by the employee, including test and overall course results. It will also include performance reviews in which managers qualify the employee's self-assessment and add their own evaluations. Peer assessments, projects completed, awards received, external recognition and other pertinent information will all be added to the employee's profile. Tests and assessments to gauge the employee's skills and knowledge in specific areas, as well as psychometric or personality testing, can be added. By these means, an organization can develop an exceptionally deep knowledge of its workforce, including skills, interests, aptitudes and capacity.

Figure 7.3: Developing a 360° View of Employees

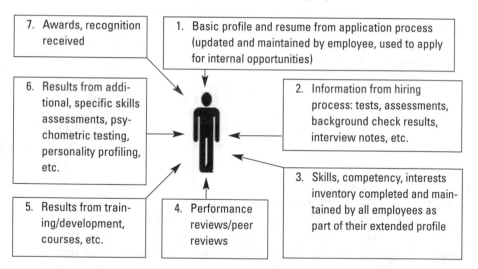

As described in the paragraph above and illustrated in Figure 7.3, TMS technology can facilitate the process of developing electronic profiles of employees. Beyond the simple self-assessments that electronic profiles and resumes typically provide, this approach validates the employee's self-assessed skills and competencies by adding test results, performance and peer reviews, training outcomes, developmental assignments and recognition the employee may have received for superior performance or otherwise. With this level of detail about employees, organizations can better redeploy staff and optimize their workforce. HR departments can aggregate the information to form an accurate picture of current capacity for use in corporate strategic planning.

Organizations will not have the same depth of knowledge about external candidates as they have about their own staff. Nevertheless, the section of the talent pool that contains external, potential candidates will be many times larger than the internal pool. Organizations that use the Internet to source and build talent pools are almost always astonished at how quickly their talent pools grow. An organization that fills one thousand jobs per year through its corporate career site can easily amass a resume pool of five hundred thousand candidates in less than a year. If it also uses large public job boards to advertise, it might pull in additional thousands of resumes per day in response to just a few job postings. The use of public resume databases and deep Web mining can bring in thousands more.

When the economy is struggling, building a large pool of resumes is not difficult. The difficulty is in creating valuable pools of true potential employees; in other words, separating the wheat from the chaff. Without spending an inordinate amount of time, organizations must filter and keep only the resumes and profiles of the people they might hire if positions were open. Then they should concentrate on marketing and relationship-building efforts with that group.

The figures below illustrate what is meant by selective talent pool creation. In Figure 7.4, all sources for external candidates pass through the same automated screening and filtering tools. These might include screening questionnaires accessed when applicants apply for positions. It might also include TMS filters that look for the best candidates by matching skills, experience and competencies to corporate requirements. Depending on an organization's sophistication in terms of required skill sets, the automated filters will range from highly porous (retail and fast food, for example) to very fine (R&D, medical and IT, among others). Candidates without the baseline skills, experience, education, competencies, etc., will be filtered out automatically, sent automated (but personalized) e-mails to that effect and will never enter a talent pool.

In this example, those that meet the baseline criteria enter the "C" pool. Depending on the sophistication of the automatic screening tools and the source of the applicant (select alumni and some employee referrals, for example), an organization might wish to direct some candidates directly to the "B" pool. However, as is implied in Figure 7.4, the "A" and "B" pools should contain only existing staff ("A" pool) and prequalified external applicants ("B" pool).

Figure 7.4: Building the Talent Pools

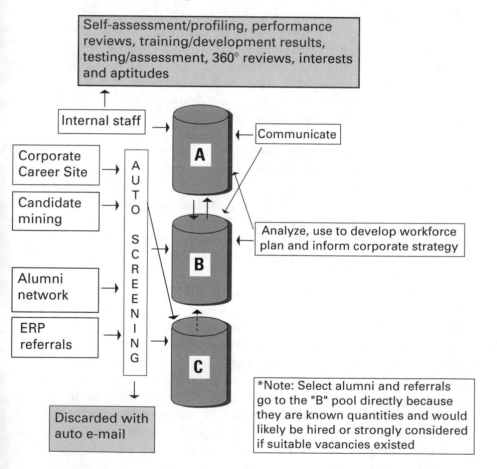

The argument for restricting the candidates in these pools is twofold. The organization will rely on the "A" and "B" pools for workforce planning. The data, therefore, has to be meaningful and reliable. To obtain and maintain quality data, resources are required. Internal applicants, as discussed above, will eventually have profiles that tell the organization a great deal about them in terms of their skills, competencies and career aspirations. "B" pool external applicants will likely have had human contact with the organization. This may be because they are previous, valued employees (alumni), were referred by a trusted employee, or have made it through several stages in a previous hiring process. Less clear-cut alumni and referrals should be directed to the "C" pool, but in most cases these decisions will require human judgment.

The "C" pool will be the largest talent pool. It is used to house promising potential candidates who meet minimum requirements but are still unknown quantities to the organization. This pool can be used to invite candidates to apply for open positions. Automated, opt-in messages concerning the organization, such as those containing company achievements and milestones, should be sent to these candidates to keep them "warm." Exceptional and costly efforts to communicate and build relationships with them, however, are not likely to pay off. The main purpose of the "C" pool is to feed the "B" pool with select candidates that have been assessed as having true potential to become employees.

Figure 7.5 below is resurrected from Chapter 4 for three reasons. First, to illustrate the effort organizations put into sourcing, screening, assessing, testing, interviewing and hiring candidates; second, to show how the "B" pool of candidates should be developed; and third, to reiterate how the "A" and "B" pools can be used to avoid costly recruitment advertising, shorten time to hire and provide much of the data required for effective workforce analysis.

After an organization has built its requisitions and advertised them in numerous sources, it expends additional effort in screening applicants and shortlisting them for further testing and interviews. Candidates that pass through manual screening have done so presumably because they are people that the company might seriously consider hiring, pending interview(s) and background checks. These candidates, whether they are placed on an interview list or not, should go into the "B" pool. Similarly, candidates who are interviewed and not selected for positions should go into the "B" pool, unless they were revealed to have been dishonest during the interview process or are rejected outright as potential employees. Finally, as illustrated in Figure 7.5, the selected candidate goes directly to the "A" pool as an employee. All employees should reside in the "A" pool.

Figure 7.5: Talent Pool Rationale

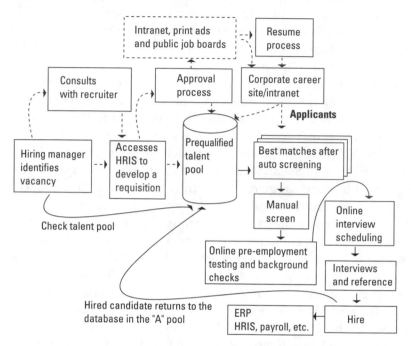

Figure 7.5 illustrates the many paths through a hiring cycle. The ultimate achievement of talent pools is that they can shorten the hiring cycle, as represented by the solid line.

The "A" pool is for employees (and should be further subdivided in conjunction with performance and incentive management initiatives). The "B" pool is a highly selective talent database that contains profiles of candidates that are known to the organization through human contact or at least manual screening. As described in Chapter 5, the "warmer" these candidates are, the more likely the organization is to be able to hire them as soon as a position opens, thereby saving enormous time and money by avoiding the costs of an empty position, recruitment advertising, recruiter fees and other staffing costs.[1]

---

[1] Standard estimates for replacing candidates into professional, salaried positions is 1.5 to 2.5 times salary. These estimates are based on average employee productivity, average time to fill and average recruiting costs.

The "B" pool can also be developed through employee referrals and select alumni. Employees, as they depart, should be interviewed and their profiles moved from the "A" pool to the "B" pool, ideally with their exit interviews eventually attached so that users will know the circumstances of the employees' departure and their attitude toward the company. The next best candidates for the "B" pool may be referrals from trusted sources (usually current employees). Referrals from the employee referral program should be assessed manually (if they pass initial, automated screening) and deposited in the appropriate pool even though they might also be selected for an interview.

More to the point of this part of the discussion, because the "A" and "B" pools represent actual and real potential talent, they are invaluable sources of data for accurate workforce planning. The "C" pool, and external resume databases, the Internet itself and various research sources, can and should be used to estimate general worker supply. But, for the purposes of knowing what talent capacity exists and what can likely be obtained rapidly, the "A" and "B" talent pools are vital. They are well worth creating and maintaining for these reasons. As alluded to above, the "A" pool can be further subdivided into strong, average and weak performers among existing staff to facilitate release of underperformers and intense retention efforts for those determined to be "A" players.[2]

Eventually, organizations should integrate performance management technologies so that they can fully understand who the strong, average and weak performers are. This will enable alignment of recruitment and training with incentives, retention efforts and past employee performance. This approach allows for the further subdivision of the "A" pool into more granular groups of employees, such as those that divide them on the basis of performance or potential. The theme is constant: the more an

---

[2]General Electric is well known for having instituted a policy by which employees are classified into top 15 percent, middle 75 percent and bottom 10 percent categories. Pay, perks, bonuses and other retention efforts are directed more to the top performers. The bottom 10 percent are expected to move up to the average range or eventually leave the company. The "forced ranking" approach has come under fire from several experts and observers, mainly when it is performed in a manner that could be perceived as arbitrary or unfair. Nonetheless, it works well when done correctly. See www.fairmeasures.com/whatsnew/articles/new237.html and, for alternative practices, see www.ddiworld.com/pdf/forced_ranking_alternatives_wp.pdf.

organization knows about its employees and candidates, the better it can become at building and managing internal and external "talent communities" and the better it will be at selecting and retaining top performers.

Conclusions

In summary, workforce planning in the context of e-recruitment cannot be separated from talent relationship management. Both rely on the development of talent pools and both provide highly compelling reasons for organizations to spend the resources necessary (within reason) to become proficient in this leading-edge best practice. Talent management, as opposed to applicant tracking, is defined by the ability of an organization to execute strategically in every aspect of the talent life cycle, from sourcing, screening and hiring through development, retention, redeployment and release—and all of it must be informed by workforce planning.

CHAPTER 8

Legal, Ethical and Fairness Concerns in E-Recruitment

Organizations must exercise due diligence in their selection and use of screening tools. Almost 100 percent of the companies polled in 2001 by Global Learning Resources cited legal considerations as an area of concern in adopting online screening technology.[1] This is partially due to the newness of the technologies and the fear that their use can be legally challenged and might be difficult to defend. Although in reality, online screening is no more legally perilous than other forms of screening, and may in fact limit an organization's liability more than is possible with manual screening, it is important that organizations do at least two things to avoid the inadvertent use of inappropriate screening methods:

1. As discussed in Chapter 5, ensure that each element of the screening criteria relates directly to a requirement for the job and that you employ a standard and documented process for selecting employees. You need to be able to show screening criteria validity, reliability of process, job relatedness and "lack of adverse impact" (all described in more detail below). For example, depending on your jurisdiction, it may be illegal to run a

---

[1] Global Learning Resources Inc., "Screening & Assessment: Best Practices" (Fall 2001).

credit check on a candidate unless good credit is necessary to job performance.[2] Personality or psychometric tests should not delve into potential medical conditions, for example, but be restricted to questions that directly test candidates' suitability for positions. For example, if the position requires that the incumbent be capable of placing fifty or more calls to potential customers each day, a question probing his or her attitudes toward cold-calling and rejection may be appropriate. A question that asks them whether they have frequent colds, flu or even laryngitis, for example, would be inappropriate.

This requirement need not be particularly onerous. Often common sense is as good a guide as is needed. Can you defend a screening criteria or can't you? For instance, if you are hiring a programmer, a test designed to assess the candidate's ability to write clean code is appropriate, while asking if he or she attend church regularly is not.

2. Thoroughly review your choice of software, whether it is purchased as a stand-alone product or integrated within a talent management system. Companies have been successfully sued based on the type of screening criteria they used. Walt Disney, for example, was alleged to have used racially biased criteria for screening because the software looked for words and phrases not often used in a particular minority community.[3] The implications for employers are clear, such that it is critical that tests and other screening tools be examined from the perspective of many different candidates. Test and screening tool providers should be questioned about the validity of their tools and whether they have screened them for potential bias against various potential users.

Choosing the Right Tests

The following list of ten questions are reprinted with permission from *How to Hire and Develop Your Next Top Performer*, by Herb

---

[2] Peter Cappelli, "Discrimination: A Serious Risk in Online Recruitment," *Harvard Business Review* (March 2001).

[3] Gillian Flynn, "E-Recruiting Ushers in Legal Dangers," *Workforce Magazine* (April 2002).

Greenberg, Harold Weinstein and Patrick Sweeney of Caliper Management Inc. These are questions that management should ask about any test before deciding to use it. The book recommends that "If the answer provided by the test provider to any of these questions is no, or noncommittal, that test should not be used under any circumstances."

1. Is the test specifically job-related? Does it measure qualities required for your particular job?

2. Does the publisher of the test provide published proof that the test does not discriminate against individuals by sex, age, race, color, religion or national origin?

3. Does the publisher provide published proof that the test has a high level of predictive validity across the industry and specifically in a situation at least closely related to the position for which the test is being given? Is there proof that people actually do perform as the test predicts they will?

4. Is the database from which the test is developed, and on which the test's reliability and validity are measured, large enough and compiled over enough years to provide dependable evidence of its reliability and validity? In other words, has the test publisher tested enough people and followed actual performance over enough years to prove that the test works?

5. Does the publisher provide a list of customers you can contact who have used the test long enough to accurately judge the results?

6. Are the test results related specifically to a company, or are they generalized results? The key here is whether the test is evaluated against a company's particular requirements, i.e., job descriptions.

7. Are results of the test provided promptly so that management will not lose good applicants as a result of waiting?

8. Does the company provide a trained test evaluator who is a specialist in your field? Will the evaluator discuss the test results with you and provide assistance in relating those results to the other steps of the assessment process?

9. Will the testing company provide ongoing help if problems or questions arise relating to poor initial performance, slumps, future promotions, training and management issues?

10. Are the qualities measured by the test those that are essential to performance in the job for which the test is to be used? If, for example, the test does not measure ego-drive (persuasion motivation), it probably would not be appropriate for use in sales selection. It is important that the test clearly measures exactly those qualities that management wants to assess in its developmental, promotion or hiring decisions.

Nevertheless, despite the caution and due diligence that must be taken, it is important for organizations to also consider that given the deluge of resumes they can expect after taking their hiring process online, the *only* way that it might be practical to give even cursory attention to each candidate is through automated screening and assessment tools.

Accessibility

Many organizations are slow to adopt Web-only policies for recruitment because they fear that doing so would disadvantage some segments of their workforce or the external candidate population. It is true that, in general, older persons are less familiar with the Internet and use it less often than younger persons (though the gap is decreasing every year). It is also true that economically disadvantaged persons may have less convenient access to the Internet. In exceptionally rare cases, some potential applicants (rural poor or the housebound, for example) may have no practical way to access the Internet at all. Persons with some types of disabilities may also be at a disadvantage, though others, particularly the less mobile, may greatly prefer online job searching.

Internally, a large organization may have workers in dozens of locations doing hundreds or thousands of different jobs. Workers performing administrative and office-related tasks may have more convenient access to the Internet than those on the road, on the shop floor or in factories, for instance. Due to the nature of job postings, however, more convenient access to the Internet does not necessarily convey an advantage. Organizations should establish minimum posting times and, where necessary, common Internet access facilities or kiosks to ensure that all staff have adequate access and time to view and apply for internal postings.

Workers with Disabilities

For disabled candidate access, organizations should refer to international standards set by the World Wide Web Consortium (W3C). These guidelines can be accessed at: http://www.w3.org/WAI/. Beware that the U.S. government has altered the W3C guidelines very slightly in its policy for its own Web sites at www.section508.org (see Figure 8.1 below). In summary, the guidelines speak to the avoidance of certain HTML codes and the use of applets, frames and other tools used in Web site construction, as these elements often interfere with devices such as text readers used by the blind. Some organizations address these issues by offering two different versions of their career site; both offer the same information but it is delivered in a slightly different way for users with disabilities.

Figure 8.1: Section 508 Guidelines

Section 508
www.section508.gov

| Buy Accessible | About 508 | 508 & You | 508 Training | 508 Coordinators | Accessibility Forum | FAQs | Events |

Search

Enter Search Words

⦿ Buy Accessible Products
○ Buy Accessible Services
○ Section 508 Website

Search   Clear

Additional Links
◦ Advanced Search
◦ Communications/Media
◦ Resources & Links
◦ AT Showcase
◦ Contact Us

Breaking News

Government Web sites must still be accessible to the disabled, despite a recent court ruling and the ongoing debate over accessibility for commercial sites, according to the Access Board. View the article at http://www.gcn.com/vol1_no1/daily-updates/20325-1.html

Home

Section 508 requires that Federal agencies' electronic and information technology is accessible to people with disabilities. The Center for Information Technology Accommodation (CITA), in the U.S. General Services Administration's Office of Governmentwide Policy, has been charged with the task of educating Federal employees and building the infrastructure necessary to support Section 508 implementation. Using this web site, Federal employees and the public can access resources for understanding and implementing the requirements of Section 508.

| Back to Top | Section 508 Home | Comments for the Webmaster | Privacy Statement |

GSA is committed to Section 508 compliance and accessibility of websites. We welcome any ideas or comments from our clients that may help us to further improve upon the accessibility and usability of our website.

http://www.section508.gov/index.cfm?FuseAction=Content&ID=3

    The scale of systemic discrimination against persons with disabilities in North America is nothing short of appalling. In the U.S., up to 70 percent of the disabled (depending on their disability) are unemployed and less than 10 percent own their own homes.[4] By making the employment site accessible, employers can enhance their employment brand by demonstrating their desire to form a diverse workforce. This in turn demonstrates to all types of candidates that their differences are valued and they will not be subjected to a monoculture or "groupthink" type setting at work. Most importantly, organizations also stand to gain by accessing relatively untapped segments of the talent market.

Privacy

Talent management systems collect and store personal information from applicants and so they must consider privacy laws and ethics. This concern can usually be overcome with a legally vetted privacy policy (see example below) that explains to candidates exactly how their information will be used and stored. In general, candidate information should be used solely for the purposes the candidate authorized when submitting the application.

Candidates should be in control of their personal information, meaning that they supply it voluntarily, control its distribution and availability, and can remove it or ask that it be removed from the database completely whenever they choose (obviously this does not apply to hired candidates whose information passes through to the HRMS. As discussed previously, it is a best practice to let candidates apply for positions anonymously if they wish. Only after the organization has expressed an interest in interviewing are the candidates asked to reveal their names and necessary contact information. This strategy is considerate of candidates' privacy and might also attract a higher caliber or wider range of interest, especially where the internal job market is concerned. This is so because it alleviates candidates' concerns around their supervisor learning prematurely that they are considering alternative employment.

The privacy policy page at GE provides a good example of a privacy statement directed at job seekers. It conveys all of the necessary information, as well as the statement that GE will respect candidate rights when depositing their resumes via the corporate career site.

---

[4] U.S. Census, 2000.

Figure 8.2: GE Privacy Statement

> Candidate Privacy Policy

At GE we are committed to protecting your privacy. Your personal information will be used by GE for recruitment purposes. It will be protected internationally according to GE's Candidate Data Privacy Guidelines outlined below.

By submitting your personal information you agree that GE may process it for recruitment purposes and transfer it worldwide consistent with GE's Candidate Data Privacy Guidelines.

Your consent to provide this information is required in order to complete the submittal process. If you do not agree, click on the "x" button in the upper right hand corner and the submittal process will discontinue.

Candidate Data Privacy Guidelines

These guidelines are derived from the GE global Guidelines on Employment Data Protection and Privacy. They are intended to provide candidates with information about the processing of Candidate-related data. For the avoidance of doubt, these guidelines do not form part of your contract of employment (where applicable). GE may amend these guidelines from time to time, should it become necessary to do so.

GE respects the privacy rights and interests of its candidates and the following principles will be applied when dealing with information that relates to identified or identifiable candidates in connection with your interest in a GE position. This type of information will be referred to as "Candidate Data".

Data Privacy Principles

- Data will be collected for the purposes specified below and used accordingly. The collection and processing of the data will be limited to these purposes and you are hereby informed in advance of the purposes and uses of such data.
- Data will be adequate, relevant and not excessive relative to the purposes for which they are processed.
- Data will be as accurate as possible and, where necessary, kept up to date.
- Data will not be kept longer than is appropriate or necessary for the purposes for which it is being processed or local legal requirements

http://www.gecareers.com/GECAREERS/jsp/jobsearch/experienced_professionals/candidate_privacy.jsp

Organizations should develop their privacy policies along similar lines as those used by GE. Generally, the policy should state why the information is being collected, how it will be used, how it is protected from unauthorized view/use, who it will be shared with, who may access it and how they will use it, how long it will be kept, how the depositor can remove their information at an earlier date if they wish and precisely how they can be sure their personal details have been thoroughly expunged from the system. Candidates should know who they can call or e-mail if they have concerns about any of the above. Links to the privacy policy should be placed on the footer of every page of a corporate career site.

Organizations that recruit internationally, especially for positions based in foreign countries, must know and understand the local data privacy laws in force. These laws, particularly in Europe, can be much more complex and rigorous than those in North America. Where transnational layers of government exist, such as within the European community, multiple layers of legislation may have to be observed.

Equal Employment Opportunity, Affirmative Action and Talent Management Systems

The U.S. government may be the world's largest buyer of contract goods and services. For example, it spends well over US$200 billion annually on things like construction, supplies, military equipment, services and IT. The Government Electronics and Information Technology Association currently estimates that the federal government spends more than US$74 billion annually on information technology alone.

For a wide spectrum of companies, the government might be a good bet in terms of pursuing business. In order to secure federal and many state and local government contracts, however, bidders must be equal employment opportunity (EEO) compliant. The Office of Federal Contract Compliance Programs (OFCCP), under Executive Order 11246 as amended, requires that contractors with fifty or more employees and government contracts of US$50,000 or more develop and implement a written affirmative action plan (AAP). They must engage in self-analysis for the purpose of discovering any barriers to equal employment opportunity. In practice, this means that you must not only have an AAP, but must collect and report on data such as the number of women and minorities in your workforce, their pay, and level and years of service, and generate an analysis of the types of applicants who apply for work in your company. Further, you must keep your records, in case of audit, for at least two years.

Making It Easy

Of course there are very good reasons for wanting a diverse and representative workforce that have nothing to do with getting government contracts or complying with OFCCP rules. No matter the motivation, collecting EEO information, analyzing it and producing reports either for government, investors or internal use can be time-consuming and difficult.

Talent management systems are the ideal tool with which to collect, process, analyze and report EEO/AAP information. With a TMS in place, most organizations begin to standardize their application processes. Candidates are usually encouraged to visit the corporate career site, browse jobs and complete a standard profile that includes the option to self-identify by gender, race and disability. Standardizing the application procedure is among the first steps organizations can take in complying with OFCCP requirements, as it allows them to track candidates through their process.

Furthermore, the e-recruitment toolset often provides the means to proactively source women and minority candidates, whether by distributing positions to specific women- and minority-related job boards or by using Web-mining tools to source candidates from resume pools and the Web itself. Several of the sourcing techniques described in Chapter 6 can be fine-tuned to search for or appeal to minority candidates, for example. Large, well-known job boards like LatPro.com and others can assist in this regard.

Best-of-breed talent management solutions sometimes include full-blown EEO/AAP compliance modules. These tools, in conjunction with reporting tools, can help track affirmative action goals, alerting the organization, for instance, when it is in danger of missing goals. The TMS can also export the data necessary to produce ready-formatted reports at the end of the year for government or internal use.

Select the Right TMS for the Job

If the organization has different teams for recruiting and diversity initiatives, it should be able to better integrate the two using its talent management system. This can enable the flow of real-time and just-in-time information so that the organization's plans for a diverse workforce become intelligently embedded in the day-to-day work of recruiters and hiring managers. In turn, data created from their progress is constantly available to EEO planners as they need it to adjust and fine-tune company efforts in real time.

There are several good reasons to formalize the organization's endeavors at creating a diverse and representative workforce. The first is in order to field the best possible talent, which logically can only be done by tapping into the widest possible pool of applicants. Another good reason is in order to get and keep government business.

A TMS vendor should be able to demonstrate how its software aids in the automatic collection of EEO data assists in EEO/AAP compliance management and helps build a diverse workforce. Potential buyers should ask to see the reports and data the TMS tools generate and ask to hear about problems it has solved for other customers, including cases in which audits were conducted and how the software helped clients through it successfully. Potential buyers should also ask to see how the vendor partners with others in the recruitment supply chain to ensure that using it, the organization can reach the audience it must in order to attract as wide and diverse an applicant pool as possible. For example, does the vendor integrate job distribution networks that include sites for diversity candidates?

The e-recruitment/talent management system might contain integrated and automated employee referral software (as described in Chapter 6). If so, it should also be plugged into and integrated with the organization's EEO tracking and AAP. Employee referral plans often account for 25 percent or more of new hires in many companies. Unfortunately, due to their nature—employees referring persons in their immediate social and professional circles—they can perpetuate the lack of diversity in an organization and undermine the progress of diversity initiatives. When integrated with the AAP, however, employee referral plans can promote the opposite. Organizations can separately track the number of women and minority candidates that the employee referral plan is responsible for. Organizations should make their workforce aware of its EEO goals and AAP with respect to their referral activity and also consider bonus objectives when AAP placement goals are achieved. The TMS should be able to automate and help track this.

Establishing EEO Capture in Your TMS Workflow

TMS makes it possible to address EEO and AAP issues in an automated fashion such that candidates can choose whether or not to participate. The system can then track their progress through the hiring cycle and produce insightful reports. By building EEO/AAP data collection into the TMS workflow, it is also possible to comply with any official definition of applicant that the OFCCP may announce (as discussed previously) because all online candidates can be treated as applicants.

The following steps are necessary in building EEO/AAP data capture into the TMS workflow.

1. Rather than worry a great deal over the definition, or lack thereof, of an applicant, leverage the TMS right at the beginning of the application process. By adding a voluntary EEO data collection section to the online profile, organizations can capture information on their candidates right up front.

2. A percentage of your applicants will elect not to complete the EEO section. The applicant data collection process is required to include a voluntary request for self-identification of race and gender with respect to EEO/AAP guidelines in hiring. Insert a short message to candidates that communicates the organization's desire to find the best candidates possible in order to build and grow a diverse workforce, etc. Assure candidates that provision of the information is voluntary and is collected only for the purposes of tracking diversity initiatives at the aggregate level. Completion of the EEO section should be made mandatory only in the sense that candidates cannot simply skip the section altogether. Rather, they should be required to select a check box with words to the effect of "I do not wish to self-identify." This will better enable the organization to track the percentage of applicants/candidates that complete the EEO section.

3. Track candidates through every stage of the hiring process. Among other things, this lets the organization study the impact of selection decisions and produce reports that will comply with the requirements of the EEOC and OFCCP. The TMS may reject some candidates immediately and without human involvement based on the screening tools operated. As described above, be vigilant in making sure that automated screening tools filter candidates based on clear requirements that are directly related to the position advertised (normally accomplished through a job analysis exercise). Automated screening tools must be free of bias toward any candidate

types; even prescreening questionnaires must be scrutinized. If automated screening tools are used, the TMS should be capable of matching EEO information against the resumes/profiles screened and reporting accordingly. If candidates pass through to a latter stage and are screened out manually because they fail an assessment or a component of a background check, the TMS should record the reason and report it as well. All candidates interviewed and offered positions must also be tracked by the TMS. Interview notes and the reasons for rejection (where applicable) should be attached. Note that EEO information must follow the candidate only through the selection process (as recommended above) for the purposes of reporting for regulatory compliance. Tracking diversity candidates for other reasons is normally prohibited by law.

4. In addition, the TMS should be capable of allowing for the extraction of external data for benchmarking. To create an AAP, organizations must know what their community looks like in terms of the availability of qualified women and minorities for the positions that make up the organization. This type of data can be purchased from research organizations like the Saratoga Institute or possibly obtained for free from regional governments or the Bureau of Labor Statistics. Knowing this, the organization can compare its workforce, as well as its talent pool of potential employees (see below) against the general availability of women and minorities in its recruitment areas.

5. As described in Chapter 7, the TMS should be used to create partially prequalified talent pool(s) of candidates that meet minimum standards and have expressed an interest in working in the organization. The talent pools offer an excellent window into the success of diversity sourcing efforts because they can be analyzed at an aggregate level to see what level of diversity-candidate interest there is in the organization. Be aware that regular searches of the talent pools or of public boards and the Internet should be free of any bias that might inadvertently discriminate against minority groups. The TMS should save searches so they can be analyzed in future for their effectiveness and adherence to affirmative action and equal employment opportunity principles.

Figure 8.3: Recording EEO Data through the E-Recruitment Process (One Example)

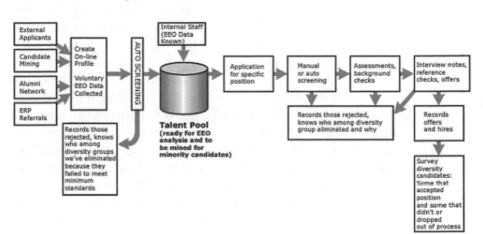

6. The TMS solution should allow the organization to input its targets (if applicable) and be alerted when those targets are in jeopardy. For example, depending on the numbers of people hired each year, the solution can send alerts to managers on weekly, monthly or quarterly bases and by company, division or possibly even workgroup. Better yet, it can alert recruiters and hiring managers to jobs and job groups that are of particular importance in the diversity plan as soon as they open a requisition. This way, they can adjust their sourcing and selection processes accordingly, if necessary.

7. With the vendor, organizations should ensure that their TMS is capable of producing the reports they need internally and for a government compliance review in formats ready for submission and/or use. Data from the TMS should also be capable of export in a variety of formats (at a minimum, .csv, .txt and .xml) for use in other reporting systems or spreadsheets. Some vendors offer easy to use and understand key performance indicators (KPIs) in a dashboard format so that users can see at a glance whether they are meeting their goals. These are useful in conveying the organization's progress and status quickly. At the very least, the TMS should be capable of producing data that can be easily extracted for use in affirmative action planning.

8. Many TMSs offer integrated candidate sourcing tools, including the ability to distribute job postings to hundreds or thousands of fee and free job boards. As described in Chapter 5, be sure to include fulsome job descriptions in postings that clearly state requirements. This will help candidates self-assess and it will make the job of screening easier and more valid. Make sure that the list of boards capable of receiving distributed jobs from the TMS includes large diversity candidate boards (such as LatPro.com and Diversity.com) and niche boards (such as Blackvoices.com). Also look at integrated resume mining tools to ensure that minority resume banks can be accessed. Ask the TMS vendor about other ways to source diversity candidates through e-recruiting; some vendors have in-house expertise on hand. If an organization has any doubts about its ability to source sufficient women and minority candidates online, traditional sources, including women and minority-targeted newspapers and magazines, should be accessible through recruitment advertisers that can also be integrated into the TMS.

Figure 8.4 below is a typical EEO/AAP capture template placed in the online application workflow. Note the employer's requirement that each applicant respond, even if only to select the "I do not wish to self-identify" box.

Figure 8.4: Sample EEO Data Collection

Job Application Process: Step 3 of 3
We are required to compile the following information for statistical purposes in order to comply with certain federal regulations relating to Equal Employment Opportunity and Affirmative Action Requirements. The information you provide is strictly on a voluntary basis and the content of the information will not effect your eligibility for employment. Likewise, if you choose not to provide this information it will not effect your eligibility for employment in any way.

Gender [　　　　　　　　　↓]

Race   [　　　　　　　　　↓]

Disability: ○ Yes   ○ No

Veteran: ○ Yes   ○ No

I do not wish to self-identify

Conclusions

Ethical hiring processes are important for a number of reasons, including legal considerations and employers' responsibility to societal standards of decency.

In terms of compliance, the latest OFCCP AAP regulations state that federal contractors must be able to identify the race, ethnicity and gender of each employee, and "where possible" to collect race, ethnicity and gender for each applicant. For employers who leverage TMS, living up to this standard, even though not legally required, is a simple task.

Equally or more important than compliance with government regulations, however, is the organization's competitiveness. It is at risk if it is unable to field a workforce that reflects the diversity of its customer base and takes advantage of the skills, creativity and outlooks that a diverse employee pool brings. If all segments of the entire workforce cannot be accessed, employers simply cannot reach the best available talent every time.

An effective EEO/AAP initiative requires methodical record-keeping and analysis and a plan. The TMS provides the most efficient means of collecting data from applicants, producing reports, sending alerts and helping to analyze progress against goals. Moreover, it can help employers source women and minority candidates and survey their opinions concerning the recruiting process. It is, in fact, difficult to imagine how a large organization can afford not to integrate its TMS with its EEO/AAP. Given the ambiguity around the definition of an applicant, employers can be sure they are compliant only if they place the collection of EEO data right up front in the application process. If voluntary collection isn't part of the online application process it can only be done at a later stage or by costly and inefficient off-line methods. The same is true for reporting on diversity candidates' progress through each subsequent step in the hiring process and in producing compliant records and reports.

By integrating EEO/AAP initiatives within the TMS, organizations will be in a better position to evaluate the effectiveness of their sources for candidates and hires overall. This will improve their general recruiting effectiveness by giving them insight into where to allocate or shift additional sourcing. Moreover, the process will give recruiters a comprehensive view of their efforts and how successful they have been in attracting candidates regardless of race, ethnicity or gender.

As for privacy and accessibility, employers should adopt standards of personal data collection and management that place the candidate's privacy and needs at the forefront. And while Internet access is increasingly ubiquitous, employers should ensure that their job postings work for candidates with limited access and those with disabilities.

Few of today's talent management/recruiting systems ship with everything suggested in this chapter. Potential buyers may need to work with their vendor to configure or customize the tools they need. Better yet, if an organization is still in the process of selecting a vendor, it should find one that can supply the features it needs with the minimum pain, delay and cost.

CHAPTER 9

Contingent, Contract, Temporary and Hourly Workers—Total Workforce Acquisition

Until recently, e-recruitment solutions such as job boards have concentrated for the most part on sourcing workers who are considered to be skilled or highly skilled. Professionals, managers and administrative personnel who make up the salaried 30 percent of the workforce have been the main focus.

The "hourly" workforce, including, in general, the 70 percent of the workforce that is classified as non-exempt[1], is only just starting to be addressed through e-recruitment. In addition, there are about 12 million contingent (contract and temporary) workers in North America, representing a roughly US$110 billion industry. Employers' use of contingent labor and workers' willingness (and increasing desire) to be "free agents" or independent contractors have been on the rise over the past ten years or so.

To date, very few talent management solutions handle the total workforce. Job boards and corporate career sites can certainly advertise any type of position, but to handle the applicants efficiently, different tools and functions are necessary on the back end, including time and expense modules to track contingent workers' hours and pay them efficiently. This chapter discusses the integration of

---

[1]The "non-exempt" classification for employees means that they are subject to either their state's labor code or the federally mandated Fair Labor Standards Act (FLSA). It also means that they must be paid for working overtime.

hiring-management tools into one seamless product in order to achieve the ability to acquire the total workforce from the desktop.

Contingent Workforce Management Automation

The contingent workforce, including temporary workers, consultants, contractors and certain professionals represents between 17 percent and 30 percent of the total labor force in the United States (depending on the industry).[2] According to more recent forecasts by the Bureau of Labor Statistics (BLS), the U.S. annual employment market for contingent workers is expected to grow by 15 percent per year. The BLS expects the number of temporary workers, including those that are attached to agencies as well as independent contractors, to increase by 49 percent this decade compared to an expected 15 percent increase in permanent workers during that time.

Services e-procurement, or the use of Web technologies to acquire all forms of temporary, contingent, professional, project-based and independent contractor services, is a sprawling industry that includes, but is not limited to, staffing organizations and agencies, online talent exchanges, overseas and domestic outsourcing, professional employment organizations (PEOs), vendor management systems (VMSs), vendors on premises (VOPs) and managed service providers (MSPs), all of which are discussed in this chapter.

According to Gartner Research, more than US$250 billion in temporary services were purchased worldwide in 2002. Gartner believes that this number will increase to US$300 billion in 2004, and that related software sales worldwide will increase to about US$2 billion by 2006. More than half of total purchasing spending in large organizations is on services. Having firm control over this expense is enormously important to corporate competitiveness and shareholder value. For these and other reasons, Gartner foresees growing demand for services e-procurement applications, with 30 percent of Fortune 1000 enterprises using a services procurement solution by 2007.

---

[2] Ron Hanscome—META Group, "Winning the Battle of the Contingent-Labor Bulge" (June 18, 2002).

Contingent workforce acquisition, management, administration, fees and wages paid represent the majority portion of overall corporate services spending. Soft dollar costs—including the time spent recruiting and tracking workers and dealing with vendors— is enormous also. There is no doubt that for large organizations, contingent workforce management (CWM) represents a massive opportunity for efficiency-driven value. By most estimates, CWM, accompanied by an effective vendor management system, can save 10 percent to 20 percent of overall contingent workforce spending and generate enormous soft dollar savings on top. In very large companies, this can easily translate into annual savings of between several million dollars in hard dollar savings alone (e.g., in fees paid to staffing firms, billing errors, etc.).

Vendor management system (VMS) is the name most commonly associated with contingent workforce acquisition software. With rare exceptions, organizations and staffing agencies were not using sophisticated VMSs until the latter part of the 1990s. Nevertheless, there are at least fifty distinct players in the market today, most with only a small handful of clients. This means the supplier landscape is crowded with unprofitable and marginally viable vendors. Pricing models and the philosophies around their approach to the market are varied and confusing. For example, some suppliers sell and support VMS software. Others give their software to organizations in return for the right to take a percentage of the amount they pay to staffing agencies. Some discount or give away their software in return for a contract to manage all of the receiving organization's contingent workforce activities. As discussed in detail below, there still exists considerable disagreement between pure-play VMS software providers, staffing-firm-owned VMS providers and the staffing agency industry itself.

In short, the VMS industry is considered immature even though, in terms of the "technology adoption life cycle" defined by author and consultant Geoffrey Moore, VMS is safely past the innovator and early adopter stages and just past the "chasm" stage where organizations observe the success or failure of the early adopters before implementing the solutions themselves. Today, large organizations (typically the Global 2000 largest companies) with annual contingent workforce spending of over US$15 million or US$20 million are good prospects for VMS, as they have the most to gain financially from streamlining their contingent workforce acquisition and management processes.

The State of the VMS Industry

As of mid-2003, there were only a few hundred VMS implementations worldwide and the largest solutions providers still had less then fifty systems implementations under their belts. No suppliers that offer VMS solutions exclusively, known as pure-play suppliers, can yet claim profitability. The suite players, who offer VMS either as part of larger human capital management (HCM) technology platforms or components of large staffing companies, are no better off, even though their losses are buried in the larger balance sheets of mostly profitable companies.

Despite the claims of VMS providers whenever they sign large new clients, the actual business that is processed through the VMS (known as "spend through") is likely to be smaller than the number quoted in the press releases. A Global 2000 company may spend over US$100 million per year on its temporary workers, contractors and consultants, but only a portion of that is likely to be passed through the VMS, at least initially. The combined spend through of all VMS implementations in the United States is likely to be no more than US$6.5 billion as of the start of 2004.

The VMS industry's problems also result from the confusing array of options and philosophies being marketed to organizations by vendors that are structured in vastly different ways. VMS pure plays preach the strength of their solutions, their focus on buyers (organizations) and the fact that they are truly and structurally vendor neutral (not biased in favor of or against any staffing agency). Suite players, including ERPs like PeopleSoft, and human capital technologies and services firms like Peopleclick, speak of the importance of an integrated approach to "total workforce acquisition." What they are talking about is permanent *and* contingent hires. Other suppliers, Ariba for example, present opinions from Gartner and other analysts that cite the gradual trend away from VMS to total services e-procurement (of which VMS is a part) and ultimately to "total procurement" solutions for virtually all services *and* goods. Staffing firms that have created their own VMS spin-offs, meanwhile, cite their financial viability and years in the business as factors that buyers should consider foremost when choosing a VMS.

As might be expected, staffing firms that have not developed VMS solutions of their own are either partnering with VMS pure plays or sitting on the fence. Many resent VMS suppliers for eating into their margins and profits (as we will see below). Many large staffing firms are forced to learn and use multiple VMSs in their day-to-day operations because their various clients have adopted the use of different tools. In a February 2003 survey of staffing firms conducted by Jordan Group, Inc., staffing firms reserved their worst criticism for the MSPs.[3] A majority felt that MSPs, firms that manage contingent workforce spending for organizations, were using their privileged positions as managers of their clients' VMSs to unfairly "gatekeep" between staffing agency vendors and hiring managers, and were keeping an inordinate amount of the business for themselves. These charges are in many cases well-founded. Allowing a staffing agency to act as an MSP can be like allowing the fox to guard the henhouse[4]— they sometimes have an inherent bias to channel work to themselves while blocking opportunities for competing firms.

VMS Value

In spite of the immaturity of the industry, the confusion, the battles and the variety of approaches VMS providers take, there is no doubt that effective VMS technologies and CWM through what is sometimes defined even more broadly as services e-procurement can shave millions of dollars off large organizations' contingent workforce spends. Most Web-based VMS can be implemented in a month or so, with minimal interruption and initial expense. There are virtually no ongoing costs, and a VMS can deliver hard dollar ROI very quickly.

Unlike almost everything else about the VMS industry, its value proposition is among the clearest and easiest to understand in the entire HCM technologies spectrum. It is also among the least disputed.

---

[3] The Jordan Group Inc., "VMS Providers' Scorecard" (February 2003).

[4] Elaine Taylor—Taylor-Harris Consulting, "Evaluating Vendor Management Systems" (2003).

Most large organizations today work with contingent worker staffing companies in the traditional sense. Thousands of hiring managers work with hundreds of vendors directly. Due to the decentralized approach taken, management of overall contingent workforce spending is often lax. There is little or no coordination among managers. HR is minimally involved and there are few standards, which often means that widely different rates are paid for very similar skills from unit to unit and department to department. Time and attendance is often loosely tracked, and billing mistakes caused by manual calculations and subsequent disputes are frequently rampant. This is to the detriment of the employer, as are instances where contractors work well past their end dates before anyone notices. Vendor performance is not monitored systematically and suppliers often wait months for payment.

Spending on temporary workers, independent contractors, professional services and specified projects is not under control in the majority of large organizations. Moreover, many organizations are in improper relationships with their contingent workforce on many levels. Because they may be breaking labor regulations by employing contractors that the Department of Labor would define as employees, they risk further costs in time and money because they may be exposed to audits, IRS penalties and independent contractor lawsuits.

Finally, in an era of heightened security concerns, VMS technology, especially when integrated with third-party background checking tools, can help organizations reduce security threats and limit associated risks such as hiring contractors and temps that may commit offences on the job. VMS can also integrate with other solutions to ensure that pass codes and other entry tools are automatically cancelled when a contractor or temporary worker's contract expires. This is a disaster waiting to happen in organizations with a high turnover of temporary and contract workers.

By reducing maverick spending, negotiating discounts and standardizing job descriptions and pay rates across every region in which it does business, an organization can realize fast and significant savings from VMS-enabled contingent workforce management. Most of the work relies on human decision-making, negotiation and process re-engineering, but the data provided by VMS is essential in order to drive the discussion, justify rate reductions and enable performance monitoring. Similarly, a preferred vendor program must be developed offline and early pay discounts negotiated in person, but the technology is necessary if payment is actually to be made early, and agreements are to be tracked, reported on and adjusted as necessary.

As described above, effective CWM with VMS technologies properly deployed and managed can reduce fiscal waste, mismanagement, and legal and security risks significantly. However, whether they are companies seeking a VMS for the procurement and management of the contingent workforce or staffing firms seeking a strategic VMS partner, organizations must perform diligent selection processes in order to make their initiatives successful.

VMS providers approach the market from a variety of angles. The majority are pure-play software companies (IQNavigator and Fieldglass, for example), others are part of HCM suite technology players (Peopleclick, Recruitsoft and VirtualEdge, for example), some are owned by staffing firms (Chimes and Beeline, for example) and a few are part of large ERP software companies (e.g., PeopleSoft). Several companies, such as Nitorum and XiSource, have gone out of business and others have been acquired (SkillsVillage, White Amber and itiliti, for example). They demonstrate the importance of the choice in terms of financial, product and overall viability.

Specific VMS-Enabled Cost- and Time-Savings Potential

With VMS-enabled contingent workforce management, organizations can improve processes and save money in a variety of ways. The following are key ingredients in doing so. The symbols below indicate the degree to which each saves money and/or time and improves quality (e.g., $$ means more cost savings than $).

$ = Hard cost savings
☆ = Time savings
✓ = Quality improvements

Requisitions: $$/☆☆/✓   As with hiring management systems for the salaried and hourly workforces, job requisition or job posting creation and distribution is a core component. VMS saves hiring managers' time by standardizing job descriptions, pay rates, approved vendor lists and other variables. Staffing firms are less likely to "lobby" hiring managers when they know that the key to doing long-term business with the company is to get on the preferred vendor list rather than encourage maverick spending (unauthorized spending by hiring managers outside the parameters of the CWM program and the VMS). Requisitions, once built, can be distributed to multiple vendors simultaneously, saving additional time and facilitating faster response and time to hire. Online requisition building reduces or eliminates data errors and standardizes inputs into the system.

Standardized Pay Rates: $$/☆   The implementation of standard pay rates calculated using the prevailing averages in the organization's region for specific skills and job types will reduce overbilling and eliminate the need for hiring managers to negotiate with vendors or conduct research into wages. VMS can include pay rates or ranges so that hiring managers cannot overpay for workers (except through maverick hiring). Many VMS providers have experts on staff that can assist in establishing hourly pay ranges based on benchmark data for the region.

Preferred Vendor Lists: $$$/☆/✓✓   VMS should enable users to reduce the number of vendors they deal with in order to negotiate volume discounts for tier-one suppliers, those staffing firms that have been classified among those the organization wants to do significant business with. Costs are reduced through VMS by streamlining the organization's roster of vendors (staffing agencies) and often slotting them into "preferred" and secondary or even tertiary groups. This can be accomplished without VMS, but automation makes sophisticated tracking, reporting and analysis practicable, while its absence makes it nearly impossible.

Armed with statistics on vendor performance and expertise on prevailing margins (the rate staffing firms charge above the actual hourly rate of the temporary worker), organizations should be able to eliminate significant costs by negotiating volume discounts from preferred vendors. There may have been several hundred vendors before the exercise but now there are many less. Those remaining can expect much greater business volume and will likely be eager to offer discounts rather than be removed from the preferred list. Moreover, vendor performance data helps organizations to obtain better, faster results and higher quality submittals (candidates) because vendors know they are being systematically monitored and compared with their competitors. They understand that the consequences of bad performance could mean their removal from the preferred vendor list.

Organizations should, if possible, reduce the number of their vendors during the VMS implementation stage and require those selected to train individuals in the parts of the VMS they will need to use. Some VMS providers and MSPs can assist or lead in the development of a preferred and tiered supplier network.

Time and Expense/Automated Reconciliation: ☆/✓ Online invoicing and timekeeping will result in significant reduction in discrepancies, errors and disputes with vendors. The solution will reconcile expected expenditure versus actual billing, flag overtime and may alert organizations to peculiarities, such as overbilling, before they become disputes or errors.

Early Pay Discounts: $ Before VMS, vendors (staffing firms) weren't often paid until many weeks or months after they invoiced. With automated time and billing reconciliation, checks can be processed in hours or days and be posted to or auto-deposited in vendors' accounts. This ability to pay vendors faster can be used to negotiate early pay discounts with them.

Auctioning: $$ Many VMSs offer built-in tools to advertise projects and assignments in an auction-like manner. A rough scope of work or requisition is posted along with details such as expected duration, required skills, etc. Staffing firms, individuals or teams of contractors can "bid." The employer is usually able to collect and compare the responses online and choose a winner based on price plus a number of other factors, including the quality of the worker's bid. Auctioning can be used for project-based work or even for individual temporary worker assignments. For example, an organization that has identified the need for a temporary team of various professionals for a project can post the project and its needs to vendors of its choice. The vendors may propose a team, provide worker details and bid a price. The organization can choose to make the bidding blind so that the vendors cannot see others' bids, or it may display the bids but block information on who made them.

Auctioning is defended by many and scorned by others because in some ways it treats workers as commodities. In some cases this argument has merit; in others, such as bulk hiring for light industrial work, call centers, etc., auctioning can work (in the manner described above) to temper high markups for what should be a fairly standard set of skills.

Reporting and Analytics: $$$/☆☆/✓   VMS solutions usually contain powerful reporting tools that can be used to track everything from total spending in a given time period to vendor performance against requisitions and service level agreements. Reports enable an organization to negotiate better rates from vendors based on volume, performance and improved time to pay, as described previously. Reports can also point to weaknesses in the process, such as bottlenecks in the workflow that should be improved.

A Note of Caution

Organizations using VMS should be concerned with the relationships they build with staffing vendors. In a poor economy, employers may have the edge in the recruitment of most types of contingent workers. When the economy improves and labor markets tighten, organizations will need to look harder to get their necessary share of qualified temporary help. Good relationships with staffing agencies, even though that might entail elements of cost reduction and performance monitoring, will pay off when the pendulum swings back to labor shortages. That said, it is important to note that through the late 1980s and 1990s, bull and bear economies included, margins for big staffing industry players like Kelly and Manpower came down steadily and significantly. This is a positive trend for employers and a sign that the staffing industry, at least in the non-exempt worker categories, is maturing. This may be aided by technologies like VMS.

If VMS can been seen as beginning with contract and temporary workers, the next phase, just emerging, will extend online procurement to encompass the full range of services procurement, including retainer-based services such as legal, media and public relations. A future stage may emphasize the unified handling of all procured resources, including services *and* goods.

Management of the Process and Technology

There are three or four ways VMS is currently delivered in an organization. At one end of the spectrum are pure-play software vendors whose only business is developing, maintaining and selling their solution. These vendors will install or host the software and train their clients in its use. Normally the client establishes an in-house team to manage the processes and technology. Alternatively, most pure-play VMS providers will provide these services as part of the deal, either from their own professional services divisions or in partnership with another vendor, usually a staffing firm or consulting organization.

Organizations must decide whether they can manage the process and the technology in-house with existing or recruited resources. The advantages include more control of the process and true vendor neutrality. Appropriate structure can be determined such that hiring managers' interaction with staffing agencies is restricted or open (organizations sometimes seek to limit interaction with staffing agencies to one or a few people, ostensibly in an effort to control the process and reduce opportunity or temptation for maverick spending). Disadvantages include the work that is necessary to develop staffing vendor networks and the relationship management necessary on an ongoing basis. The organization also assumes responsibility for monitoring vendor performance, time and expense, payment, and the analysis of data associated with any metrics the organization wishes to track.

Alternatively, organizations can work with one of their preferred staffing vendors in a master vendor or MSP setup. This arrangement outsources the work described above to an organization (typically a large staffing firm) that may have decades of experience in the industry and deep knowledge and expertise it can tap in building the network and processes.

Staffing agencies are eager to enter into no-cost MSP relationships with large clients, provided they gain first crack at the staffing business from that company. This is a disadvantage for the organization. The staffing agency MSP will establish a network of vendors with itself at the top and the rest as subcontractors. Vendor neutrality, along with some of the ROI outlined earlier in this chapter, may disappear in many cases. This scenario might restrict the ability for organizations to cast the net wide in searches for contingent workers in order to get the best talent at the lowest prices. There are grades and degrees of vendor neutrality, so organizations should be careful selecting their MSP. An MSP led by a national firm like Manpower, for example, may differ widely from MSP services offered by a regional staffing company like Nelson (WorkforceLogic) because Manpower is able to find workers for nearly any position, anywhere in the U.S., while Nelson is far more limited. To some degree, however, the organization will be able to minimalize these effects by setting parameters within which the MSP can operate. This usually means that the MSP is required to source a set percentage of requisitions from firms and agencies other than its own, or in some cases is prohibited from supplying any workers at all.

Pricing Models

VMS can be sold to an organization or "leased" in an application service provider (ASP) format. In deals involving software VMS providers, customers typically pay for implementation (US$50,000–US$200,000) and pay their suppliers a fee based on the percent of "spend" that goes through the VMS. Depending on the amount considered, 1 percent to 3 percent is common. The most common payment model, however, is one in which organizations are provided VMS software and managed services free of charge. The buyer may or may not pay for the VMS solutions provider to implement the software, depending on the negotiation, duration of agreement and how valuable the supplier perceives the account to be. The buyer, or an MSP, then manages the VMS and charges staffing firms a fee or "toll" as a percentage of spending through the VMS. As one would expect, each method of payment has its pros and cons.

Clearly, cost is the main downside to the first option. However, paying for VMS software provides ultimate control over the solution and how it will be applied. All negotiated rate reductions, including volume and early payment discounts, accrue directly to the organization without the complications added by MSP providers trying to impose their toll on top. Paying for a true vendor-neutral software is the cleanest, best approach to contingent workforce management through VMS. If an organization does not wish to, or cannot administer the VMS and/or the relationships with vendors, it should hire an independent service provider. This would be one that understands the staffing industry well but is not itself a staffing firm and can be trusted not to show favoritism toward any provider in particular. A knowledgeable service provider will build the most favorable structure of vendors and negotiate advantageous discounts. It will manage communications between the organization, its hiring managers and the vendors so that maverick hiring is reduced and eventually eliminated, requisitions are vetted and compliant, referrals are excellent and hiring managers are shielded from vendors to the degree desirable.

If an organization chooses a VMS provider that also offers MSP services and is affiliated with a staffing firm, it must address questions of vendor neutrality. The advantage in this case is the organization gets VMS software with minimum cost and pain. It can be reasonably sure that the MSP service will be conducted by personnel who are experienced in the staffing industry. Unfortunately, experience thus far suggests a broad dissatisfaction with the way VMS provider and staffing firm MSP is carried out, particularly when the two are combined. Organizations that go this route must put in place careful measures to eliminate overt favoritism toward the VMS provider's staffing firm parent. These measures might include the elimination of the parent staffing firm from the list of preferred vendors or at least rules as to the percentage of requisitions that can be filled by the parent firm. The organization also bears some responsibility to ensure that the VMS provider is not appropriating proprietary information gathered from competitors using the VMS, such as markup rates and resumes. In short, if an organization hires a staffing firm MSP, it is unreasonable to expect that it will operate completely without bias unless clear rules, such as those listed above, are negotiated and enforced.

Other CWM Technologies and Tools

Included in the realm of CWM tools are Web-based exchanges on which independent professionals, contractors and teams can bid for project-based work and temporary assignments. Readers might remember the ascendancy of exchanges in the late 1990s when the valuation of companies like Verticalnet were massive and every type of company from airlines to automobile manufacturers were banding together to build online marketplaces for supply-chain-related procurement. Consumer-based exchanges like eBay also sprung up, but despite eBay's success, few business to consumer or business to business exchanges remain vibrant and profitable today. This is in part due to the general dot-com collapse but also due to the difficulty in building the critical mass of users (buyers and sellers) needed to make an exchange viable.

Nevertheless, several enterprising individuals and companies have brought the exchange concept to human capital management. These tools are separate from VMS but are sometimes integrated components, as is the case with the eWork Exchange and eLance. In summary, the tools allow organizations to describe temporary assignments and projects and post them on the exchange for individuals and teams to bid on. Unfortunately, most exchanges are poorly regulated and loosely managed (due to the expense of doing so), which has led to the demise or irrelevance of the majority of these services.

The problem many employers experienced with exchanges is the free-for-all atmosphere that ensues when respondents are not screened for qualifications and/or do not have to pay a fee to use the exchange. As employers become frustrated with the number and quality of responses they receive on exchanges, they stop posting to them, which leads very quickly to the exchange's demise.

Nonetheless, some exchanges are well run and can be an important aspect of CWM and cost control. If an organization can access qualified independent contractors and teams for its projects directly, it stands to save a great deal by avoiding the markups charged by staffing firms.

Staffing Exchanges

Of the main players (past and present) in the staffing exchange industry, many, including Guru.com and Ants.com, are out of business. Some, most notably ProSavvy, eLance and eWork, are succeeding. ProSavvy advertises large, project-focused work from several hundred corporate clients, most of which are Fortune 500 and/or Global 2000 firms. It claims to carefully screen and qualify all of its suppliers, requiring references from at least five satisfied customers. The advantage for employers is receipt of a very manageable response from a handful of qualified contractors. ProSavvy monitors its suppliers' activity and will work with them to find suitable projects to bid for. It will also intervene if it determines that suppliers are submitting bids for assignments and projects they are clearly not qualified for.

eLance offers a greater volume of assignments than ProSavvy but, on average, they are much smaller in terms of dollar value. Bidders tend to be individual contractors or "free agents." Like ProSavvy, eLance charges an annual fee to suppliers/contractors but it does not screen them. Some exchanges, such as eLance, offer billing and payment services and private messaging tools, as well as a means to evaluate suppliers for future reference.

In summary, exchanges can be an important component of CWM because they offer the potential to save on margins charged by staffing firms. Unfortunately, organizations that hire independent contractors directly can expose themselves to Department of Labor compliance issues and suits brought by long-term contractors seeking back pay, benefits and stock options based on having done similar work as full-time employees. Employers must ensure that they comply with regulations and guidelines when hiring contingent workers directly.

Professional Employment Organizations

IRS penalties for misclassification of contractors (paying a worker as a contractor when they are in fact, an employee) can be steep. They include fines for failure to withhold income taxes equal to 1.5 times wages plus 20 percent of the social security and Medicare taxes that should have been paid by the employee.

Professional employer organizations (PEOs) can alleviate the risks associated with hiring independent contractors directly because they act as employers of record for contractors, making them, in effect, "W-2"—regular employees of the PEO. PEOs may also offer contractors back-office support including billing and collection; tax calculation, deductions and preparation; liability, health, life and other insurance administration; and reporting to track billings, income, retirement accounts and taxes paid, among other features. Typically, contractors pay their PEO a small percentage (less than 5 percent) of their income for these services. Organizations often refer previous employees and others that they would like to hire as independent contractors to PEOs in order to transfer risk and increase compliance.

The PEO industry has fallen on hard times recently, with IRS rulings putting some of their retirement plans' legality in doubt. Workers' compensation scams in Florida, embezzlements in Michigan and missing pension funds in Arizona all allegedly by, or associated with, PEOs haven't helped the reputation of the industry, nor have several bankruptcies among formerly large players.

Regardless, PEOs continue to play a role in the CWM arena. And they will probably continue to as long as organizations need the flexibility of a contingent workforce and government rules exist to regulate their use of it.

The PEOs listed below represent some of the main players (past and present) in the PEO space as defined for these purposes (there are at least two different types of organizations that always or occasionally refer to themselves as PEOs). Note that several formerly large players have exited the business, some accompanied by alleged embezzlement of benefits plans or retirement funds. This reflects the instability of the PEO landscape.

Table 9.1: Professional Employment Organizations

Company and URL	Focus	Comments	Status (2003)
MyBizOffice www.mybizoffice.com	General	Almost 2,000 independent contractors. Partnership with BrassRing. Charges contractor 4 percent of billings. Employers pay roughly 18 percent markup.	In business
ZeroChaos www.zerochaos.com	General	Charges contractors US$275/ month. Also offers a VMS and a talent exchange.	In business
Independent Professional Services (IPS) www.iprofessional.com	General	PEO for independent contractors	In business

FreeAgent.com www.freeagent.com	General	eOffice PEO for independent contractors. Integrated with exchange	Out of business. Previous users referred to Yurcor.com
Simplified Employment Services URL no longer available	General		Bankrupt
HR Logic www.hrlogic.com	General		Out of business
Employee Solutions	General		Out of business
Peopleworks www.peopleworks.com	General		Out of business

Implications of CWM for Human Resource Professionals

In the majority of organizations, human resources departments have so far been content to let others handle CWM. For several reasons, they should take a strategic position toward the acquisition and management of contingent workers. Too often, CWM is controlled exclusively outside HR, mainly in procurement departments and collectively among hiring managers. There is an obvious role for procurement and finance in that CWM implies cost savings through procurement efficiency and control. HR, however, must increasingly view the contingent workforce as a strategic asset.

For many organizations, the contingent workforce includes not only light industrial, clerical and administrative workers. As often as not, senior technical specialists, professionals, project managers and other high-level contingent workers work on-site and many of them are engaged in mission-critical assignments lasting months or longer. HR must balance procurement's tendency to overlook the importance of selection in favor of cost savings. As introduced in Chapter 7 on workforce planning, HR should also understand the makeup of the contingent portion of the organization's workforce—the skills it brings, its proportion of the total workforce, and whether decisions to outsource are effectively made versus staffing internally, recruiting externally (for full-time talent), converting current contingent workers to employees or training existing staff where contingent worker hiring is done primarily to obtain specialized skills.

Among the most important factors in making VMS pay is the reduction and eventual elimination of maverick spending. Organizations that are successful in driving all contingent workforce spending through their VMS will maximize ROI associated with VMS and CWM. Similarly, organizations that effectively manage their network of preferred vendors and the interaction between vendors and hiring managers will extract the most value and achieve the best returns associated with CWM and VMS.

For all of the reasons discussed, CWM technologies, particularly VMS, are a must for any large organization with significant expenditures on temporary workers, contractors and consultants. The benefits are clear and obvious enough that several industry analysts believe VMS adoption by the Global 2000 will grow exponentially over the next three to four years. Indeed, Ron Hanscome of META Group predicted in 2002 that use of best-of-breed and ERP-based VMS by the Global 2000 will increase to approximately 80 percent from 20 percent of the Global 2000 by 2008.

A revitalized economy will not do away with the demand for the advantages VMS provides. Employers will become more willing to pay higher rates for temporary staff as the labor market tightens in the future, but will still demand systems to help them manage contingent labor or will at least choose staffing firms that offer the most competitive prices and services. Those firms will likely be the ones that have mastered VMS.

As stated at the beginning of this chapter, contract labor is usually an organization's largest indirect spend, yet it remains one of the most loosely managed. VMS technology and effective contingent workforce management processes can improve this situation dramatically, saving large companies millions of dollars each year.

Hourly and "High Volume" Workers

With the exception of skilled workers (e.g., tradespersons), full- and part-time employees that are paid on an hourly basis are often massed at the low end of the labor market, primarily in the retail and services industries. They include fast-food workers, sales clerks, "associates" and other workers who earn minimum wage or close to it. Turnover among these workers is usually very high, which adds to the enormous costs of hiring and retaining them. Estimates associated with replacing hourly workers range between US$400 and US$3,000 each. This becomes a very substantial number when multiplied by hundreds or thousands of workers hired each year by large retailers and fast-food chains. While it may be next to impossible to greatly reduce turnover among this segment of the workforce, e-recruit technologies are playing an important role in saving time and money both through improvements to retention and by lowering staffing costs.

Talent management systems can help standardize the process for accepting resumes, screening, and processing hourly workers into jobs. Rather than accepting resumes and/or applications on paper, organizations should develop their application forms online, use automated screening technologies and test potential personnel using valid tools offered by companies such as Test.com, ePredix, Brainbench and others. Because positions like sales associate, cashier, food service, call center operator and many others require standard skill and personality sets, organizations can purchase tests off the shelf and use them by the thousands. This approach can quickly and legitimately find better-suited candidates, thereby lowering turnover and saving staffing costs.

Several retailers, fast food chains, call centers and staffing firms in the business of requiring hourly workers have developed kiosks to aid in recruiting. Kiosks can sit in an organization's reception area, or in the case of a retailer, near the entrance to stores. They can also be placed in malls and movie theaters, and be taken on the road to career fairs, high schools, college campuses and elsewhere. Kiosks can contain marketing and branding messages and engage the user with voice, video and interactive exercises such as aptitude tests. They can collect candidate information and integrate with the talent pools created through TMS. Several TMS providers, such as Unicru and Deploy, have versions of their software that sit on kiosks and can synchronize over the Internet with the organization's recruiting databases and talent pools.

In high-volume, hard-to-fill areas, managers can interview promising candidates on the spot. In other words, when a candidate applies for work and passes whatever skills and aptitude tests the organization administers via the kiosk, a manager is alerted (by the system, using e-mail) and meets the candidate right then and there. An interview and an offer (pending background check and references) can often be made on the spot.

The U.S. Department of Defense launched a kiosk project in 2002 that offers potential candidates video and sound presentations of opportunities in all branches of the armed forces (see Figure 9.1 below). The kiosks are attractive and, when placed in locations where the target audience congregates, can generate significant traffic. Note that this kiosk looks like a video game. This is in part to attract young potential recruits, and in part to convey a modern message about the armed forces. The kiosk is interactive both online and off. If the message compels a candidate to seek more information, they can pick up the attached phone and speak to a recruiter directly.

Figure 9.1: E-Recruitment Kiosks

The Department of Defense has developed and deployed kiosks like the one above in shopping malls, movie theaters, employment offices and elsewhere.

Many employers of hourly workers use specialized TMS providers like Recruitsoft, Unicru, VirtualEdge and Recruitmax. These TMS providers take a broad-based approach—utilizing kiosks, corporate career sites, a public job board for its clients, integrated skills and personality tests, integrated background and drug testing, and integrated tax credit eligibility screening (Work Opportunity Tax Credit and welfare-to-work)—which greatly improves time to hire, increases applicant quality and reduces costs. Furthermore, they help employers with multiple locations in the same area to share applicants more effectively. Some solutions provide candidate-specific interview guides, as well as assistance in complying with employment equity requirements. They might also have components for exit interviews and statistical reporting.

Hourly type job seekers should be able to search across employers' sites using a simple zip code search. Employers receive applicants from this source and through their corporate career site and kiosks.

Figure 9.2: Hourly Worker Recruitment

Candidate Job Search	All ↓
Type of Position:	↓
Shift Desired:	Evenings ↓
Your Zip Code:	How far will you travel? 10 ↓

29 Jobs Met Your Criteria

Posted	Job	Company	Category	Pay/Hour	Hours	Distance	Start	Apply
04/08/03	Store Clerk	Propos	Customer Service	$8	FT-Evenings	7.5 miles	Immediate	Apply
04/08/03	Customer Service Rep	Tier One	Customer Service	$8.25	FT-Evenings	4 miles	Immediate	Apply
04/08/03	Shift Leader	Caligo	Management	Competitve	FT-Evenings	9.8 miles	Immediate	Apply
03/08/03	Sales Rep	The Pail	Customer Service	$7+comm	PT-Evenings	3.2 miles	Immediate	Apply
03/08/03	Cook	Phil's	Kitchen	$10.50	PT-Evenings	6.9 miles	01/09/03	Apply
04/08/03	Waiter	Phil's	Customer Service	Min+tips	FT-Evenings	6.9 miles	01/09/03	Apply
03/08/03	Host	Phil's	Customer	$7+tips	FT-	6.9 miles	01/09/03	Apply

Refine Search   Access Help

Integrated Contingent, Hourly and Permanent Workforce Acquisition.

Large employers have been using applicant tracking or talent management systems for several years to improve their processes around hiring permanent staff to save money and time. Some have purchased and use separate TMSs for the hourly (non-exempt) and salaried (exempt) workforce. Blockbuster Video is an excellent example. Blockbuster uses Recruitsoft's best-of-breed TMS for the salaried workforce and Unicru's best-of-breed solution for hourly workforce needs. As it and increasing numbers of other organizations look to contingent labor as an area to increase efficiencies and lower costs, a third solution, this one a VMS, will be necessary in order to manage acquisition of the entire workforce. A few progressive suppliers, such as VirtualEdge and PeopleSoft, have already developed all-in-one solutions that enable salaried, hourly and contingent workforce acquisition.

Organizations are saving significant time and money with VMS and TMS (hourly and salaried) but greater efficiencies are possible by combining all three. A carefully integrated solution combining access to VMS and TMS at the user interface level for hiring managers, yet maintaining sufficient separation at the back end for compliance reasons is necessary. This total talent acquisition system would provide greater ROI by reducing the number of separate solutions needed to acquire and manage the complete workforce. Total workforce planning, analysis and reporting would also be possible by having data from vendor management, hourly recruiting and permanent recruiting in one system.

Many TMS providers claim to offer vendor management modules. What these modules typically do is allow hiring managers and recruiters to post their requisitions to preferred staffing vendors and independent recruiters from the system. Some give vendors a secure window to the TMS so they can submit candidates for consideration, communicate, and generally collaborate with internal staff to fill positions. This is where they tend to stop. Similarly, several VMS providers offer permanent hire modules, which also tend to lack back-end functionality, appropriate workflow capabilities and robustness. A few vendors, such as Unicru, Oracle and Recruitsoft, offer integrated hourly and salaried workforce acquisition tools that appear promising but are as yet untested. Perhaps two or three (e.g., VirtualEdge) offer combined hourly, salaried and contingent workforce management solutions that are also untested insofar as a critical mass of customer use is concerned. The reason for the lack of integrated tools so far is simple—e-recruitment is new and customers have only recently become used to it. The market is saturated with vendors, most of whom are struggling to survive let alone reach out in new, expensive and risky directions. As customer demand and sophistication meets the vendor's search for competitive differentiation, more combined, total workforce acquisition tools will emerge.

Total workforce acquisition solutions should enable an organization to use one system to post a requisition for permanent, contract or temporary workers. This would include the flexibility to hire a combination of the above under one requisition, for example, if a company is looking for five technical writers, two of which will be full-time and the other three on three-month contracts. The hiring manager needs to be able to configure workflows on the fly so that the full-time hires go through their necessary approvals and stages while the temporary hires follow a different workflow, perhaps involving both HR and procurement.

In an integrated, seamless approach, the hiring manager would select where the requisition is to be distributed for the full-time hires (intranet, corporate career site, job boards, recruiters, etc.) and for the temporary hires (the organization's approved staffing agency vendors). The hiring manager should also be able to use the system to hire someone into the job temporarily and quickly (through a staffing agency) while the lengthier process of filling the position permanently is launched at the same time. If hourly workers are required, the process should be streamlined and capable of hiring en masse with entirely different workflows. Moreover, it should be possible to place the hourly components on a kiosk and for the hiring manager to route the positions accordingly.

The system would track hourly, salaried and temporary candidates through the process—interview scheduling, tracking correspondence, decisions, etc. These three segments of candidates would route to different parts of the integrated systems for payroll, time sheets, attendance, performance pay, reporting and so on.

The VMS portion of the integrated tool would consolidate invoice reconciliation and payment to the vendors. For reporting, it would be possible to benchmark against other similar organizations

202 Chapter 9 • Contingent, Contract, Temporary and Hourly

to compare vendor rates, contingent worker salaries and process efficiencies. As with TMS, the VMS portion of the system will track related budgets and use alerts to warn procurement or HR managers when contracts are expiring, or diversity targets are not being met, for example. ROI calculators should be able to determine time and cost savings continuously. The system should contain an element of vendor and worker evaluation, though for contingent workers, evaluation should be "pushed" to the staffing agency where applicable.[5] By requiring the staffing agency to maintain contingent worker evaluations, the organization shields itself from the appearance of treating contract and temporary staff like employees.

All salaried, hourly and contingent worker data should merge at the back end for complete workforce statistics, analytics, ad hoc reporting, affirmative action planning, workforce planning and cost/ROI information. This is the second major benefit of integrated TMS and VMS—a much more holistic and complete view of the entire workforce.

An integrated total workforce management platform should also seamlessly connect EEO/diversity systems and workforce planning components with VMS and TMS (including internal and alumni). Along with performance and learning management, this might give organizations the first automated 360° view of their entire workforce. This might allow them to monitor performance against diversity targets, time and cost-to-hire goals, and retention efforts, and to track skills and competencies, determine which positions are better to staff full-time versus with temporary staff, assess the performance and quality of staffing agency vendors as well as the candidates they refer, determine training and development needs and, in effect, properly align corporate objectives to available human capital once and for all.

Though at least two different parts of the organization need to be involved in administering and "owning" the integrated software, their different interests might actually aid in the process. The procurement or purchasing departments care about contracts, prices and legalities, etc. The HR function cares more about people, quality of hire and best fit. Neither is usually interested in

---

[5] Organizations should avoid conducting and keeping performance reviews of contingent workers. Doing so may constitute a strong indication that the employer treats contract workers like permanent workers. This may lead to investigation and possible sanctions.

doing the other's job. Therefore, both departments' strategic goals can be achieved while eliminating the conflicts caused by operating disparate systems or processes (i.e., those run by HR and procurement, in this case).

It is becoming clear that workforce management decisions should be reshaped to maximize the total workforce. Whether in the market for a TMS or a VMS, it would be prudent for organizations to plan for platform integration, immediately or down the road. The first generation of fully integrated TMS/VMS are becoming available. PeopleSoft, for example, has recently integrated its VMS (PeopleSoft purchased SkillsVillage in May 2001) within its HCM platform and workforce acquisition modules. PeopleSoft's total workforce acquisition solution is also tied to workforce planning tools to create a powerful end-to-end platform. Unfortunately, PeopleSoft HRMS is required to operate it along with the separate purchase of several modules, all adding up to a large expense (typically in the millions of dollars for large organizations). On the other end of the price spectrum, TMS provider VirtualEdge announced an integrated contingent, permanent and hourly worker recruiting solution in late 2003. It appears solid in demonstrations but it is too new to have developed a track record with live customers. The same can be said of Oracle's, Recruitsoft's and Unicru's integrated hourly and salaried TMS solutions.

Total workforce acquisition and management is a platform that will grow in popularity unless it is sidelined by regulatory and compliance issues (which is unlikely). Common wisdom is to keep permanent and contingent hiring processes as separate as possible in order to reduce real or perceived similar treatment of the two types of workers. If total workforce acquisition software is to take hold, it will have to streamline recruiting on the front end while managing the processes separately and distinctly in the back end. This might be accomplished, in part, by using portal-like graphical interfaces for hiring managers with separate databases, tracking and record-keeping in the back end. The solution will have a front end that is capable of interfacing seamlessly with physically separate systems in the back office, in other words.

Conclusions

It is important for organizations to consider the whole workforce in their talent management planning and strategy. The contingent workforce is large and growing faster than the permanent workforce. Hourly workers, especially in retail, are becoming harder to find and increasingly difficult to retain. VMS technologies can save organizations millions of dollars in the first year of use. Integrated, total workforce acquisition solutions can streamline staffing right across the organization and facilitate better workforce analysis and planning.

Outsourcing

O rganizations have been outsourcing elements of the HR process for decades. At least 70 percent of companies outsource at least one component of HR. The broad topic of HR outsourcing is beyond the scope of this book as only some of it deals with talent management and only a very small part has to do with technology. Recruitment outsourcing, however, is of interest as it presents the option of removing a key component of talent management outside the organization.

Recruitment outsourcing can encompass everything from engaging a staffing firm to assist in filling difficult hires to moving everything from sourcing through actual hiring out of the organization and into the hands of a third-party outsourcer. Organizations like BrassRing, Kenexa and Bernard Hodes are TMS solutions providers that also offer recruitment outsourcing services. In doing so, they can offer all of the sourcing, selecting and hiring components of best practice talent management. This might include all or some of the following: job description writing, requisition building, job distribution, employment branding and advertising, screening, interviewing and selection or hiring.

Few companies appear to have gone so far as to outsource the entire recruitment process, but several have turned over everything but the final decision on who gets hired. In these cases, outsourcers should be required to conduct their sourcing, screening and selection according to policy set by their clients. For example, the organization may still want to set employment equity goals and compensation bands. Recruitment outsourcing may be a good idea for organizations that have not developed recruiting as a core competency, or for those that have done so but find it too expensive to maintain. Others ripe for outsourcing include companies that have a tremendous amount of hiring to be done in a short period of time. For example, a new casino that must hire and screen hundreds of dealers, security guards, tellers and managers on top of an entire hotel staff might require at least the temporary assistance of a third party.

Organizations should be careful to retain all strategy- and policy-making around talent management, however. In the case of final candidate selection, it may be practical to give this responsibility to outsourcers when the type of hiring is high volume and in an industry with high turnover. The salaried workforce and those who are in senior positions especially should be interviewed and ultimately selected by the organization itself.

A somewhat better outsourcing option for talent management may be found with human resources business process outsourcers (HR BPOs). These organizations, until recently, have focused almost exclusively on very large companies. business process outsourcing contracts involve the outsourcing of multiple HR processes—payroll, health and benefits, compensation, HRMS, recruiting, training, and performance management to name a few. Typically, an HR business process outsourcing relationship involves the outsourcing of several and sometimes all HR processes. The size and length of business process outsourcing contracts are much larger than those won by niche outsourcers (e.g., payroll, recruiting). HR BPOs aim to bring about strategic and process improvements in addition to cost savings, and normally assume a higher portion of the risk and ownership of the results.

The HR business process outsourcing industry is in its infancy but is growing at a fast pace. High-profile deals involving British Petroleum, Bank of America, Kellogg and others for large components or all of HR are worth up to over US$1 billion each over a span of up to ten years and these are just the tip of the iceberg. Various analysts estimate the potential size of the market to be US$30 billion to US$60 billion among Global 2000 companies by

2005. At present, there are probably no more than fifty true HR business process outsourcing deals worldwide but the associated contracts are likely worth an aggregate US$15 billion or more. Aon Consulting, one such HR BPO, signed a deal in 2002 with AT&T that encompasses almost all HR processes for about seventy thousand employees. Aon is contracted to provide its services through at least 2009 and will likely collect somewhere in the neighborhood of a billion dollars to do so. Exult, another BPO, has seen the most success. It has signed deals with more than a dozen Global 2000 companies, including British Petroleum, Bank of Montreal and International Paper, for HR outsourcing deals spanning up to ten years and worth, overall, at least US$8 billion.

As the industry proves its worth by delivering consistent cost savings in the 10 percent to 20 percent range and by generating satisfied customers who can attest to improved and faster processes, more organizations will outsource increasing shares of their HR functions and many will decide to outsource everything except strategy, policy-setting, governance and vendor management (managing the relationship with the outsourcer). The figure below from Exult describes its recommendations for what a client should consider in outsourcing. While many HROs and BPOs would be happy to take on strategy and policy-setting, organizations should retain these responsibilities because they are ultimately accountable. Such things as determining what types of workers to hire, pay rates, leave and benefits policies, grievance procedures and how the organization responds to complaints of harassment, for example, are better kept in-house even though the advice of the outsourcer may be sought. Similarly, the organization will need to keep or develop competencies that allow them, as a smaller HR division, to consult to the other business units that make up the organization. Being free of the transactional and administrative elements of HR, remaining staff will have time to take on more strategic roles within the organization.

BPO differentiation boils down to who can provide the greatest cost savings guarantees and who can promise the greatest process improvements and positive transformations to processes.[1] Despite solid service level agreements (SLAs) and proof of cost savings and

---

[1] Most HR BPO vendors speak of their ability to "transform" processes. By that they mean real change, not just tweaking processes but altering them fundamentally to generate significant efficiencies, improvements and cost savings.

Figure 10.1: Exult's BPO Pyramid of Responsibility

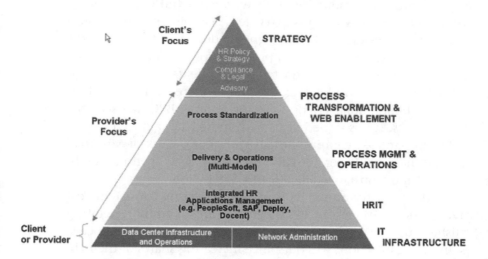

Reprinted with permission from Exult. Copyright Exult 2000.

process improvements, real evidence of success can only come from customer experience and testimonials. Unfortunately, in a market with only fifty or so customers, most of which are new and many of which are secretive, obtaining reliable testimonials is difficult.

At least until the market matures, organizations considering HR business process outsourcing should be very careful in the selection of a partner. This will include doing an assessment of the providers' reputation, viability, technology, flexibility and overall fit with the organization considering the outsourcing. The selection process should be intensive because so much is at stake and contracts are typically lengthy (between three and ten years). Even market leader Exult, who as a seller could be expected to favor shorter sales cycles, recommends taking up to one full year to complete the selection process.[2]

Organizations have to ask themselves whether they are ready for a commitment on the scale of a typical HR BPO deal. At a minimum, the HR department will have assessed itself as capable of managing vendor relationships, maintaining ultimate responsibility for all outsourced functions and playing a strategic role in the organization. This means it has the staff and expertise necessary.

---

[2] Exult "Freedom to Focus" presentation on June 6, 2003.

The organization must know exactly what it wants to outsource and what it wants to retain and it must have a clear understanding of what it expects to gain. Many organizations struggle to assess the full costs of providing their HR services, and are therefore unable to properly compare the costs of outsourcing HR to an external provider. Finally, the organization must know how it will define and monitor vendor performance and success overall. It should have a baseline comparison for the outsourced process and vendor.

Table 10.1: HR BPO Selection

Reputation	Fit	Viability	Technology	Technology
• References • Word of mouth/word on the street/analyst opinion • Customer satisfaction • Evidence of cost and process improvements for clients • Commitment to best practices and continuous improvement	• Customers of similar size and scope • Relationship—is it a long-term partner? Can it be relied on? Do you connect with the company on a personal level? • Can it assist in change management and training? • Does it have expert staff?	• Financial and overall vendor viability • Performance and ROI data should be available	• Best-of-breed, integrated technology platform. Exult, for example, has partnered with best-of-breed solutions providers for CWM software (IQNavigator), recruitment solutions (Deploy) and e-learning (Docent), to name a few • Evidence of sustained service, technology investment and innovation • Comprehensive demonstrations and proof of capabilities/functionality • Flexible solutions (can change with customers' needs and shifting priorities over the life of the agreement) and flexible staff • Flexible SLAs and metrics	• Guarantee of ROI in the 10 percent to 20 percent range

The organization will have completed a thorough cost/benefit analysis and will have determined that it can expect appreciable cost savings (normally in the 10 percent to 20 percent range or better). As above but bears repeating, the organization must understand what its full costs are prior to outsourcing a process or the entire HR function. It should also be prepared to enter into a long-term partnership with a vendor and should have built a compelling business case such that all of the key players in the organization (VP, HR, CFO, CIO, CEO) are behind the initiative. Staff must be briefed and there should be a transition plan in place for affected employees. The company should have clear (if not universal) buy-in at operational levels, especially in mid-management. Organizations should appoint a cross-representative team to lead the initiative. Finally, the processes to be outsourced should be in reasonable shape. Extremely flawed processes may set the outsourcer up for failure or at the very least cost the organization more because the outsourcer will have more to fix.

SLAs and defined metrics that describe the expectations organizations have of their BPOs are extremely important to negotiate, legalize and monitor but they do not render a detailed selection process unnecessary. Organizations must study business process outsourcing business models, customer lists (to ensure appropriate, relevant experience), infrastructure, track record in delivering on SLAs and negotiated metrics, staff expertise, culture and values (for fit), financial viability and any reference customers that can be provided.

A less discussed but quite critical element is the BPO's technology platform. Unlike the first years of the industry when BPOs often purchased their customers' facilities and assets and hired most or all of their staff, today most deals involve the customer inheriting their BPO's HR technology platform. This is important because customers' staff will use components of the technology, as may business partners, customers, job candidates and other vendors. Outdated, proprietary, insecure, difficult to use or functionally deficient technology may result in bad impressions, lost business, lost job candidates, a decline in employee retention and a host of other problems that will harm the brand and cost money and time to resolve despite the SLA.

Ideally, BPOs will leverage their economies of scale to construct world-class technology platforms by integrating best-of-breed solutions such as those referred to above for e-learning and staffing.

Like large organizations, BPOs will be tempted to standardize using one or a few technology vendors for the sake of cost and convenience. In organizations, a decision to do so is often justified for time and cost reasons. For BPOs, however, the decision should be easy. BPOs should choose only best-in-class technologies (sometimes offered by ERPs and sometimes offered by pure plays) that can be integrated into a seamless world-class HR and talent management platform for customers. In this way, the BPO will be able to differentiate and offer something that very few organizations can afford on their own.

For buyers, selection of the best BPO rests on multiple factors (see Table 10.1 above), one of which should be the BPO's defense of its technology platform. Is it world-class in every respect? Or does it appear to have been selected for other reasons that most organizations will recognize as a compromise? For example, does the BPO attempt to argue that the world's best payroll, benefits, e-learning, recruitment and performance management software all comes from one supplier? (The one it happens to offer?) Or can the BPO explain why certain technologies were chosen for different processes and despite the fact that they come from different suppliers, how they are all integrated to the degree necessary?

The importance of the HR technologies platform used by HR BPOs is sometimes overlooked or buried in other considerations such as the BPO's domain expertise and track record in process improvement. While no one advocates that BPOs' selection and integration of an HR technology platform is the most important factor in the decision to consider in BPO selection, it is vital nonetheless.

The argument for best-of-breed solutions on BPO-integrated platforms can be described well and concisely by illustrating the decision points around one critical component of many HR BPO contracts. After payroll and benefits, recruitment is among the most outsourced processes today, with a projected BPO market of US$8.3 billion by 2005 according to Gartner Dataquest.

In many ways, it is surprising that organizations outsource their recruiting functions at all. The use of an ASP to host and maintain recruiting software or a staffing agency to source difficult hires is one thing, but in a knowledge and information age with shrinking labor market growth and potential looming talent shortages, shouldn't recruitment and talent management be a core competency for every company?

Much of sourcing, selection, staffing and recruitment, though, is non-strategic in nature. A niche outsourcing service provider or a BPO may be able to perform the transactional and administrative elements of recruiting, such as requisition building, advertising and distribution, screening, etc., better and less expensively than most companies. Again, if these processes can be handed off, in-house recruiters can perform a more strategic role. An emphasis on tactical and administrative processes in HR can be costly in terms of employee relationships, solid planning and workforce optimization efforts. If organizations cannot build strong strategic capacity in HR, such as the ability to think about who they need to hire and why, then they may need to outsource the administrative and transactional processes that are bogging them down.

For the HR BPO buyer, HR technologies generally and recruitment management solutions specifically are important considerations. Organizations that may not have the resources or capacity to justify best-of-breed solution purchases can and should expect access to them through their BPOs. Best-of-breed recruitment management technologies offer competitive advantages in all economic cycles, enabling wider sourcing, more efficient screening, integrated assessment, workforce planning and recruiting metrics. Organizations can leverage their BPO's expertise to improve the entire recruitment and talent management process. This includes using the BPO's best-in-class recruiting software to enable strategic initiatives such as the development and management of talent pools, better retention, optimization of the workforce and compliance with regulatory and hiring practices guidelines. At the same time, the BPO must use the recruiting software to improve efficiencies in the transactional and clerical processes around staffing, as this is where the money will be saved.

In Figure 10.2 below, a pyramid shows the hierarchy of processes and strategy that make up the recruiting aspects of talent management. The administrative processes in the lower half give way to strategic initiatives at the top. Workforce planning and optimization, and talent relationship management (internal and external), should be retained by the organization but executed using the BPO's technology and expertise.

The administrative elements at the base of the pyramid that represent the bulk of the time HR spends on recruitment are prime candidates for outsourcing. Even screening, testing and assessing

Figure 10.2: BPO Recruitment and Staffing

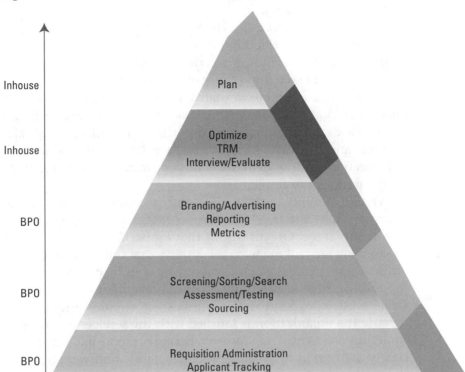

candidates (according to strategy and guidelines determined by the organization) can be handed off. More strategic functions, like positioning the organization in the eyes of job seekers (employment branding), should be done jointly. Exercises like talent optimization and TRM strategies should be the domain of the organization, with input from the business process outsourcing partners. Planning, the most strategic element of all, is purely the responsibility of the organization, though specific advice and data might be obtained from the BPO.

BPOs may be in a unique position that affords them the economies of scale to build and integrate truly world-class TM technology platforms based on best-of-breed solutions. Organizations that are suitable for and ready to outsource all or some elements of talent management to a BPO stand to gain in significant ways but should be sure to choose a BPO that is the right mix of expertise, services and technology.

In summary, a successful HRO or HR BPO strategy is linked to several things. The selection process, for example, must be thorough. It is not uncommon for this process to last one year or longer. And while the importance of a strong personal relationship based on trust cannot be overstated, organizations and BPOs must remember that the partnership has to be based and built on strong, clear and unambiguous contractual obligations. That said, balance and realistic expectations are important to success. Organizations cannot demand endless guarantees and try to track every metric, for example.

Vendor viability must be taken into account, especially as the industry is new and true HR business process outsourcing deals are rare at this stage. Organizations that embark on end-to-end HR outsourcing are still pioneers; even those that fully outsource only one strategic process, such as recruiting, can be counted among the leading edge of the trend. Cost management is also critical. Deals tend to expand under the best of circumstances, often because the organization is satisfied with the services it is getting. Sometimes costs expand, however, because responsibilities weren't clearly delineated or because processes handed off were in worse shape than previously thought. Ultimately, SLAs and contracts can protect only to the degree that the organization is willing to walk away from the arrangement.

Again, look carefully at the technology the outsourcer brings to the table and its track record and commitment to owning best-in-class tools. Does it integrate HR technologies into a seamless platform or is that work at least underway? How does it store and protect data? What is the scope and capacity of its network? What are its disaster recovery processes and capabilities? Technology and scalability are key to the success of your project, and, at this stage in the industry's development, cannot be taken for granted.

The amount of time and effort organizations and their HRO/BPO partners put into dealing with change management is directly correlated to the success of the project overall. This includes the way the transition is handled with affected and retained HR staff. Is there a plan for staff who will lose their jobs? Have they been communicated with? Finally, the capacity of the organization to manage the outsourcing relationship is vital to success. Are there individuals in the HR department who have vendor relationship management skills and experience? Have they managed SLAs and resolved issues with suppliers on this scale in the past?

Offshore Outsourcing

Outsourcing is of course not limited to HROs and BPOs. The options for organizations to contract with workers, staffing agencies and BPOs in other countries for everything from call centers to software coding and even investment banking are growing. The trend has accelerated so much, in fact, that some elected officials are calling for regulations and limits. As it stands today, however, in addition to determining what type of worker should be engaged (salaried, hourly, contingent, etc.), organizations must consider whether the work they need done can be best accomplished by domestic or foreign-based workers.

It is worth looking at the phenomena of offshore outsourcing in the context of talent management planning in organizations. Though technology plays only a small part, offshore outsourcing can be a key lever in acquiring and using talent competitively. Offshore outsourcing is no longer restricted to administration, call centers and rote code writing. Research and development, investment banking, radiology, and other high-end knowledge work is being outsourced to countries such as India, China, the Philippines and throughout eastern Europe where the requisite talent is available at lower costs.

Offshore outsourcing flourished during the talent shortages of the last decade partially because skilled workers were so hard to find locally. Its growth has not abated. It is increasing because of the significant cost savings made possible. Reduced costs will always be a key reason organizations outsource work offshore. Just as importantly, though, countries like India have an abundance of high-level talent that organizations may be scrambling for in a few years. The engineering profession, for example, is growing at a much higher rate in India and many other developing countries than it is in developed countries. When a talent gap for these individuals reappears it will occur in an era of enhanced security and greater barriers to immigration, at least in the United States. As such, the shortfall will likely be made up from outsourcing projects more than importing people. This is true also because the countries in question are typically much more interested in keeping talented individuals in jobs at home than in contributing to a brain drain when they emigrate.

In light of the possibility that immigration will be less an option in the next talent crisis, some organizations will be well-served by developing an offshore outsourcing component to their recruitment and overall talent management plans. These companies must know and understand the global market, including where the workers are, their competencies, their costs and the logistics of doing business in any particular jurisdiction. With Internet and Web-based recruiting technologies, it will be possible and practical for employers to outsource work to individual contractors overseas, as well as to overseas organizations and BPOs.

There is a trend away from using very temporary offshore labor on discrete projects to using large teams involving combinations of local and offshore workers for long duration or ongoing projects with much wider scope. This is due in part to the higher value-added work that is flowing offshore. A decade ago it was data collection, now it is debt collection, tax management, trend analysis, sales, mortgage processing, benefits management, payroll and resume processing, travel management and much more. Forrester Research, for example, estimates that 3.3 million services jobs will move offshore from the U.S. over the next fifteen years.

Organizations that engage offshore workers become global employers to varying degrees and must manage new challenges associated with an international workforce. Here, selection of the right talent management software pays off again. A TMS equipped with multiple language interfaces, currency and exchange rate calculators and converters, international tax tables, flexible workflows and other features are needed to accommodate the varying employment laws and regulations, culture and other differences among jurisdictions. Back-end tools to track and manage applicants should also be translated so that local administrators can use the solution where needed, worldwide, and get support in their own languages (provided the TMS supplier has this capacity).

In preparation for talent shortages, to save costs and to ensure the right choice of TM technologies, organizations should chart the types of projects and work they might outsource overseas and where. This is a significantly complex and lengthy process, especially since the market shifts constantly as countries and jurisdictions compete to attract business. Companies interested in developing knowledge and capacity in this area should consider engaging consulting firms that know, understand and track the market.

The Disadvantages

The main negative consequence of offshore outsourcing may turn out to be the damage that it can do to an organization's employment brand and overall perception with the public. Dozens of companies have felt the backlash of affected domestic workers, the press and politicians over their announcements of domestic layoffs with simultaneous increases in offshore outsourcing. It is not a stretch to imagine consumer boycotts during poor economies when the domestic employment situation is bleak and an organization is perceived as having made particularly egregious or cold decisions with regard to the domestic workforce versus that engaged overseas.

Other, more mundane problems associated with offshore outsourcing include difficulties in managing projects, quality, expectations and timelines. Language, cultural and distance barriers often impact the project. Organizations cannot simply look at the cost of a Java developer in Hyderabad, India, for example, versus a similar developer in New York. The hourly rate difference might be as high as five to ten times but the total costs of getting productive work delivered from the developer in India will normally cut the margins considerably. First, organizations must invest time in selecting an offshore vendor or partner. This will take time and money and the partner will expect a fee, perhaps 1 or 2 percent of the value of the work. If the organization is currently doing the work at home, it will face transition costs as the project gradually shifts offshore. These costs can include bringing foreign workers to the U.S. to learn the organization's processes and applications, as the case may be. Organizations cannot hand off a process or a chunk of work and expect that it will be handled efficiently by people who have not had the benefit of any orientation. Some of this orientation can be done by telephone and remote demonstration software such as WebEx, but organizations should expect to bring at least a small team "onshore" for at least two to three months or longer depending on the scope and complexity of the work transferred.

If the organization plans layoffs it will have to compensate the individuals affected and pay severance and employee outplacement costs, among other things. This is on top of a potential dip in performance and productivity due to the effect outsourcing often has on remaining employees' morale. Productivity is further affected by cultural differences and lack of institutional knowledge. No longer can the organization expect to describe something minimally and have a veteran developer, for example, run with it. A company that is used to doing things loosely or by the seat of its pants, so to speak, will find that it must become a detailed, precision-oriented company quickly in order to produce specifications and instructions that offshore contractors can use to deliver to expectations. Moreover, the organization will find it necessary to establish solid communications between employees at home and abroad. The considerations above, and the other costs of managing contracts with overseas workers and partners, obviously add up. Organizations must perform thorough cost estimates and compare them against their current costs of doing business. In the end, organizations should not expect to save more than 20 percent by contracting work overseas, and even this is only possible when the contracts are managed expertly.

Conclusions

Outsourcing to onshore or offshore individuals and companies is an increasingly compelling option for organizations that wish to decrease costs, concentrate on strategic activities and return to their core competencies. Even for organizations that can boast world-class talent management capabilities, the option of outsourcing to a BPO that can do the work equally well, and at less cost, is something that must be considered. It is vital, however, that outsourcers are selected carefully and that the organization fully understands its own processes and total costs before it engages an HRO or BPO. Similarly, organizations that assume they can save enormous money by using low-cost overseas workers must estimate the true costs, hard and soft, as well as the potential damage to their brand should there be a backlash from workers and customers.

CHAPTER 11

卍

Usability, Implementation, Data Security and Reporting— Talent Management System Essentials

T he preceding chapters have provided how-to advice and a description of best practices in an attempt to describe the range of technology-enabled options available to organizations to manage their workforce. Where chapters on outsourcing, workforce planning and talent relationship management represent optional best practices, this chapter returns to mandatory components of TMS, as initiated in Chapters 3 through 6, which described necessary components for corporate career sites, candidate sourcing, screening and searching.

All TMS buyers should concern themselves with how their systems will be used by hiring managers, recruiters and administrators and how change management processes can ensure that the system is used to its fullest extent across the organization and not abandoned after the initial interest following implementation.

Ease of Use

Talent management technology must be easy to use or implementation across an enterprise is likely to fail. Different users have different needs. For instance, some hiring managers will become familiar with the system through regular use, but others will access it very rarely, perhaps only to approve requisitions.

Talent management systems should ship with role-based interfaces for various users of the solution. Heavy, power, occasional and light describe various users in some systems. More commonly users are described by their function: hiring manager, recruiter, approval manager, administrator, super administrator and analyst, among others.

For recruiters (typically the power, or everyday, users of the system), hiring managers (occasional users, e.g., when they have positions that they need to fill) and administrators (intense users of portions of the system), there must be specialized interfaces that aggregate the tools and information these users access most often. For hiring managers especially, the tools must be intuitive and simple because the time between uses might be long and any familiarity they have gained from previous use might be completely or partially lost.

Better solutions providers will not stop with specialized interfaces. Super administrators within the organization should be able to configure access levels and user interfaces for an unlimited number and type of other users. If, for instance, there is a hiring manager who is very active and behaves more like a recruiter, that person can be given a unique interface with access to tools beyond what ordinary hiring managers see. Senior managers, on the other hand, may never need to access the system or even be aware of its existence if the vendor has incorporated or embedded sufficient e-mail processes so that senior managers can make approvals and participate in interviewing, for example, using e-mail interfaces that work seamlessly with the solution.

It is becoming standard for HR systems to use Web browsers as the user interface and navigation instrument. Using Web tools takes advantage of the fact that most users will be very familiar with the interface. Leading vendors are also incorporating contextual help screens so that users can get information about the page they are on without having to search through help menus. PeopleSoft's eRecruit solution, for example, lets users build on top of the help tool to create personal or shared knowledge libraries. Others, like Recruitsoft, offer e-learning modules so that hiring managers, recruiters and others can learn how to use the TMS online and at their own pace.

As above, it is becoming common practice to offer e-mail interfaces with TMS so that infrequent users will never require any training or orientation and can perform their tasks via e-mail without having to actually access the system. This is an important feature to look for, especially if a large number of individuals will interact with the hiring process minimally but will perform essential and time-sensitive tasks such as approvals, interview scheduling and post-interview evaluation of candidates. Some vendors have incorporated job requisition building into e-mail in such a way that the hiring manager receives an e-mail that either contains the requisition form or directs him/her, with one click, to the portion of the tool for building requisitions. This type of navigational aid improves productivity and user acceptance enormously—especially among casual users.

Most leading systems offer role-based access to the recruiting solution. Trained super-administrators at the client end are able to configure access for every user so that when they log in, they see only the tabs, buttons, tools and features that they have access to and are authorized to use. This personalizes the experience and reduces clutter on the desktop, making the system more user friendly.

Employee portals and role-based self-service modules streamline tasks and provide one-click access to functions that would otherwise have to be found by navigating through a series of Web pages. Hiring managers and recruiters access portal-like pages (i.e., managers' and recruiters' desktops) that alert them to their outstanding tasks and the activity on their various requisitions (e.g., expiration of posting, approvals received, etc.). Other alerts can tell them when a requisition has become stuck somewhere in the process or when a highly qualified candidate has applied for one of their positions.

Vendors such as Kenexa and Webhire offer live chat sessions enabling users to get help from technicians during business hours. Others offer e-mail support and, in many cases, unlimited toll-free telephone support for administrative and technical users. Training and orientation can be costly so it is advisable to look for vendors that offer hands-on training for trainers and/or Web-based training.

Ease-of-use factors impact change management, which, as stated in previous sections, is often the key factor in the ultimate success of an e-recruit or TMS project. Buyers (organizations) should look for:

- clean, easily navigable, flexible and role-based interfaces that are necessary to facilitate adoption by all types of users in the organization;

- interfaces that are inviting, intuitive and uncluttered;

- administrative tools that allow changes to the appearance of and access to the solution depending on who is using it;

- thorough documentation and online help features;

- vendors with experience in handling change management and that can provide examples of customers of similar size and with similar challenges.

Buyers should ask references what level(s) of training were required. How did they overcome resistance? Were pilots or limited live tests of the TMS necessary? How long did it take for the organization to implement the solution across the enterprise? Buyers must verify any case studies with the customers involved.

A simple but useful test is to gain access to the vendor's hiring manager interface. Is it as easy to use, navigate, understand and learn as setting up and using an online banking service or advertising something on a site like eBay? If so, the solution is probably simple enough that the vast majority of casual users will be able to get by with minimal orientation, some online instruction and perhaps an occasional call to a help desk. If not, buyers are asking for trouble, including lengthy and ultimately unsuccessful training exercises. In short, by selecting a difficult-to-use system, organizations invite a failed project.

Most talent management technology projects are successful (or not) depending on whether the recruiting team uses the solution or, in self-service organizations (in which the recruiting function has been pushed to hiring managers), whether hiring managers can. In the former case, it is relatively easy to check recruiter satisfaction during reference checks and during preliminary testing of a mocked-up or live system. The recruiting team is many times smaller than the number of hiring managers in an organization and will use the tools on a frequent basis. Formal training for recruiters is, therefore, possible and practical given the limited size of the group.

Where an organization has internal recruiters, the successful introduction of a TMS should be easier. Key elements to look for in addition to the list above are highly configurable workflows and flexible portal-like user interfaces for recruiters. If the toolset slows them down in any way, there is a greater likelihood that it will be bypassed to the extent possible. Recruiters tend to work on relationships and volumes; any system that is going to be adopted will have to prove its capacity to make recruiters' lives easier, not more difficult. Recruiters, therefore, should be represented on the TMS selection committee and be instrumental in user group testing and acceptance. Buy-in from this key user group is essential.

In organizations without recruiters, in which hiring managers have responsibilities normally associated with recruiters, the change management challenge is greater. First, there are many hundreds or thousands of managers in large organizations. They may not hire more than once or twice per year and will not use a TMS frequently. Formal training on the TMS for hiring managers does not make sense in most cases due to the numbers and the likelihood that many will have forgotten what they learned in training by the time they have occasion to use the TMS in a real hiring process.

In organizations without recruiters it is necessary to keep the TMS as simple as possible at first and to train a number of internal trainers, such as HR assistants, who can work with hiring managers as needed to answer their questions and walk them through the steps, for example, in creating and distributing a requisition. As in recruiter-driven systems, solutions should be Web-based and intuitive, with contextual help and self-service access to online training. Again, the closer it is in ease of use to online banking, travel, auction or shopping systems, the more likely it is to be easily understood and used by infrequent users like hiring managers.

Employee Portals/Self-Service

The term "portal" is used to describe many Web-based user interfaces and services. In TMS, they are configurable browser-based workspaces that aggregate all of the key features and tools the employees use in their daily work. This makes it easier for users to find the information and tools they need and therefore has a consequent positive impact on system adoption. Organizations that use employee portals do so in order to provide frequently accessed and referenced information and tools on one interface. Normally, things like access to benefits, leave balances, electronic pay stubs, knowledge repositories and the like are offered through the portal. With TMS, the portal will also contain access to job postings, career information, to do lists, components of an HR management system and perhaps key workforce metrics if the user is a manager or analyst.

For TMS, the portal or a basic intranet is the method by which to encourage employees not only to look for jobs but also to complete profiles on their skills, experience and aspirations. This process eventually leads to a better understanding of the workforce and can facilitate effective redeployment of staff inside the company.

As far back as mid-2002, more than half of all Fortune 500 firms were in some stage of employee self-service portal development and, according to a more recent MetLife study, 40 percent of U.S. firms with more than one thousand staff had some form of employee self-service solution in place as of 2003. Other research suggests that this number will be close to 80 percent in 2004.[1] Staff self-service portals provide a single Web interface to applications and information that workers use daily, including e-mail, calendars, HR information (benefits, training, vacation balances and job postings) and legacy databases.

Much of what is discussed above and in previous chapters contains elements of employee self-service—managers building and publishing requisitions, and staff locating, reading about, applying for and referring friends to jobs, for example. Self-service portals encompass more than human resource functions but are part of the talent management discussion because their purpose is to increase efficiency, "do more with less," and boost employee satisfaction and retention. Some portal vendors refer to their solutions as employee relationship management (ERM) tools due to their ability to empower and improve employee access to information, and to generally improve communications.

Employees can normally tailor portals to create their own personalized experience by selecting from a menu of options

---

[1] According to Paul Hawking, School of Information Systems, Victoria University, Australia in 2003. See his paper titled "B2E Portal Maturity: An Employee Self-Service Case Study," page 2.

including the display of key performance indicators (KPIs) relevant to their role, quick access links to information and tools they use frequently, and personal items like news, weather, Internet search tools, favorite sites and more.

From the HR point of view, portals can provide streamlined access to employee profiles and access to job postings, temporary assignments, course calendars, benefits enrollment, vacation balances, shift swaps, time and attendance, the employee referral program and much more. Managers and recruiters can also be provided streamlined access to additional tools that assist them in e-recruitment and hiring. Some solutions offer a form of vendor management—modules that allow external recruiters, employment advertising firms and others self-service access to appropriate portions of the solution so that they can collaborate with internal staff more efficiently.

Essentially, whether they are offered as add-on options in a talent management system such as PeopleSoft, are purchased separately from vendors like Plumtree or Workbrain, or are built in-house, self-service portals offer ease of use and aesthetic advantages that can speed HR systems adoption rates, increase systems usage in an organization, boost productivity, reduce administrative costs and have a positive impact on staff retention rates. For these reasons, their benefits are not to be overlooked.

Though in most cases, employees can access all relevant portions of a TMS's functionality without the use of a portal, the portal presents preconfigured paths to popular tools, tailored to individual preferences. A portal can provide one-click access rather than requiring employees to navigate various menus and screens. Because portals allow for personalization and aggregation of disparate sources of information and tools, they are popular with users and normally become the "dashboard" from which employees organize their work. HR departments, furthermore, can save staff resources where the portal answers everyday staff HR questions and gives them easy access to their own vacation balances (and perhaps the vacation balances of those who report to them), benefits plans and other personal information. For these reasons, even though the responsibility for employee self-service and portals may fall outside HR, the strategic HR department will be sure to play a central role in any enterprise-wide portal initiative and its ongoing delivery.

Employee self-service is especially important in organizations that have downsized the role of HR specialists who know the company culture, rules, regulations, policy, and state and federal employment law and possess other specialized knowledge. Self-service portals become more valuable when they embed intelligence so that users can be prompted with additional information, help and tips depending on what they are doing in the system. For example, users browsing course calendars for training dates might be presented with their own schedule overlaid for easy comparison. The system might alert them to any conflict if they try to book a course for themselves or their staff. Beyond this, the system might compare a course curriculum to their skills/competency profile, or those of their staff, to tell them quickly what value they can expect from the course and whether it furthers their learning goals and career objectives.

Beyond digital dashboards that let staff and managers track KPIs, employees can be alerted to the implications of certain decisions. For instance, those considering relocation to new positions within the company and making local or out-of-state moves might be shown the tax and cost-of-living implications. Employees browsing their HMO or managed health care options might be told the larger implications of moves, births, spousal employment status and other factors that might impact on eligibility and premiums.

Managers who are interviewing job applicants should be able to access skill and competency profiles and parameters for salary and benefits, for example. Managers selecting new employee start dates should be prompted if there are any significant pay, bonus or benefits differences depending on whether the employee starts next week or the week after. In the past, when terminating an employee, a manager might consult extensively with HR. In a smart self-service environment, the manager can be told the rules and legalities in the context of what they are doing and where they are in the process. The system can calculate the employee's severance pay and perhaps the average cost to replace him/her. In the end, the manager will probably need to consult with someone in HR but they might do so briefly at the end of the process rather than throughout and perhaps only to ensure compliance with company policy and the jurisdiction's employment law.

In short, the best self-service portals will be dynamic in that they will offer related information in anticipation of user needs. If users access the vacation request module, for example, why not present their leave balance automatically and inform them of any employee discounts available for flights through particular travel sites and agencies or negotiated car rental discounts?

Employee self-service can be referred to in portal terms or under the acronym ERM. Either way, the objective is to reduce administrative costs, improve efficiencies and boost employee satisfaction, morale and retention.

Configuration and Customization

Rules and procedures around recruiting vary among organizations and industries. Talent management systems should be extensively configurable so that each organization's unique needs can be accommodated easily, inexpensively and without customization of the software itself. The best solutions offer broad configuration options that can be performed by trained staff at the customer end. For example, if there is a need to change a workflow so that another level of approval is inserted for job requisitions, it should be possible for the customer to do it themselves.

The latest versions of solutions from Recruitsoft, Deploy, VirtualEdge, Recruitmax and Unicru, for example, offer configuration down to the database level so that customers can create sub-career sites and change not only workflow, look and feel but also the information they collect and search on. This level of flexibility protects an application against future obsolescence by allowing it to change with the strategies and directions of the organization. It should offer enough flexibility for most organizations such that customization to the actual software code can be avoided or greatly reduced.

Configuration differs from customization in that it requires no code or software changes. Keep in mind that hosted (ASP) solutions are often less flexible where customization is concerned because there are many customers subscribing to the same version of the code and the vendors do not wish to support multiple, customized versions. Buyers who anticipate significant alterations requiring custom programming to their vendor's solution beyond what configuration can allow may have to eliminate ASPs as an option and instead customize a vendor's licensed solution via access to its source code. This might occur in heavily regulated environments, for example, where employment policy has been unchanged for several years and cannot easily adapt to Web-based or online best practices.

While it is not unusual for organizations to require changes to off-the-shelf software, it is good practice to put sufficient effort into vendor selection up front so that the solution best suited to the organization's needs is selected. Customers should look at vendors who have a track record in their industry and with other organizations of comparable size and challenges (e.g., multiple language requirements, global usage or decentralized operations in which hiring managers perform the role of recruiters).

E-recruitment projects should include an analysis of current recruitment processes with a view to adopting the more efficient practices that technology can facilitate. Unbridled customization to a vendor's software in order to make it fit with legacy workflows may cause integration problems when upgrading to future versions and may make it difficult for the vendor to provide support. In very rare cases where a strong requirements match cannot be found, an organization may be better to develop its solution in-house or negotiate access to a vendor's source code (as a condition of purchase) so that it can be modified and customized (and ultimately maintained) in-house with the assistance of the vendor.

Increasingly, forward-looking vendors are making their solutions flexible through advanced configuration tools that can be used by non-technical administrators at the client-end who are trained and certified by the vendor. Alternatively, the vendor may use the same tools to manage reconfiguration on behalf of the client. Either way, buyers should pay special attention to the "configurability" of their solutions and place this component in the must-have column of their RFP. Very few organizations should have such specific and unusual recruitment/talent management processes that one of today's configurable solutions cannot be made to fit with minimal customization.

Planning, Change Management and Implementation

Whether an organization leases its solution from an ASP, purchases and installs the software on its servers or purchases and hosts with the vendor, the supplier should be able to demonstrate that it has a reliable, proven and repeatable process to implement its solution. Vendors should supply experienced project leads that have led several successful implementations. They should have documentation that explains their approach and methodology, as well as a project plan with milestones, timelines and a critical path. Some vendors have instituted recognized processes around software implementation including Six Sigma and total quality management (TQM). Others, such as Recruitsoft, have established in-house audit teams that dissect each implementation and document the results to inform future projects. Buyers should ask for and check references specific to the implementation capacity of their shortlisted vendors.

Often vendors will send their professional services consultants to meet with prospective clients before implementation so that they can map the client's processes and workflow to the software. They will work with the client to define an implementation plan that includes training and orientation for all users. It bears repeating that change management is often the central component of the overall project that makes or breaks the initiative. Vendors presumably have a great deal more experience in this regard than their clients and should play a leading role in ensuring that their clients are ready for the new processes and technology.

Prior to launching the new solution, organizations should have completed an evaluation of existing recruitment and talent management processes, and determined, with their vendor, where areas for improvement and opportunities to implement best practices exist. The vendor should be able to recommend best-practice methodologies and processes based on its work in the field, accumulated expertise and research it has conducted. In areas where an organization cannot adhere to its vendor's vision of best practice, the software must be highly flexible so that, in most cases, it can be quickly configured or slightly altered to meet the client's needs. Only in rare cases should it be necessary to delay the project to wait for extensive changes to the code or architecture itself.

ASPs should be able to have their solutions up and running within four to sixteen weeks provided there are no large data migration requirements (movement of resumes, job descriptions and other information from another system) or the necessity to integrate with other HR systems. Installed software will normally take longer but should be ready, on average, within eight to twenty-four weeks (of course, this can vary widely). As discussed above, efforts made to select the best vendor will reduce or eliminate the need for customizations, speed the implementation process, reduce costs and make it easier to upgrade and implement new features as they are offered.

Vendors should also offer flexibility to license only the components of their solutions that clients need and will use. Most tier-one vendors and ERPs offer systems integration, resume processing, reporting and analytics, hiring manager and recruiter desktops, and other components. Clients may already own similar tools or have no need of them. The flexibility to purchase or lease components à la carte, with the option of adding more later as they are needed, is important in order to lower costs and speed ROI.

Integration and Open Source Software

Large organizations with legacy HRMS or ERP solutions will, in most cases, want to integrate their talent management systems with the rest of their enterprise HCM suite or ERP. If so, they should proceed with caution when selecting a vendor. Companies like Hire.com, Recruitsoft, Deploy, Yahoo! Resumix, Recruitmax and Webhire, for example, have a track record of successful integration with other systems. The e-recruit components of ERP systems (Lawson, PeopleSoft, Oracle, SAP) are built, more or less as integrated components of the larger enterprise solution, potentially eliminating the concern altogether (though buyers should be very cautious in assuming this).

Smaller or newer (and less expensive) vendors, however, may never have attempted full integration. If integration is important to an organization, it should ask for reference customers that have integrated the TMS in question with the systems the organization wants to interface with (e.g., PeopleSoft, Oracle, SAP, etc.).

Daily data exchange via one-way or two-way transfer may be sufficient for the needs of most organizations. If it is only a matter of keeping records and data consistent or passing information about hired candidates between the TMS and an ERP solution or HRMS, non-real-time data transfer is often sufficient. Reducing integration needs to what is truly necessary will reduce costs and implementation time, while reducing the complications that can arise when disparate systems are unnecessarily or overly integrated.

True, real-time integration is complex. Even when an organization chooses its ERP vendor to supply its talent management software, it should query the vendor on the type of adaptors, connectors and tools they use to integrate with HRIS and ERP, and the professional services teams they deploy to accomplish it. Generally, the more the vendor has invested in integration tools and the more documented and tested its methodology, the faster, less expensive and more successful will be the integration project. Some point solutions vendors are certified integrators, such as Kenexa (with Oracle) and Recruitsoft (with SAP).

To determine their needs, organizations should look at what data they have and where it is located. For example, if it has developed a vast and up-to-date library of job descriptions in an HRIS and wants it to be available to hiring managers and recruiters when they are building job requisitions, the organization may be able to accomplish what it needs with one-way, on-demand data exchange. If, on the other hand, there is a need for records to be updated between the HRIS or ERP and the TMS several times per hour or day, real-time or full integration is probably necessary.

As often as not, however, the issues in integration for e-recruit projects have less to do with batch data transfer versus real-time integration and more to do with the number of "points" of integration. Projects are obviously made more complex depending on how many connections are necessary between the TMS and other HR or enterprise systems. One way to minimize the pain around integration now and in future is for buyers to choose vendors that are evolving their solutions in step with HR-XML standards, advances in XML APIs, the Web services architecture including .Net and J2EE, and open standards. Eventually, disparate systems will be much more easily integrated as their designers build on Web services architectures and comply with industry XML standards.

Integration is often complex and time consuming. Buyers should expect that vendors will provide separate time and cost estimates beyond those for normal implementation.

Application Service Providers

Many organizations, particularly large ones, struggle with the question of whether to outsource hosting and maintenance of TMS to ASPs versus buying the software outright for installation on premises. Placing recruitment, candidate and employee data into the hands of a third-party vendor (hosting is usually subcontracted by TMS vendors to professional data centers) can be a difficult decision to make. Nonetheless, most ASPs are likely able to demonstrate to your satisfaction that the facilities they use are sufficiently secure. For some, the ASP will offer much greater security than even the largest organizations could replicate in-house. ASPs like Recruitsoft, BrassRing, Peopleclick, Hire.com and others have a multiyear track record of successfully hosting some of the world's largest organizations. Concerns about an ASP's ability to meet an organization's security and scalability needs can be addressed by completing a short threat risk assessment (TRA) to identify risks to data, system availability, vendor viability and other issues. A TRA normally attempts to identify what could go wrong, such as information leaks, security breaches, loss of data due to system failure, viruses, hackers, etc., and strategies to protect the organization and its data against those eventualities. The TRA can aid enormously in choosing the right TMS vendor, as it provides an objective standard against which to assess ASPs and their hosting environments.

No matter the vendor, no organization should enter into a third-party hosting agreement without performing its own due diligence, and this usually means visiting the host with its own in-house or hired experts and making an assessment firsthand (see Security of Data in the next section). Large organizations should also conduct privacy impact assessments (PIAs) to ensure that the vendors they choose can meet their own privacy-of-data policies and those set out by law in the jurisdiction(s) the organizations operate out of. Like a TRA, a PIA is conducted to reveal potential problems and deal with them beforehand. Typically, organizations map the flow of their data (in a PIA process) and document precisely who will have access to data, when, where and for what reasons. Every time personal data is accessed, there should be a reason for doing so that is directly related to the purpose for which the information was originally provided. For example, it is permissible for a hiring manager to retrieve a profile in order to assess a candidate's suitability for a position. It is not acceptable for that hiring manager to access a profile in order to find likely candidates for a product focus group or to complete a marketing survey.

Beyond security issues are cost factors. ASPs typically charge less up front. Their model operates on recurring revenue of fees paid by their customers year after year. Organizations save money at first and can test the waters somewhat without buying a solution outright. Costs are likely to be higher with an ASP in the long term, but clients save themselves the time, expense and headaches associated with maintaining the solution on-site. Furthermore, ASP customers get upgrades automatically and usually with little or no pain. Licensed and installed solutions have to be upgraded manually. ASPs' interests might also be better aligned with their customers' because ASPs know they have to satisfy their customers even after their solutions are installed. After all, the customer can cancel the contract during (for cause) and after the term of the agreement. This arrangement often results in better customer service and technical support than customers might receive when they purchase software outright.

In the past, ASP software has been less flexible, meaning that clients could not easily change it to their own liking (because many other customers were sharing the solution's code base). As discussed earlier, ASPs have recently developed means of configuring their tools for each different user without having to make code changes to their software. Nonetheless, some organizations will have requirements that are beyond the capacity of any off-the-shelf solution to satisfy. If heavy customization needs are anticipated, the organization is better off purchasing a system outright so that it can make the changes necessary. In very rare cases, it may have to build the solution in-house.

Generally, small and mid-size organizations that need to focus on their core competencies should strongly consider outsourcing to an ASP. Large organizations with the capacity to manage the application on their premises might gravitate toward purchasing the software in order to potentially save money over time, but more often than not, even they are probably better off outsourcing the hosting and maintenance of their TMS to an ASP. This is evidenced by the fact that after examining the pros and cons, most large organizations opt for the ASP model instead of installing and maintaining the e-recruit solution or TMS themselves.

Security of Data

If an organization is considering an ASP to host its TMS solution, it must consider security. The data it will be entrusting to its vendor is the lifeblood of the HR department and the organization. Some ASP customers have complained of their data being held hostage while various disputes with their vendor are worked out. Others have seen their data disappear or be temporarily unavailable when their vendor has closed due to bankruptcy or been acquired.

Maintaining servers, administering databases and providing adequate security are specialized competencies. One school of thought argues that vendors of talent management solutions should focus exclusively on developing their software and servicing their clients. They should outsource hosting to professional data centers that do nothing else. Another believes that large TMS vendors can do as good or better a job of hosting than commercial providers. For one thing, they presumably host only workforce and recruitment data, not financial data, credit card information or something else that might present a more tempting target to hackers and thieves.

In either case, a visit to the data center for the selected TMS provider as a final condition before signing the contract is a good idea and a detailed conversation with the CIO or CTO is mandatory. A data center, even for recruitment data, should be physically secure. The data center should operate like a prison in some ways. Access to the servers should be severely restricted with a pass system at a minimum and ideally something more advanced like palm or retinal scanning. Visitors should sign in and be escorted at all times. The data center should not be easily identifiable as such from the outside. Customer data servers should be isolated (contain no other customer's data) and should be stored in a locked compartment. There should be robust back-up power generators capable of providing power for twenty-four hours or more. Obviously the facility should be as close to fire-proof as possible, and data centers must use monitored smoke, heat and flame detectors and server-safe methods to suppress flames and contain fires.

As for network security, leading data centers use the latest in hardware- and software-based firewalls. They have multiple connections to the Internet through at least two different Internet backbone providers (in case one goes down). They maintain multiple redundant servers (for hosting the same data and applications in case one fails) in different physical locations. For transmission of data, look for 128-bit encryption security. Personnel with physical or virtual access to the data should be screened via criminal, drug and background reference checks. The data center should conduct regular audits of physical, network and personnel security and make the results available to customers. A disaster plan should be in place and documented for customer reference.

Finally, your SLA should stipulate that you own your data outright and can request copies of it with reasonable notice. The SLA should stipulate planned downtime, if any, and a guaranteed level of uptime with documented penalties for non-compliance. You should also require that your ASP hold a copy of its latest source code in escrow with a mutually acceptable third party in case it exits the business and you require the code to keep your system going.

Reporting and Metrics

In 2001, at least 68 percent of Fortune 1000 firms measured HR productivity and assessed HR strategic goals against overall business goals.[2] More and more, HR is attempting to prove its value in quantifiable terms rather than being viewed as overhead. Talent management systems can be among an organization's best sources of strategic HR intelligence.

---

[2] PricewaterhouseCoopers, *Human Resources Benchmarks and Best Practices Survey, 2001.*

It is typical for TMSs to include canned reports that ship standard with the system. These reports normally include cost and time to hire, best sources for recruitment (for example, number of hires resulting from posts to Monster versus to HotJobs), Web site traffic and even ROI calculators. These types of reports facilitate metrics-based recruitment advertising budgeting and can project talent acquisition timelines against corporate growth strategies. TMSs usually ship with between twenty to one hundred or more standard, built-in reports. This means that to generate a report, a user can simply click on that report's title (and perhaps indicate a data date range).

Organizations should also look for an ability to generate ad hoc reports—reports that can be created according to the organization's needs, when it needs them, and ideally by its own administrators or analysts. A good solution will allow for the creation of reports on all of the data collected, either through an integrated tool or by allowing the export of data to an external program for analysis. Because it is not possible to foresee all of the potential uses of data collected by the system to meet the demands of managers for reports, ad hoc reporting tools are critical. To accommodate the need, many TMS vendors have integrated very powerful analytics tools such as Cognos and Business Objects into their solutions.

Leading vendors such as PeopleSoft and Hire.com go further. As workforce planning becomes more important (see Chapter 7), it is vital to have a firm grasp of what talents and skills are crucial to the organization and where those skills, competencies, experience and knowledge reside—both within the organization and in its broader talent supply chain. These vendors are beginning to offer full workforce analysis modules, some of which are tied to enterprise-wide tools like the Balanced Scorecard.[3] Others, like BrassRing, Recruitsoft and Recruitmax, integrate Cognos or Business Objects so that their customers can export data to those systems for advanced reporting and workforce analytics.

At its best, analysis from data produced by TMSs should combine with performance measurement efforts to determine the quality of hires and where the best recruits are coming from. It should assist and support workforce planning.

---

[3] The Balanced Scorecard was developed in 1992 by Harvard professors Robert Kaplan and David Norton as a more holistic means of measuring performance in organizations.

At a minimum, organizations should attempt to measure the success of their e-recruitment methods. Typically, organizations track the increase in traffic to their Web sites and the decreased cost and time to fill positions. Other measures, such as the percentage of hires from various e-recruitment sources, quality of candidates and how well e-recruitment performs against initiatives such as diversity hiring goals, should be conducted. Organizations should know which sources—job boards and resume databases, for example—are providing the most (and best) candidates and hires. Speed and success in building partially prequalified talent pools should be tracked and organizations should attempt to gauge employee retention against efforts to deliver more and better career and job information to existing staff. Increasingly, organizations should turn to their vendors for support in proving and documenting the hard cost savings their systems can generate—ROI reporting, in other words.

Finally, and as discussed in the chapter on workforce planning, data should be captured for the purposes of understanding and analyzing the internal and external workforces. Many TMS providers now integrate useful workforce planning tools in their solutions. Most others allow for the export of data to business intelligence tools like Cognos and Business Objects for flexible and extensive analysis.

Customer Service and Technical Support

Vendors of e-recruitment and full TMS technologies can offer a range of customer support. The better (and usually more expensive) services offer dedicated account managers and professional services teams. These individuals consult with customers pre-sale to determine their needs, and supply further assistance at implementation to determine customer workflows and ensure that the solution is configured or customized to their needs. After implementation, the dedicated account manager acts as the liaison between customer and vendor to resolve issues, answer questions and track progress, including ROI.

Organizations should look for a vendor that supplies appropriate levels of in-house or Web-based training and materials during and after installation. The "train the trainer" approach, discussed earlier in the chapter, is a good idea both to develop in-house expertise and to reduce training costs. Most vendors offer toll-free help lines during business hours and many are starting to offer chat-based live help, page-sensitive online help and automated tools like RoboHelp (to assist users in finding the help information they are looking for and to create help pages dynamically). For technical support, organizations must demand a comprehensive SLA tailored to their needs. Buyers should also make sure that their SLA provides 24/7 access to technicians in case of serious events such as site or system failure. There is a big difference between a guarantee of 99.5 percent uptime and a promise of 99.9 percent uptime—the former may be relatively easy to accomplish, the latter very difficult for the ASP and expensive for the buyer. There is also a difference between statements of uptime that refer to business hours rather than those that average in non-peak times.

The TMS Team

The importance of selecting a vendor who is not only a software supplier but also a service organization is vital to implementing change management and user adoption. It cannot be stated too often: the success or failure of TMS projects and e-recruitment initiatives has at least as much to do with change management issues and information in general as it does with excellent software.

Organizations should ensure that the vendor they select receives excellent reviews from its customers as can be determined during reference checks and reading materials from analysts and others. The vendor should have expert staff on hand that can assist clients with all of the issues around e-recruitment best practices, legal issues, trend awareness, employment equity tracking, reporting and compliance, forming partnerships with third parties in the e-recruit supply chain and so on. Vendors must also be capable of deep involvement, if not leadership, in the implementation and change management processes.

Internal Resources

Inside the organization, there is likely to be a good level of knowledge among some HR staff and recruiters about talent management solutions and e-recruiting. Organizations should identify those individuals who are highly interested in the project. Expertise in TMS technologies and best practices can be acquired by these individuals, in part, by reading and reviewing the vast body of information available, most of which is free on sites like HR.com, Erexchange.com, Interbiznet.com, Workforce.com, HRonline.com, SHRM.org and many, many others.

Obviously a project manager and one or more assistants will be required to lead the discovery and RFI stages. The project manager should form volunteer teams that include technicians, recruiters and hiring managers from throughout the organization. These teams will provide advice on the elements required in RFIs, RFQs and RFPs. A core team might be comprised of the project manager, assistants, technical and legal representatives and perhaps a vendor-neutral (unaligned) external consultant with deep domain knowledge and experience in TMS selection and implementation. These individuals can be found using the same Internet resources listed above.

The marketing or public relations department may have a role to play in communicating the new solution to staff, management and external users. A technical writer may be required to prepare the initial material for the corporate career site. Depending on whether the solution will be outsourced to an ASP or installed on site, the IT department will be engaged very minimally or quite heavily.

As for those who will run the system after installation, an organization's general recruiters are often given primary responsibility for online recruitment in addition to their responsibilities for other forms of recruitment. Recruiters are provided passwords to the job boards that the organization subscribes to and can place their ads directly or through an established workflow. Many companies are also adding specialists such as Internet sourcing experts to the mix.

Internet researchers schooled in the techniques of online searching (such as flipsearching, peelbacks and X-ray, as taught by AIRS and others) can assist generalist recruiters in making the most of job boards and the Internet as a whole.[4] Internet recruiting specialists

---

[4]Flipsearch uses search engines with the syntax "link" in the URL followed by the name of the company, etc., you wish to search for resumes. Peelback involves removing the latter parts of long URLs to reveal more sources for resumes after you have found a likely source. X-Ray uses the command "host" or "url" before a sourcename (company, etc.) with keywords (e.g.,"java") to find resumes or leads within an organization on pages that may not be public.

have deep knowledge of sources for candidates, including the large and niche job boards. They are also experts in creating complex Boolean searches and in using meta search engines and deep Web mining tools. They are also familiar with sites (job boards, industry associations, alumni networks and others) where specialist candidates can be sourced.

While not yet an established best practice, companies may have to look at employing recruiting researchers or "sourcers" in future to maintain an edge. When talent pools stretch thin again, companies may need to research the depths of the Web, looking for active and passive talent both at home and abroad. This strategy complements the concept of developing prequalified talent pools discussed in Chapter 7.

Every TMS project should have identified trainers who receive "train the trainer" instruction from the vendor. Depending on the size of the organization, one or more individuals should become expert in the vendor's technology. They should understand all of the components of the tool (most other users will learn only the parts they use) through training, complete familiarization with the documentation and learning about the changes in new upgrades. These individuals become resources to all other users and management. They can help ensure that the usefulness of the solution and ROI is maximized. These individuals can do double-duty by filling the role of "super administrator"—that is, the person(s) who receive special training in order to reconfigure the solution after implementation and create and manage accounts for users.

In some cases, it will be necessary or cost advantageous to establish a tier-one help desk on-site, staffed with persons who are familiar with the system. These persons can triage users' questions about the solution, answering simple ones and referring those that are more complex to the vendor.

Choosing a TMS Vendor

In that the majority of this book has concentrated on the themes of best practices in talent management and vendor selection, this section is meant mainly to offer some final advice. As discussed very briefly earlier, it is very worthwhile to perform a threat risk assessment and due diligence before selecting a vendor. The stakes are high and the industry is immature. Risk mitigation is essential and that usually means the selection of a stable vendor with an excellent track record and numerous clients that are similar in size, industry and scope to the organization that is considering the purchase. Unless an organization's needs are truly unusual (requiring that they look at customization) or budgets are extremely tight (making the discounts offered by new and eager vendors attractive), it is better to err on the side of caution than to be an early or first adopter of unproven technology or vendors.

Organizations should check the references supplied by their shortlisted vendors, but they must go beyond that, if possible, and interview customers that have cancelled or not renewed their contracts with the vendors to find out why and what the problems were. This information may be hard to come by unless they also consult buyers' guides, white papers, the results of general customer surveys and speak with industry experts. Trade shows can be useful in terms of browsing the show floor to see all or most of the key vendors in one place and to discuss the merits of each with other delegates.

When a vendor is ultimately selected, buyers should perform site visits as a final condition to signing the contract. Technical personnel or hired consultants should assess the data center and Internet facilities. The project manager and consultant should assess the operations and project management capacity of the vendor. Overall, the organization should have a comfortable and trusting relationship with the vendor it chooses.

CONCLUSIONS

Effective talent management is essential to the success of organizations over the next several decades. The reasons range from cost savings to employee retention and maintaining an ability to source and attract external candidates in tight labor markets. Effective talent management in organizations of several hundred or more people is impossible without the use of modern technologies.

E-recruitment and automated talent management continue to evolve at a fast pace. To keep up with the demands of the workplace, systems vendors will need to further consolidate each of the elements in the talent supply chain into one seamless system. This means that recruiting solutions will become capable of managing total workforce acquisition efforts and that these systems will incorporate workforce planning, performance, learning and incentive management tools, among others.

In 1995, automated talent management best practices meant using Web-based job boards to attract as broad a range and as large a number of candidates as possible. By 1999, organizations began to recognize the importance of integrated employment branding and providing a focal point for recruiting through corporate Web sites where all online traffic could be funneled. This realization led to the rapid and near universal adoption of corporate career sites among large companies.

Today, most large organizations use database- and workflow-driven talent management systems behind their corporate career sites to track applicants and requisitions, analyze e-recruitment activity, expand sourcing capabilities and shortlist candidates. Now and in future, organizations will build prequalified talent pools of internal and external candidates so that recruitment becomes more proactive and continuous. Vendors and their customers will demonstrate that this is the way to achieve virtuous cycles in recruiting and to become a true "employer of choice." Vendors will build on their efforts to integrate everything from candidate mining to online assessments and from ERP to alumni networks into one seamless plug-and-play system. VMS and TMS (including salaried and hourly workers) will merge and then combine with performance and learning management tools and workforce planning software.

Screening, sorting and assessment tools will gain an even deeper acceptance as one of the primary means of decreasing recruitment costs and time to hire. With vendors, employers will work toward discovering and implementing better selection methods to build true talent organizations. Advanced screening and sorting technologies, combined with thorough and ongoing job evaluations (to determine what makes an outstanding employee for a particular job), will prove to be a significant part of the answer.

Organizations will accelerate the trend to Web-only application policies for all but the most senior positions. In spite of potential talent shortages, employers will happily risk the chance of losing the shrinking percentage of candidates who do not wish to search and apply for jobs online, reasoning that few within this population are of interest anyway.

Talent management solutions that offer global recruiting capability, meaning localization in everything (language, currencies, culture, laws and idiosyncrasies) but integration for central roll-up and reporting, will become the norm in sales to multinational organizations. Large companies will look increasingly to outsource the transactional and administrative components of talent management to HR outsourcers and BPOs. Mid-to-large and even some small companies will outsource more and higher value-add work overseas and acquire temporary and long-term project-based talent from countries like India, China, the Philippines and others in eastern Europe, the Caribbean and Latin America.

A great deal has already been accomplished through automated talent management systems and e-recruitment. These solutions are enabling organizations to reach out to and communicate with far more people. Job boards, corporate career sites, Web crawlers (spiders) and resume databases allow employers to attract many more applicants with much less effort. Primary screening tools and advanced skills matching, online testing and assessments allow them to filter, screen, rank and sort candidates instantly. Applicant tracking tools streamline the management of applicants as they make their way through an organization's processes, relieving hiring managers, recruiters and HR administrators of tedious filing and record-keeping.

The same systems trigger alerts and messages and can generate letters to candidates automatically. Quality of hire is undoubtedly being impacted, even if a means to prove it has not completely materialized in the technology to date. In short, if we step back for a moment and consider all that e-recruitment and TMS technologies have enabled in the decade or so they have been in existence, we realize that the industry has come a long way, and that without these tools it would be difficult for an organization to cope or compete.

TMS tools and software promise to free recruiters and hiring managers from mundane tasks necessary in recruitment and talent management. Technologies are eliminating clerical functions and elevating organizations' capacity to spend more time with candidates and employees. As much as ever, human involvement in the process is critical. More time must be spent evaluating, pursuing and retaining the best candidates, creating the environments that will attract the best and brightest, and then getting the most out of them.

We are not all the way there yet, but by making talent management more efficient and productive, technology can enable a better future for the workforce for both workers and employers. Indeed, no organization will be able to compete and prosper in the twenty-first century without a strategic and tactical talent management capacity, and this can only be accomplished where talent management technologies play a central role.

INDEX

HR.com

HR.com is the largest Web destination in the world dedicated to senior HR professionals. With up-to-date news, surveys, research, HR tools, careers, events, benchmark data and so much more, this is the best place to find HR information you need!

HR.advertising

Over 145,000 members look to HR.com for unbiased, for up-to-date information, advice and resources for the HR industry. What better place is there to promote your business ... Brand your organization ... Generate sales leads ... Make news announcements ... Educate and inform ... your target audience?

HR.education

Our educational **Online Learning Seminars,** are free to all HR.com members and are an excellent way to build your reputation in the marketplace. Call your sales rep for complete details on this new sponsorship opportunity.

HR.events

HR.com is proud to offer **HR.com Events**, the largest HR series of its kind, which brings senior HR decision-makers, HR vendors and the entire HR community all face-to-face.

HR.research

ICG (Intellectual Capital Group), a division of HR.com, provides cutting-edge research reports (Redbooks™) on topics that are important to HR decision makers. From HR technology purchases and departmental cost control to strategic HR issues and access to our analysts, you'll get all the HR facts you need to make the best decision possible for your organization.

HR.communities

Share your expertise and learn from like-minded individuals. HR.com hosts a number of communities based on areas of expertise. Whether you are buying an Enterprise Performance Management System, implementing a Talent Management System, or sharing best practices on talent retention, these communities connect you to other organizations and your HR peers. You can network, learn and contribute within the communities.

HR.marketer

The marketing and PR solution for companies selling to HR professionals. HR.Marketer is an all-in-one Web-based marketing tool dedicated exclusively to the HR industry.

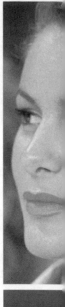

Human Capital
I N S T I T U T E

A PREMIER MEMBERSHIP ORGANIZATION WITH RESEARCH, EDUCATION AND INFORMATION FOR HUMAN CAPITAL PROFESSIONALS

Knowledge
- Human Capital Library
- Monthly Bulletins
- Original Research
- Leadership Forums

Recruiting Directories
- Job Boards
- Employment Classifieds
- Diversity
- Colleges
- Organizations
- Communities
- ISPs
- Employers

Networking
- Local Chapters
- Daily Forums
- Members Directory

Career Tools
- HCI Job Board
- HCI Career Portal

Education
- Skills Certification
- Degree Programs

Events
- Webcasts
- Regional Summits
- Annual Conference

Marketing Your Services
- Recruiter Directory
- Consultant Directory
- HCI Marketplace